C000131327

MCSE 2000 JumpStart™:
Computer and Network Basics

Lisa Donald with
Patrick Ciccarelli and
Dan Newland

SYBEX®

San Francisco ✦ Paris ✦ Düsseldorf ✦ Soest ✦ London

Associate Publisher: Neil Edde
Contracts and Licensing Manager: Kristine O'Callaghan
Developmental Editor: Linda Lee
Editor: Sharon Wilkey
Production Editor: Bronwyn Shone Erickson
Technical Editor: Scott Warmbrand
Book Designer: Maureen Forys, Happenstance Type-O-Rama
Graphic Illustrator: Tony Jonick
Electronic Publishing Specialist: Maureen Forys, Happenstance Type-O-Rama
Proofreaders: Carrie Bradley, Alison Moncrieff, Laurie O'Connell, Suzanne Stein
Indexer: Lynnzee Elze
Cover Designer: Archer Design
Cover Illustrator/Photographer: Archer Design

SYBEX and the SYBEX logo are trademarks of SYBEX Inc. in the USA and other countries.

Jumpstart is a trademark of SYBEX Inc.

Some screen reproductions produced with FullShot 99. FullShot 99 ©1991–1999 Inbit Incorporated. All rights reserved.
FullShot is a trademark of Inbit Incorporated.

Some screen reproductions produced with Collage Complete.
Collage Complete is a trademark of Inner Media Inc.

Internet screen shot(s) using Microsoft Internet Explorer 5 reprinted by permission from Microsoft Corporation.

Microsoft, the Microsoft Internet Explorer logo, Windows, Windows NT, and the Windows logo are either registered trademarks or trademarks of Microsoft Corporation in the United States and/or other countries.

SYBEX is an independent entity from Microsoft Corporation, and not affiliated with Microsoft Corporation in any manner. This publication may be used in assisting students to prepare for a Microsoft Certified Professional Exam. Neither Microsoft Corporation, its designated review company, nor SYBEX warrants that use of this publication will ensure passing the relevant exam. Microsoft is either a registered trademark or trademark of Microsoft Corporation in the United States and/or other countries.

TRADEMARKS: SYBEX has attempted throughout this book to distinguish proprietary trademarks from descriptive terms by following the capitalization style used by the manufacturer.

The author and publisher have made their best efforts to prepare this book, and the content is based upon final release software whenever possible. Portions of the manuscript may be based upon pre-release versions supplied by software manufacturer(s). The author and the publisher make no representation or warranties of any kind with regard to the completeness or accuracy of the contents herein and accept no liability of any kind including but not limited to performance, merchantability, fitness for any particular purpose, or any losses or damages of any kind caused or alleged to be caused directly or indirectly from this book.

An earlier version of this book was published under the title MCSE JumpStart: Computer and Network Basics copyright ©1999 SYBEX Inc.
Copyright ©2000 SYBEX Inc., 1151 Marina Village Parkway, Alameda, CA 94501. World rights reserved. No part of this publication may be stored in a retrieval system, transmitted, or reproduced in any way, including but not limited to photocopy, photograph, magnetic or other record, without the prior agreement and written permission of the publisher.

Library of Congress Card Number: 00-101926

ISBN: 0-7821-2749-5

Manufactured in the United States of America

10 9 8 7 6 5 4 3 2 1

This book is for the woman who taught me self-confidence. If I could do this, so can all of you! Thanks, Mom. That's Terry Whinery to all of the people she corners in the bookstores.
—Lisa Donald

To my brothers and sisters, you have been an inspiration to me. Thanks for the support and the late night basketball games.
—Patrick Ciccarelli

To my sister Nancy, who is always there for me.
—Dan Newland

Acknowledgments

This book was first inspired by all of the people I have met who are interested in the MCSE program but don't know where to begin.

As always, a book is not the work of an individual but rather a team.

I would like to thank Neil Edde, associate publisher, and Linda Lee, acquisitions and developmental editor, for bringing together a great team to revise *MCSE JumpStart* for Windows 2000, and for being there to answer questions; production editor Bronwyn Shone Erickson for deftly carrying out the unenviable task of keeping us all on a schedule; and editor Sharon Wilkey for her valuable advice and assistance with the writing and editing process. Her skilled handling of the text, graphics, and JumpStart design made the book-building process fruitful instead of frustrating. Thanks also to technical editor Scott Warmbrand for his thorough edit and speedy turnaround.

Revisers Patrick Ciccarelli and Dan Newland deserve special thanks for their contributions. Patrick revised the first three-quarters of this book, making sure that all the material was up to date with current technologies and standards. Dan Newland wrote the last four chapters on Windows 2000, making the book relevant to the requirements of the Windows 2000 MCSE track. Both met seemingly impossible deadlines, helped create a high-quality book, and never lost sight of the readers' needs.

Maureen Forys acted as the designer for the book and served as the electronic publishing specialist. She was the creative force behind this book and did an excellent job with the design.

The nature of this book required a great deal of artwork. Tony Jonick acted as the illustrator and did an excellent job of creating artwork that was appropriate for the book. They say a picture is worth a thousand words, and his art is an essential part of this book.

The book you hold in your hands was the result of not only this book team, but also that of the previous version, *MCSE JumpStart*. Thanks go out to Bonnie Bills, the original acquisitions and developmental editor, who encouraged the writing of this book. Others members of the original team who deserve thanks are Guy Hart-Davis, Brianne Agatep, Debby English, James Tower, Shannon Murphy, Jeff Wilson, and Nancy Guenther.

Dan Newland also thanks the kind folks at Moxie Java, where he did most of his work on this project (in collaboration with a ThinkPad and dozens of cups of strong coffee!).

Finally, I want to thank my family for all of their support.

Contents

Contents

Chapter ◆ 10 Networking the Computers   198

Chapter ◆ 11 Moving Data: Network Layer Protocols   216

Chapter ◆ 12 Network Operating Systems: A Comparison   228

Contents

Contents

Introduction

One of the greatest challenges facing corporate America today is finding people who are qualified to manage corporate computer networks. Many companies have Microsoft networks that run Windows 95 and 98, Windows NT, and other Microsoft BackOffice products (such as Microsoft SQL Server and Systems Management Server). Windows 2000, Microsoft's newest operating system, is also increasing its presence in the corporate world.

Microsoft developed its Microsoft certification program to certify those people who have the skills to work with Microsoft products and networks. The most highly coveted certification is the MCSE, or Microsoft Certified Systems Engineer.

Why become an MCSE? The main benefits are that you will have much greater earnings potential and that an MCSE carries high industry recognition. Certification can be your key to a higher salary or a new job—or both.

So what's stopping you? If you don't know where to begin, this book is for you. The first step in Microsoft certification is a good understanding of the prerequisite information. Microsoft defines the prerequisites but assumes you will acquire this information on your own.

This book takes all the prerequisites and puts them in a single book that specifically targets MCSE candidates. This book is designed for the novice user who wants to become Microsoft certified but doesn't know where to start. When you are done with this book, you will have the foundation you need to study for the MCSE exams.

The next step in the certification quest will be preparation for each Microsoft exam. This can be accomplished by taking Microsoft-approved training classes or by purchasing the Sybex MCSE books that will prepare you for each exam.

What This Book Covers

Before you begin the MCSE or any Microsoft certification, Microsoft recommends that you have this prerequisite information:

- ◇ A working knowledge of an operating system such as DOS, Unix, Windows 3.x, Windows 9x, Windows NT, or Windows 2000
- ◇ Proficiency with the Windows interface and a working knowledge of Windows Explorer
- ◇ An understanding of networking concepts such as networks, servers, clients, network adapter cards and hardware, protocols, network operating systems, and drivers
- ◇ An understanding of computer hardware, including processors, memory, hard disks, communication ports, and peripheral devices

This book covers the MCSE prerequisites in easy-to-understand language with graphics to illustrate the concepts. Information is presented in small chunks so that it won't be overwhelming.

Based on the knowledge you need to begin your MCSE preparations, this book is organized as follows:

Chapters 1–4   These chapters deal with computer hardware. They cover computer processors, data storage, input/output devices, and hardware configuration issues.

Chapters 5–7   These chapters cover software. You will learn about the different local operating systems, get a good overview of DOS, and learn the basics of the Windows 9x interface.

Chapters 8–12   These chapters cover common networking concepts such as the OSI model, peer-to-peer and client-server network models, network topologies, networking hardware, network protocols, and common network operating systems.

Chapters 13–17   These chapters focus on Windows NT and Windows 2000, covering their history, the platforms, user and group management, and file and print resource management.

Understanding Microsoft Certification

Microsoft offers several levels of certification for anyone who has or is pursuing a career as a network professional working with Microsoft products. These certifications include

- ◇ Microsoft Certified Professional (MCP)
- ◇ Microsoft Certified Systems Engineer (MCSE)
- ◇ Microsoft Certified Trainer (MCT)

The one you choose depends on your area of expertise and your career goals.

Microsoft Certified Professional (MCP)

This certification is for individuals with expertise in one specific area of the Microsoft product line (for example, Windows 98). MCP certification is often a stepping stone to MCSE certification and allows you some benefits of Microsoft certification after just one exam.

By passing one of the current core exams, you become an MCP.

NOTE

Only four exams are considered the core exams. The core exams are ones that cover Microsoft operating systems. The current exception is Microsoft Windows 2000 Accelerated Exam for MCPs Certified on Microsoft Windows NT 4.0; this does not count toward the MCP.

Microsoft Certified Systems Engineer (MCSE)

The MCSE certification for network professionals requires commitment. You need to complete all the steps required for certification. Passing the exams shows that you meet the high standards that Microsoft has set for MCSEs.

NOTE

The following list applies to the Windows 2000 track. The Windows 2000 track exams will be available beginning the second quarter of 2000.

To become an MCSE in the Windows 2000 track, you must pass five core exams and two elective exams:

1. Installing, Configuring, and Administering Microsoft Windows 2000 Professional

2. Installing, Configuring, and Administering Microsoft Windows 2000 Server

3. Implementing and Administering a Microsoft Windows 2000 Network Infrastructure

4. Implementing and Administering a Microsoft Windows 2000 Directory Services Infrastructure

NOTE

In place of the first four core exams, you can also take the Microsoft Windows 2000 Accelerated Exam for MCPs Certified in Microsoft Windows NT 4.0. This exam is only recommended for those with a significant amount of experience. If you're reading this book, you'll likely be better off taking the individual exams.

5. One of the following three design exams: Designing a Microsoft Windows 2000 Directory Services Infrastructure, Designing Security for a Microsoft Windows 2000 Network, or Designing a Microsoft Windows 2000 Network Infrastructure

6. Elective

7. Elective

Some of the electives include:

- ◆ One of the design exams, other than the one taken as your fifth exam
- ◆ Upgrading from Microsoft Windows NT 4.0 to Microsoft Windows 2000
- ◆ Administering Microsoft SQL Server 7.0
- ◆ Designing and Implementing Databases with Microsoft SQL Server 7.0
- ◆ Implementing and Supporting Microsoft Exchange Server 5.5
- ◆ Implementing and Supporting Microsoft Proxy Server 2.0
- ◆ Implementing and Supporting Microsoft Systems Management Server 2.0

NOTE

Many of the electives are from the MCSE Windows NT 4.0 track. Be sure to check Microsoft's site for updated information on what electives are current.

Microsoft Certified Trainer (MCT)

As an MCT, you can deliver Microsoft-certified courseware through official Microsoft channels.

You need to submit an application that Microsoft must approve and you must pass the exams for each course that you plan to teach. As of January 1, 2001, you must also be certified as either an MCSE or as an MCSD (Microsoft Certified Solution Developer is a certification program for programmers).

TIP

For the most up-to-date certification information, visit Microsoft's Web site at www.microsoft.com/train_cert.

Preparing for the MCSE Exams

To prepare for the MCSE certification exams, you should try to work with the products as much as possible. You can learn about the products and exams from a variety of resources:

- ◆ You can take instructor-led courses.
- ◆ Online training is an alternative to instructor-led courses. This is a useful option for people who cannot find any courses in their area or who do not have the time to attend classes.
- ◆ If you prefer to use a book to help you prepare for the MCSE tests, you can choose from a wide variety of publications. These range from complete study guides (such as the Sybex *MCSE Study Guide* series, which covers the core MCSE exams and key electives) to test-preparedness books.

After you have completed your courses, training, or study guides, you'll find the *MCSE Exam Notes* books an excellent resource for making sure that you are prepared for the test. You will discover whether you've got it covered or you still need to fill in some holes.

NOTE

For more MCSE information, point your browser to the Sybex Web site, where you'll find information about the MCP program, job links, and descriptions of other titles in the Sybex line of MCSE-related books. Go to www.sybex.com/certification.

What Types of Questions Are There?

Until recently, the formats of the MCSE exams were rather straightforward, consisting almost entirely of multiple-choice questions appearing in a few different sets. Prior to taking an exam, you knew how many questions you would see and what type of questions would appear. If you had purchased the right third-party exam preparation products, you could even be quite familiar with the pool of questions you would be asked. All of this is changing.

In an effort to both refine the testing process and protect the quality of its certifications, Microsoft has recently begun introducing adaptive testing and new exam elements. These innovations add new challenges for individuals taking the exams. Most importantly, they make it much more difficult for someone to pass an exam after simply "cramming" for it.

Real skills and in-depth knowledge are now needed much more than they were before. Because Microsoft has a policy of not stating in advance what type of format you will see, let's take a look at adaptive testing and the new exam question types so you can be aware of all the possibilities.

Adaptive Exams

Microsoft is in the process of converting exams to a new "adaptive" format. This format is radically different from the conventional format previously used for Microsoft certification exams. If you have never taken an adaptive test, there are a few things you should know.

Conventional tests and adaptive tests are different in that conventional tests are static, containing a fixed number of questions, while adaptive tests change or "adapt," depending on your answers to the questions presented. The number of questions presented in your adaptive test will depend on how long it takes the exam to "figure out" what your level of ability is (according to the statistical measurements upon which the exam questions are ranked).

To "figure out" a test-taker's level of ability, the exam will present questions in increasing or decreasing orders of difficulty. By presenting sequences of questions with determined levels of difficulty, the exam is supposed to be able to determine your level of understanding.

For example, we have three test-takers, Herman, Sally, and Rashad. Herman doesn't know much about the subject, Sally is moderately informed, while Rashad is an expert. Herman answers his first question incorrectly, so the exam gives him a second, easier question. He misses that, so the exam gives him a few more easy questions, all of which he misses. Shortly thereafter, the exam ends, and he receives his failure report. Sally, meanwhile, answers her first question correctly, so the exam gives her a more difficult question, which she answers correctly. She then receives an even more difficult question, which she answers incorrectly, so the exam gives her a somewhat easier question, as it tries to gauge her level of understanding. After numerous questions of varying levels of difficulty, Sally's exam ends, perhaps with a passing score, perhaps not. Her exam included far more questions than Herman's included, because her level of understanding needed to be more carefully tested to determine whether or not it was at a passing level. When Rashad takes his exam, he answers his first question correctly, so he's given a more difficult question, which he also answers correctly. He's given an even more difficult question, which he also answers correctly. He then is given a few more very difficult questions, all of which he answers correctly. Shortly thereafter, his exam ends. He passes. His exam was short, about as long as Herman's.

Microsoft has begun moving to adaptive testing for several reasons:

❖ It saves time, by focusing only on the questions needed to determine a test-taker's abilities. This way an exam that, in the conventional format, took 1½ hours can be completed in less than half that time. The number of questions presented can be far less than the number required by a conventional exam.

❖ It protects the integrity of the exams. By exposing a fewer number of questions at any one time, it makes it more difficult for individuals to collect the questions in the exam pools with the intent of facilitating exam "cramming."

❖ It saves Microsoft and/or the test delivery company money by cutting down on the amount of time it takes to deliver a test.

NOTE

Unlike the previous test format, the adaptive format will *not* allow you to go back to see a question again. The exam only goes forward. Once you enter your answer, that's it; you cannot change it.

Select-and-Place Exam Questions

Select-and-place exam questions involve graphical elements that the test-taker must manipulate in order to successfully answer a question. For example, a question could present a diagram of a computer network with several computers next to boxes that read "Place Here." There would also be several labels representing different computer roles on network, such as Print Server, File Server, etc. Based upon information given for each computer, you are asked to drag and drop each label to the correct box.

NOTE

You need to correctly drag the correct labels to *all* correct boxes in order to get credit for the question. No credit is given if you correctly label only some of the boxes.

Simulations

Simulations are the kinds of questions that most closely represent and test the actual skills you use while working with Microsoft software interfaces. These types of exam questions include a mock or imitation interface on which you must perform certain actions according to a given scenario. The simulated interfaces look nearly identical to what you see in the actual product.

Simulations are by far the most complex element introduced into Microsoft exams to date. Because of the number of possible errors that can be made on simulations, it is worthwhile to consider the following recommendations from Microsoft:

- ◇ Do not change any simulation settings that don't directly pertain to the solution.

- ◇ Assume default settings when related information has not been provided because it is non-critical.

- ◇ Be sure entries are spelled correctly.

- ◇ Close all simulation application windows after completing the set of tasks in the simulation.

- ◇ Most important, however, is that you spend time working with the operating system.

Case Study—Based Questions

Case Study—based questions first appeared in the Microsoft Certified Solution Developer program (Microsoft's certification for programmers). The basic idea of the Case Study—based exam item is that you have a scenario with a range of requirements. Based on the information provided, you need to answer a series of multiple-choice questions. The interface for Case Study—based questions has a number of tabs with the information about the scenario appearing under each tab. The net result is that you have a rather lengthy description of a scenario, with several multiple-choice questions.

Scheduling and Taking an Exam

Once you think you are ready to take an exam, call Sylvan Prometric Testing Centers at (800) 755-EXAM (755-3926) or Virtual University Enterprises (Vue) at 800-TEST REG (837-8734). They'll tell you where to find the closest testing center. Before you call, get out your wallet, because each exam costs $100.

You can schedule the exam for a time that is convenient for you. The exams are downloaded to the testing center, and you show up at your scheduled time and take the exam on a computer.

After you complete the exam, you will know right away whether you have passed. At the end of the exam, you will receive a score report. It will list the areas that you were tested on and how you performed. If you pass the exam, you don't need to do anything else—Sylvan Prometric or Vue uploads the test results to Microsoft. If you don't pass, it's another $100 to schedule the exam again. But at least you will know from the score report where you did poorly, so you can study that particular information more carefully.

Test-Taking Hints

If you know what to expect, your chances of passing the exam will be much greater. Here are some tips that can help you achieve success.

Get There Early and Be Prepared

This is your last chance to review. Bring your books and review any areas you feel unsure of. If you need a quick drink of water or a visit to the restroom, take the time to do so before the exam. After your exam starts, it will not be paused for these needs.

When you arrive for your exam, you will be asked to present two forms of ID. You will also be asked to sign a paper verifying that you understand the testing rules (for example, the rule that says you will not cheat on the exam).

Before you start the exam, you will have an opportunity to take a practice exam. It is not related to the exam topic and is simply offered so that you will have a feel for the exam-taking process.

Be Aware of What You Can and Can't Take in with You

These are closed-book exams. The only thing that you can take in is scratch paper provided by the testing center. Use this paper as much as possible to diagram the questions. Many times, diagramming questions can help make the answer clear. You will have to give this paper back to the test administrator at the end of the exam.

Many testing centers are very strict about what you can take into the testing room. Some centers will not even allow you to bring in items such as a zipped-up purse. If you feel tempted to take in any outside material, be aware that many testing centers use monitoring devices such as video and audio equipment (so don't swear, even if you are alone in the room!).

Sylvan Prometric and Vue testing centers take the test-taking process and the test validation very seriously.

Follow a Planned Approach

As you take the test, fill in the answers to questions that you know and move on. If you're not sure of the answer, mark your best guess, then "mark" the question.

At the end of the exam, you can review the questions. Depending on the amount of time remaining, you can then view all the questions again, or you can view only the questions that you were unsure of. Double-checking all your answers is a good idea, just in case you misread any of the questions on the first pass. (Sometimes half the battle is in trying to figure out exactly what the question is asking you.) Also, sometimes a related question may provide a clue for a question that you are unsure of.

Be sure to answer all questions. Unanswered questions are scored as incorrect and will count against you. Also, make sure that you keep an eye on the remaining time so that you can pace yourself accordingly.

If you do not pass the exam, note everything that you can remember while the exam is still fresh in your mind. This will help you prepare for your next try. Although the next exam will not be exactly the same, the questions will be similar, and you don't want to make the same mistakes.

After You Become Certified

After you become an MCSE, Microsoft kicks in some goodies, including

- ◇ Access to a secure area of the Microsoft Web site that provides technical support and product information. This certification benefit is also available with MCP certification.

- ◇ Permission to use the Microsoft Certified Professional logos (each certification has its own logo), which look great on letterhead and business cards.

- ◇ An MCP certificate, suitable for framing or sending copies to Mom. (You will get a certificate for each level of certification you reach.)

- ◇ A one-year subscription to *Microsoft Certified Professional Magazine*, which provides information on professional and career development.

Making the Most of This Book

At the beginning of each chapter of *MCSE 2000 JumpStart*, you'll find a list of topics that you can expect to learn about within that chapter. As you read through the chapter, you'll notice that when a topic continues to the next page, you'll see this icon at the bottom outside corner of the page:

When a topic ends, you'll see this icon:

To help you soak up new material easily, I've highlighted **new terms** in bold and defined them in the margins of the pages. And to give you some hands-on experience, there are Test It Out sections that let you practice what you've just learned. In addition, several special elements highlight important information:

NOTE

Notes provide extra information and references to related information.

TIP

Tips are insights that help you perform tasks more easily and effectively.

WARNING

Warnings let you know about things you should do—or shouldn't do—as you learn more about the MCSE.

Introduction

At the end of each chapter, you can test your knowledge of the topics covered by answering the chapter's Review Questions. (You'll find the answers to the Review Questions in Appendix A.)

There's also some special material for your reference. If you'd like to quickly look up the meaning of a term, Appendix B is a glossary of terms that have been introduced throughout the book. If you are wondering what acronyms stand for, Appendix C is an acronym guide showing the acronyms in this book spelled out.

Chapter

1

The Computer's Brain: Processors and Memory

pro·cess *v* : to complete a series of actions

Every computer consists of a microprocessor and memory. Without the two, the computer would not function. The microprocessor, commonly referred to as the Central Processing Unit (CPU), is the brain of the computer. Like the human brain, the CPU is responsible for managing the timing of each operation and carrying out the instructions or commands from an application or the operating system.

The CPU uses memory as a place to store or retrieve information. Memory comes in several forms, such as random access memory (RAM) and read-only memory (ROM). Memory provides a temporary location for storing information and contains more permanent system configuration information.

This chapter provides an overview of these topics related to microprocessors and memory:

 Processor types

 History and evolution of Intel processors

 Intel's competition—AMD, Cyrix, PowerPC, and Alpha

 Multiprocessor computers

 Physical memory

 Bus architecture and bus types

Processor Types: A First Look

So many types of computer processors, also referred to as microprocessors, are on the market today that it can be quite confusing to wade through them all. All processors are not created equal, and each processor has its own characteristics that make it unique. For instance, a processor that is built around an architecture common to other processors of the same time period may actually operate at double or triple the speed. Fierce competition among the various chip makers lays the groundwork for new technological innovations and constant improvements.

The most obvious difference among processors is the physical appearance of the chips, meaning that many processors differ noticeably from one another in size and shape. The first processor that Intel released was packaged in a small chip that contained two rows of 20 pins each. As processor technology improved, the shape and packaging scheme of the processor also changed. Modern processors, such as the Intel Pentium II, use an advanced packaging scheme in which the processor is encased in a **single-edge cartridge (SEC)** module that plugs into a 242-pin slot on the **motherboard**. Much like an expansion card that easily plugs into the motherboard, the SEC module can easily be removed and upgraded. This design also reduces the cost involved in producing the **CPU**.

Another noticeable difference among processors is the type of instruction set they use. The instruction sets that are most common to processors are either **Complex Instruction Set Computing (CISC)** or **Reduced Instruction Set Computing (RISC)**.

CISC has been a common method of processing operations, especially in Intel CPUs. CISC uses a set of commands, which include subcommands that require additional CPU memory and time to process. Each command must go through a decode unit, located inside the CPU, to be broken down into **microcode**. The microcode is then processed one microcode at a time, which slows computing.

RISC, on the other hand, uses smaller commands that enable it to operate at higher speeds. The smaller commands work directly with microcode, so there is no need for a decode unit. This factor—along with a RISC chip's capability to execute multiple commands simultaneously—dramatically increases the processing power.

Finally, different manufacturers design processors to varying specifications. You should be sure that the processor type and model you choose are compatible with the operating system that you want to use. If the processor is not 100 percent compatible with the operating system, the computer will not operate at its best or might not work at all.

single-edge cartridge (SEC)

An advanced packaging scheme that the Intel Pentium II and later models use. The processor is encased in a cartridge module with a single edge that plugs into a 242-pin slot on the system board, much as an expansion card plugs into the system board.

motherboard

The main board in a computer that manages communication between devices internally and externally.

Central Processing Unit (CPU)

The microprocessor, or brain, of the computer. It uses logic to perform mathematical operations that are used in the manipulation of data.

2

NOTE

The terms *processor*, *microprocessor*, *chip*, and *CPU* are used interchangeably.

Deciphering Processor Terminology

For most computer novices, terms such as *microcode efficiency* and *internal cache RAM* can sound like part of a foreign language. To help you keep things straight, here are some common terms and their definitions:

Clock cycles   The internal speed of a computer or processor expressed in **megahertz (MHz)**. The faster the clock speed, the faster the computer performs a specific operation.

CPU speed   The number of operations that are processed in one second.

Data path   The number of **bits** that can be transported into the processor chip during one operation.

Floating Point Unit (FPU), or math coprocessor   A secondary processor that speeds operations by taking over math calculations of decimal numbers. Also called a numeric processor.

Level 1 (L1), or internal, cache   Memory in the CPU that is used to temporarily store instructions and data while they are waiting to be processed. Modern CPUs such as the Pentium II processor typically have at least two L1 caches of 16 or 32 kilobytes.

Level 2 (L2), or backside, cache   Memory that is used by the CPU to temporarily store data that is waiting to be processed. Originally located on the motherboard, recent CPU architectures such as the Pentium II and III have incorporated L2 cache directly on the same board as the CPU. The CPU can access the on-board L2 cache two to four times faster than it can access the L2 cache on the motherboard.

Microcode efficiency   The capability of a CPU to process microcode in a manner that uses the least amount of time and completes the greatest number of operations.

Word size   The largest number in bits that can be processed during one operation.

NOTE

All the computer's components, including the processor, are installed on the motherboard. This fiberglass sheet is designed for a specific type of CPU. When purchasing a motherboard, you should check with the motherboard manufacturer to determine which types of CPUs are supported.

Complex Instruction Set Computing (CISC)
A full complement of instructions used by a processor to complete tasks such as mathematical calculations. Used in the most common type of processors produced; Intel processors are currently based on this standard.

Reduced Instruction Set Computing (RISC)
A reduced set of instructions used by a processor. PowerPC and Alpha processors are manufactured using this standard. The reduced instruction set enables a microprocessor to operate at higher speeds.

---

microcode
The smallest form of an instruction in a CPU.

---

megahertz (MHz)
One million cycles per second. The internal clock speed of a microprocessor is expressed in MHz.

The Intel Processor Lineup

Over time, Intel has introduced several generations of microprocessors. Each processor type is referred to as a generation; each is based on the new technological enhancements of the day. With each product release come new software and hardware products to take advantage of the new technology.

Several generations of Intel processors are available today. Since the arrival of the first Intel chip in the IBM PC, Intel has dominated the market. It seems that every time you turn around, a new chip promises greater performance and processing capabilities than the previous one.

What makes Intel the market leader is its ability to bring the newest innovations in chip technology to the public, usually before its competitors, who are not far behind. Competition is fierce, and each manufacturer attempts to improve on the designs of the others, releasing similar chips that promise better performance.

The following table shows the specifications for the Intel processors issued to date. You should read the specifications and reviews of each processor to understand its capabilities and reliability.

Model	Year Introduced	Maximum Internal Clock Frequency (in MHz)	Data Path (in Bits)
4004	1971	.108	4
8008	1972	.2	8
8080	1974	2	8
8086	1978	8	16
8088	1979	4.77	8
80286	1982	20	16
80386	1985	40	32
80486	1989	100	32
Pentium	1993	200	32
Pentium Pro	1995	200	32
Pentium MMX	1997	233	32
Pentium II	1997	450	64
Pentium II Xeon	1998	450	64
Celeron	1998	500	64
Pentium III	1999	733	64
Pentium III Xeon	1999	550	64
Intel Itanium	2000	to be determined	64

bit
A binary digit. The digit is the smallest unit of information and represents either an off state (zero) or an on state (one).

Factors Affecting Performance

Many factors come together to determine the performance of any computer. All other factors being equal, faster components will give better performance, but any computer will be limited by its "weakest links." As an analogy, consider that putting a larger engine in a standard automobile will make it faster, but only if the automobile is going in a straight line. As soon as you try to make the car follow a twisting road, other components such as the drivetrain and the tires can limit the performance of the larger engine.

Within a processor family, faster processors will outperform slower processors. But when comparing processors from different families, that rule does not apply. For example, the rating of 400MHz for a processor from one family does not indicate that it will run significantly faster than a 333MHz processor from a more advanced processor family.

As you learned earlier, clock cycles and data path are two factors that can influence the performance of your computer. Other factors are:

Cache memory   Very fast memory that sits between the CPU and the main RAM. Cache memory can be as fast as 5 to 10 nanoseconds, whereas main RAM is usually not faster than 60 to 70 nanoseconds. (Yes, a lower number is better here because it indicates that the memory takes less time to move data.)

Bus speed   The rate at which data can be transferred between the CPU and the rest of the motherboard. Typical bus speeds are 50, 60, 66, or 100MHz, with 133MHz-based motherboards entering the market.

NOTE

The type of peripherals on your computer can affect system performance. If your application spends a lot of time accessing your hard disk, selecting a better-performing disk system would improve CPU efficiency. For example, Small Computer System Interface (SCSI) hard disks place a much smaller overhead burden on your CPU than Integrated Device Electronics (IDE) storage devices. Storage systems are covered in detail in Chapter 2, "Storing Your Files: Data Storage."

History of Intel Chips

Intel released the world's first microprocessor, the Intel 4004, in 1971. It was a 4-bit microprocessor containing a programmable controller chip that could process 45 instructions. The four bits meant that the chip had four lines for data to travel on, much like a four-lane highway. Because of its limitations, it was implemented only in a few early video games and some other devices. The following year, Intel released the 8008, an 8-bit microprocessor with enhanced memory storage and the capability to process 48 instructions.

millions of instructions per second (MIPS)

A measurement of the number of microcode instructions that a CPU or microprocessor can complete in one second, or cycle.

Intel then began to research and develop faster, more capable processors. From that research emerged the 8080, which could process instructions 10 times faster than its predecessors. Although the speed had dramatically improved, it was still limited by the number of instructions it could process. Finally, in 1978, Intel broke many barriers by releasing the first of many computer-ready microprocessors, the 8086. The 8086 was a breakthrough technology with a bus speed of 16 bits and the capability to support and use 1MB of RAM. Unfortunately, the cost for manufacturing such a chip and compatible 16-bit components made the chip unaffordable. Intel responded the following year with the production of an 8-bit chip, the 8088.

Intel continued to break new ground as the release of each new generation of processor offered improved functions and processing capabilities. The most dramatic improvement was the number of instructions, based on a scale of millions, that the processor could process in one second. This rate, referred to as **millions of instructions per second (MIPS)**, ranges from 0.75MIPS for the 8088 to over 200MIPS for Pentium II processors.

The second most dramatic improvement was the speed of the internal clock, measured in megahertz. All processors are driven by an internal clock mechanism that keeps the rhythm of the chip, much like the rhythm of a heartbeat. The faster the speed of the internal clock, the faster the processor can process instructions. Intel continued to increase the speed of the internal clock from 4.77MHz for the original 8088 to more than 700MHz for the newest generation of Intel microprocessors.

The First Generation: 8086 and 8088

The first major processor release from Intel was the 8086 microprocessor. The processor debuted as the first evolutionary step in a multitude of processors, each improving on the design of the original 8086. The lineage is referred to as the *x*86 family of microprocessors. Although this first release was crude compared to today's standards, it paved the way for the others to follow.

The 8088 was released a short time after the 8086 but was not as powerful as its predecessor. The 8086, a true 16-bit processor, contained 16-bit registers and a 16-bit data path. Motherboard technology had not quite reached the 16-bit level and was still costly in 1981. IBM decided to use a version of the 8088 chip, with the same design but with an 8-bit data path to accommodate the widely used 8-bit technology of the time.

The Second Generation: 80286

Intel forged a new milestone in PC processor technology with the release of the 80286, more commonly called the 286. The 286 offered a significant performance increase over the 8086 and 8088 with the unique capability to operate in a **protected mode**. The protected mode enabled the processor to **multitask** and still included its normal, or real, mode of operation.

Real mode required memory to be accessed in a linear format. This means that data being sent to RAM had to be placed in the order it was received—one application after another. With this limitation, instructions were usually processed one at a time.

Protected mode enabled multitasking to occur by allocating a specific range within memory for each task. Applications could therefore be accessed simultaneously, greatly improving performance.

NOTE

Some companies produce upgrades for 286, 386, and 486 computers. The processor upgrades are relatively inexpensive and can greatly improve the overall CPU speed. Although 286 upgrades are nearly impossible to find, upgrades for 486-based computers are available. The processor upgrade can convert your aging 486 into a speedy computer, comparable to a Pentium.

protected mode
A mode available in Intel 80286 and 80386 processors. Added the capability for the processor to allocate each application its own separate memory space. In the event that an application crashed, the rest of the system was protected.

multitask
To perform several operations concurrently.

The Third Generation: 80386

Intel's introduction of the 80386 processor reached yet a new milestone, condensing more than 250,000 **transistor**s onto a single 32-bit processor chip. (The number of transistors on a processor is an indicator of the complexity of the processor and of its ability to perform complex calculations.) This new generation of processors incorporated true, fully functioning multitasking capabilities. Protected mode was now commonly referred to as the 386 Enhanced Mode, because the 80386 was able to overcome the multitasking limitations of the 80286.

The 80386 included a new operating mode called Virtual Real Mode. This new mode created **conventional memory** space required by **DOS** programs to run within the **Windows operating system**. Virtual Real Mode, or Virtual DOS Mode as it is commonly called, is still used for running DOS-based games and applications within Windows 95 and 98.

> **NOTE**
>
> You will learn more about DOS and Windows operating systems in Chapter 5, "Desktop Operating Systems: A Comparison" and Chapter 6, "DOS 101: DOS Basics Every MCSE Should Know."

Several types of 80386 chips were issued, each with a unique combination of features. Intel offered two options: the 80386DX and the 80386SX CPUs. Both were 32-bit processors, but the 80386DX used a 32-bit data path, and the 80386SX used a 16-bit data path. Although the SX chip had smaller data paths, it was more competitively priced.

The Fourth Generation: 80486

Like the 80386, the next family of processors was released in 80486SX and 80486DX versions. Both included a 32-bit internal and external data path and an original internal clock frequency of 33MHz. The SX version was released with the numeric processor, or FPU, disabled and the internal clock speed slowed to 20MHz to offer a lower-cost processor to the consumer. Later this became a limitation with the emergence of more powerful software applications. A numeric processor was issued to complement the SX, turning it into a fully functioning DX.

A dramatic improvement was engineered into later deployments of the processor. A mechanism called a clock doubler enabled the internal system clock to run at twice the normal bus speed. Soon the 486DX-33 became the 486DX2-66, with the 2 signifying the clock-doubling technology. Eventually the idea of increasing the clock speed led to a clock tripler.

---

transistor
A microscopic electronic device that uses positive electrons to create the binary value of one, or "on," and negative electrons to create the binary value of zero, or "off." Modern CPUs have millions of transistors.

conventional memory
The first 640KB of memory, which is required by the Disk Operating System (DOS) to run. Memory above 640KB was used by operating systems such as Windows 3.1.

DOS
An operating system developed by Microsoft. DOS predominantly uses command lines to manage the operating system, applications, and files.

Windows operating system
An operating system developed by Microsoft that provides a graphical user interface for DOS.

The Next Generations: The Pentium Family

Intel released the Pentium chip to take advantage of the newly released **Peripheral Component Interconnect (PCI) bus architecture**. The new processor also consisted of 3.1 million transistors and a new 64-bit data path. The chip was originally designed to operate at 66MHz but was scaled down to 60MHz to support the new transistor design, which was experiencing heat and power problems. The first chips deployed also suffered from a bug in the microcode that hampered the processor's capability to calculate complex mathematical equations with precision. This problem was immediately fixed through a new batch of chips.

The most significant development in the Pentium was the use of two parallel 32-bit **pipelines** that enabled it to execute twice the number of instructions as previous Intel processors—a technological advancement that Intel named superscalar technology. Almost all processors today use this technology.

Released with the Pentium family of processors was **MultiMedia Extension (MMX)** technology. MMX technology is often referred to as multimedia enhanced technology, but this is not completely accurate. MMX-equipped processors contained additional instruction code sets that increased the processing speed for audio, video, and graphical data by up to 60 percent as compared to traditional Pentium processors. The MMX chips dramatically improved the response time of games and multimedia-based applications.

The types of Pentium Processors include:

- ◇ Pentium
- ◇ Pentium MMX
- ◇ Pentium Pro
- ◇ Pentium II (PII)
- ◇ Celeron
- ◇ Pentium II Xeon
- ◇ Pentium III (PIII)
- ◇ Pentium III Xeon
- ◇ Itanium (IA-64)

Peripheral Component Interconnect (PCI)
A bus standard for the transfer of data between the CPU, expansion cards, and RAM. PCI communicates at 33MHz.

bus architecture
Any linear pathway on which electrical signals travel and carry data from a source to a destination.

pipeline
A place in the processor where operations occur in a series of stages. The operation is not complete until it has passed through all stages.

MultiMedia Extension (MMX)
A processor technology that dramatically improves the response time of games and multimedia-based applications. The technology was introduced through the MMX-equipped line of Intel Pentium chips.

Pentium

The Pentium chip introduced the world to the first parallel 32-bit data path, which enabled the Pentium to process 64 bits—twice as much data as before. The Pentium was the first microprocessor chip designed to work with the PCI bus specification and had internal clock speeds ranging from 60MHz to 200MHz.

Pentium MMX

The Pentium with MMX technology included an expanded instruction code set with 57 new MMX microcode instructions. MMX enabled the microprocessor to increase the processing speed of audio, video, and graphics by up to 60 percent.

Pentium Pro

The Pentium Pro was the successor to Intel's Pentium processor. One of the unique features of this microprocessor was its internal RISC architecture with CISC-RISC translator services. The translator service was able to use the CISC set of instructions, common to all Intel chips, convert them to the RISC set, the faster of the two, and then complete the tasks as necessary using RISC.

The architectural enhancement that really distinguished the Pro from the original Pentium would influence how almost all microprocessors would later be developed. The Pro was two chips in one: On the bottom of the Pentium was the actual processor. Connected directly overhead of the processor was an L2 cache. By placing the L2 cache close to the processor, Intel was able to greatly increase the performance of the Pentium Pro.

Pentium II (PII)

The Intel Pentium II, or PII, processor is essentially an enhanced Pentium Pro processor with MMX extensions, cache memory, and a new interface design. The PII was designed to fit into an SEC that plugs into a 242-pin slot.

Celeron

The only noticeable difference between the Celeron and regular Pentium II processors is the lack of cache memory within its cartridge. Later models of the Celeron include cache memory on the same chip as the processor.

Pentium II Xeon

One of the major enhancements in the Pentium II Xeon is larger on-board cache. This processor is available with either 1MB or 2MB of L2 cache and a clock rate of 450MHz.

Pentium III (PIII)

With its faster clock rates (currently up to 733MHz), the Pentium III supports demanding applications such as full-screen, full-motion video and realistic graphics. Seventy new instructions have also been added to make technologies such as 3-D graphics, video, speech, and imaging faster and more affordable for mainstream users. Each Pentium III also contains a unique processor serial number. Intel's intent behind this feature was to enhance system security and asset tracking. However, many individuals object to the serial number as infringement on their privacy because it can be used to identify computers on the Internet.

Pentium III Xeon

The Pentium III Xeon processor challenges RISC-based servers in both price/performance and raw performance. It is available in speeds of up to 550MHz and supports configurations that have more than one processor in the same box.

Itanium (IA-64)

Previously known by the code name Merced, the Itanium processor employs a 64-bit architecture and enhanced instruction handling to greatly increase the performance of computational and multimedia operations.

NOTE

Although most of us would like to get our hands on the new high-speed processors, the reality is that it will be a while before they are affordable. Also, to really reap the benefits of those high-speed CPUs, computers will need to have equivalently high-powered hardware. That is why you will see the first high-speed high CPUs only in expensive servers.

Stacking Up the Competition

Many manufacturers are competing with Intel to produce microprocessor chips. For many years, Intel's competitors produced clone copies of its chips, often slightly altering the original design to allow for faster processing speeds. A good example of this was the release by Advanced Micro Devices (AMD) of a 40MHz version of the 386 processor to rival the 33MHz version that Intel was producing. Non-Intel, or clone, chips became popular because of the cheaper price and improved features.

In addition to clone chips, other manufacturers have produced powerful processors that are not based on Intel architecture. Digital Equipment Corporation (DEC), Sun Microsystems, IBM, and Motorola have all produced powerful CPUs. Most of these chips are RISC-based CPUs designed to meet two needs: First, RISC-type chips could meet the powerful speed demands of Unix workstations; second, companies wanted to differentiate themselves from Intel to increase sales.

When Intel released the Pentium generation of processors, the clone manufacturers adopted their own unique naming conventions that steered away from the path that Intel laid with this new release. Intel at the same time was experiencing problems with the early release of its Pentium line, with the discovery of a high-level mathematical division problem. Intel's competitors took advantage of the opportunity by releasing their chips to compete with the Pentium processor.

The subsections that follow provide an overview of these processors:

- ✧ AMD
- ✧ Cyrix
- ✧ PowerPC
- ✧ Alpha

Hardware Compatibility List (HCL)

Provided by Microsoft, the HCL lists all hardware that has been tested by Microsoft and has proved to work with a particular operating system. Hardware not on the HCL might work, but is not certain to.

WARNING

Be sure to check the Microsoft **Hardware Compatibility List (HCL)** before attempting to buy non-Intel processors.

Advanced Micro Devices (AMD)

In 1996, AMD introduced the K5 to combat the already released Intel Pentium processor. The K5 was released in a 64-bit version as a follow-up to the earlier K5x86, which resembled a higher-performance 486-based processor. The performance of the K5 equals the Pentium at a reduced cost to the consumer.

AMD soon followed the K5 generation with the release of the K6 processor. The K6 offers a boost by accelerating the audio, video, and 3-D capabilities of the chip in processing software, and adding MMX technology to compete with the Celeron, Pentium II, and Pentium III.

In addition to competing with the latest PC processors equipped with MMX technology, the AMD K6 offers a better "bang for the buck." The AMD K6 processors still plug into standard motherboards by using current technology with chipset and **Basic Input/Output System (BIOS)** support, without the need for special motherboards required by processors such as the Intel Pentium Pro and Pentium II models.

AMD's latest processor version is the Athlon (formerly the K7). Unlike earlier AMD processors, the Athlon cannot be used with standard motherboards. Instead, these processors require a special Athlon-compatible motherboard. One factor that sets this chip apart from its Intel and Cyrix counterparts is that it uses RISC technology. By using the reduced instruction set, it is able to process instructions at a more rapid rate. This capability and other improved implementations in design enable this chip to often outperform its Intel counterpart.

This table shows the specifications for the more popular AMD processors currently available.

Model	Year Introduced	Maximum Internal Clock Frequency (in MHz)	Data Path (in Bits)
K6-2-3D 266 MMX	1998	233	32
K6-2-3D 300 MMX	1998	300	32
K6-2-3D 333 MMX	1998	333	32
K6-2-3D 400 MMX	1998	400	32
K6-2-3D 533 MMX	1999	533	32
K6-III	1999	450	64
Athlon 750	1999	750	64
Athlon 800	1999	800	64

Basic Input/Output System (BIOS)
Software located in a ROM chip that is responsible for communicating directly between the computer hardware and the operating system.

Cyrix

Cyrix introduced a rival to the Intel Pentium processor in 1995. The first generation of its non-clone processor was named the MI 6x86 series. Although early releases of the MI encountered heat-related issues, Cyrix resolved the issues and produced a model that did not suffer from the initial design problem. The improved chip offered lower power consumption requirements that enabled the chip to operate at cooler temperatures. However, the 6x86 received mixed reviews about its compatibility with Windows NT.

Although the chip was originally designed to rival the Pentium, it included additional features found in the Intel Pentium Pro. One of the important features of the MI processor was the capability to predict the next instruction to process before encountering it, thereby considerably boosting processor performance.

A follow-up to the MI series of processors was the MII series, a direct competitor with the Celeron and Pentium II CPUs. The improved design included additional optimization, enabling instructions to be processed faster than by other processors. The MII processors' improved capabilities were overshadowed by incompatibilities with software that made them unable to take full advantage of the improved timing. Cyrix has since released software utilities and patches to address the timing issues. The MII features a set of 57 new instructions that are fully compatible with industry-standard MMX software.

This table shows the specifications for the more popular Cyrix processors currently available.

Model	Year Introduced	Maximum Internal Clock Frequency (in MHz)	Data Path (in Bits)
Cyrix MII 233	1997	233	32
Cyrix MII 266	1997	266	32
Cyrix MII 300	1998	300	32
Cyrix MII 333	1998	333	32
Cyrix MII 366	1998	366	32
Cyrix MII 400	1999	400	32
Cyrix Joshua	2000	to be determined	64

PowerPC

Apple, IBM, and Motorola developed the PowerPC as a new microprocessor technology. The PowerPC microprocessor uses RISC technology to produce a high processing rate. The innovative design of the PowerPC chip enables it to deliver high-performance computing power with lower power consumption than its counterparts.

The PowerPC chip is used in the IBM RS/6000 Unix-based workstation and in Apple Macintosh computers. Its design is much different from the traditional design of the Intel microprocessors. The term *PowerPC* refers to more than just a type of processor. It is also an architecture standard that outlines specifications by which manufacturers can design processors. The resulting designs that follow the specifications offer performance advantages and innovative manufacturing techniques such as those IBM created.

IBM developed one of the most significant changes in processor manufacturing, which it called **Silicon-On-Insulator (SOI)** technology. The PowerPC 750, marketed by Apple Computer as the G3, was the first chip released that used this new manufacturing method. SOI technology provided increased processor performance while using low power consumption. Low power consumption is the key to producing products such as handheld devices, which operate for long periods of time powered by a battery. Since the PowerPC 750, Motorola has released the PowerPC MPC 7400, which is more commonly known in Apple circles as the G4.

This table outlines specifications for the more popular PowerPC processors currently available.

Model	Year Introduced	Maximum Internal Clock Frequency (in MHz)	Data Path (in Bits)
PowerPC 601	1991	132	32
PowerPC 603	1994	300	32
PowerPC 603e	1995	300	32
PowerPC 604	1995	350	32
PowerPC 750 (G3)	1997	400	32 and 64
PowerPC MPC 7400 (G4)	1999	500	64

Silicon-On-Insulator (SOI)
The microchip manufacturing innovation that IBM invented. It is based on the capability to enhance silicon technology by reducing the time it takes to move electricity through a conductor.

Alpha

The Alpha is a high-speed microprocessor that DEC developed. The Alpha processor is typically found in workstations and servers that need more processing power than that found in Intel-based servers. Compaq, which has acquired DEC, has continued to enhance the speed and capabilities of the Alpha processor.

Virtual Address eXtension (VAX)
The technology built by Digital to run the VMS platform computers.

WARNING

Do not confuse the Alpha processor with the first line of DEC processors referred to as the Alpha, or **Virtual Address eXtension (VAX)**. The Alpha processor is unique and is much more advanced than the VAX.

One of the Alpha chip's selling points is that it is the only other chip besides the Intel *x*86 generations of processors that can run the Microsoft Windows NT operating system. Alpha-equipped workstations are often characterized as the fastest NT workstations on the planet. NT takes advantage of the Alpha's capability to produce or generate graphics up to eight times faster than Intel Pentium-based systems. Alpha chips are also commonly found in Unix workstations.

There are several versions of the Alpha chip available that operate at speeds from 366MHz to 833MHz. The Alpha 21264 has been recently replaced by the much faster Alpha 21264a, also known as the EV67. The EV67 is available at 667, 750, and 833MHz. The Alpha EV67 is also slated to be replaced by the EV7. EV7 will break the 1GHz (1,000MHz) barrier and is expected to eventually reach 1.4GHz in just more than a year.

NOTE

Although Microsoft and Compaq will not be supporting Windows 2000 on the Alpha platform, other operating systems, including Compaq's version of Unix and Linux, will be heavily supported. Other manufacturers, such as Samsung, will also be producing servers and workstations running on the latest Alpha processors.

Using Multiprocessor Computers

Multiprocessor computers can have more than one processor installed in them. Computers that contain more than one processor can scale to meet the needs of more demanding application programs. Microsoft Windows 2000 and its predecessor, Windows NT, are examples of operating systems that can use multiple processors.

There are two multiprocessing methods: **Asymmetrical Multiprocessing (ASMP)** and **Symmetrical Multiprocessing (SMP)**.

In ASMP, one processor is reserved to run the operating system and the **input/ output (I/O)** devices. The second ASMP processor runs the application, including the other miscellaneous tasks that the first processor does not handle. This method is often inefficient, because one processor can become busier than the other.

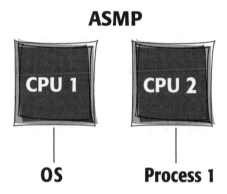

In SMP, all tasks are shared equally. The tasks are split among each processor. The Microsoft Windows 2000 operating system supports this multiprocessing method.

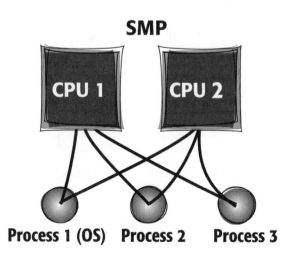

Asymmetrical Multiprocessing (ASMP)

A computer architecture that uses multiple CPUs to improve the performance of the computer. In the ASMP model, one CPU is dedicated to managing tasks (which usually involves managing the other CPUs) for the computer system. The remaining CPUs process user tasks.

Symmetrical Multiprocessing (SMP)

A computer architecture that uses multiple CPUs to improve a computer's performance. As performance demands increase on an SMP-capable computer, additional CPUs can be added to boost performance. During operation, if one a CPU is idle, it can be given any task to perform.

input/ouput (I/O)

Refers to any device or operation that enters data into or extracts data from a computer.

Physical Memory

Memory is an important part of any computer's system. Memory is used in every function of a computer, and it can have a major effect on computer performance. If you are going to get the most out of your computer, you need to understand the types of physical memory and how to select the type that is best suited to your computing needs.

NOTE

In Windows 2000, memory is more important than ever. The minimum requirement for Windows 2000 Professional is 64MB, and 128MB is recommended. Windows 2000 Server has a minimum requirement of 128MB and 256MB recommended.

Memory is basically a series of cells with an address. Each memory cell stores a small piece information. And each memory cell is identified by a unique address so the processor knows where the cell resides and can easily access it. Computers use several types of memory, each serving a different purpose.

Random Access Memory (RAM)

Random access memory (RAM), often referred to as main memory, is a temporary type of memory that the computer uses as a work area. This type of memory is dynamic, meaning that it is constantly changing because of the activity of the processor. When you shut off the power to the computer, RAM loses everything stored in it. RAM stores program instructions and related data for the CPU to quickly access without having to extract data from a slower type of memory, such as the hard disk.

The hard disk and floppy disk are more permanent forms of data storage. Programs and their output data are stored on disks for future use. When you shut off the power to the computer, the data on the storage media is intact. Accessing data and program instructions from storage media can take over a hundred times longer than from RAM.

Read-Only Memory (ROM)

Read-only memory (ROM) is a special type of memory in which data is written onto a chip during manufacturing. Information stored in ROM is permanent and cannot be changed. ROM stores the BIOS, the set of instructions a computer uses during the first stages of initialization. Without the BIOS, the computer would not have a mechanism to verify that the main hardware components are installed and functioning properly.

random access memory (RAM)

A temporary memory location that stores the operating system, applications, and files that are currently in use. The content in this type of memory is constantly changing. When you shut down the computer, all information in this type of memory is lost.

read-only memory (ROM)

A type of memory that has data pre-copied onto it. The data can only be read from and cannot be overwritten. ROM is used to store the BIOS software.

RAM Types

Every computer needs RAM, but which type? Not all types of RAM will work in a computer. Some physically won't fit in the RAM socket, and others will fit but won't work, preventing the computer from passing the **Power On Self-Test (POST)**.

Selecting the right type of RAM requires you to know your CPU type and motherboard. Some CPUs, such as the Pentium II, work only with motherboards designed for that chip. The motherboard is typically designed to meet the highest performance levels of a particular CPU and, therefore, determines which types of physical RAM can be used. RAM comes in one of two types: Single Inline Memory Modules (SIMMs) and Dual Inline Memory Modules (DIMMs).

SIMMs

SIMMs are physically different from DIMMs. Older SIMMs were designed with 30 pins that connected to a slot in the motherboard. These modules were slow and typically had to be added in groups of two or four identical SIMMs to be recognized by the BIOS. The current model is a 72-pin SIMM. On motherboards designed for the Pentium processor, the SIMMs must be added in pairs.

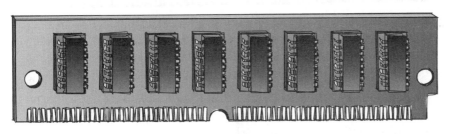

72-pin SIMM

DIMMs

DIMMs have 168 pins with a data path of either 64 bits for non-parity memory or 72 bits for **parity** memory. DIMMs have the largest data path of any memory module. The wider data path makes the chip as fast as the data path on the CPU. This means that the DIMMs can be added one at a time and in varying sizes. It is because of this improved performance and flexibility that DIMMs have become popular in today's personal computers.

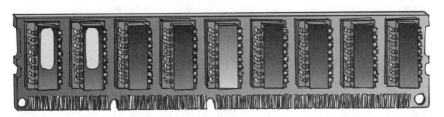

168-pin DIMM

Power On Self-Test (POST)
A set of diagnostic tests that are used to determine the state of hardware installed in the computer. Some components that fail the POST, such as bad RAM or a disconnected keyboard, will prevent the computer from booting up properly.

parity
An extra bit found on some memory modules. Non-parity memory has eight bits. Parity adds an extra bit that is used to keep track of the other eight bits. This can help prevent memory errors and is recommended for use in servers.

RAM Speed

Identifying the type of RAM that will physically fit into your computer is only one part of the selection process. You also should consider the performance of the RAM you select. Two types of RAM to choose from include Extended Data Out (EDO) and Synchronous Dynamic RAM (SDRAM). Each offers improved performance over older models. Check with your computer manufacturer to see which type of RAM is supported on your computer.

EDO RAM

EDO RAM uses dual-pipeline architecture that enables the unit to store data (write) at the same time it sends it out (reads). EDO RAM is limited to a bus speed of 66MHz, due to its non-parity design. EDO RAM can be purchased in 72-pin SIMMs or 168-pin DIMMs.

SDRAM

SDRAM is similar in design to EDO RAM in that it writes at the same time that it reads, vastly accelerating data along. SDRAM is a popular choice over EDO RAM due to its high bus speed of 100MHz and its low cost.

Other ROM Types

Besides the basic ROM chip discussed earlier, other ROM chips are used in computers and small computing devices. The ROM chips described below are programmable, meaning that information can be recorded onto them. These types of chips are important because they enable software that is critical to the computer start-up process to be updated.

PROM

Programmable Read-Only Memory (PROM) is a special type of chip that is manufactured without any configuration. Manufacturers can then *burn in*, or program, the chip to contain whatever configuration is needed.

EPROM

Erasable Programmable Read-Only Memory (EPROM) maintains its contents without the use of electrical power. The stored contents of an EPROM chip are erased and reprogrammed by removing the protective cover and using special equipment to reprogram the chip.

EEPROM

Electrically Erasable Programmable ROM (EEPROM) typically maintains the BIOS code, which can be updated with a disk that the BIOS manufacturer supplies.

Bus Architecture

When configuring the hardware for a new computer, you have to consider the CPU and motherboard, as discussed earlier in this chapter. In addition, you need to decide which **expansion card**s to install. Expansion cards include sound cards, video adapters, and **network interface cards**.

The expansion cards fit into expansion slots built into the motherboard. The most common exceptions are special types of computers such as laptop computers. Expansion cards and the slots they fit into can have several different connector types. The connector types are physically different from one another and have varying performance characteristics.

Some reasons why expansion slots are useful are:

❖ The earliest motherboards didn't have room for all the necessary components.

❖ The expansion slots add flexibility in the event that you need to replace a failed expansion card without having to buy a complete new motherboard.

❖ Most motherboards have several types of expansion slots. The older type of expansion slots, described in the next section, are available to support older expansion cards, protecting consumers' original investment in their hardware.

In most modern computers, you insert a new add-in, or expansion, card as follows:

WARNING

Before opening any electronic device, make sure that the power is turned off and that you are grounded. To ground yourself, use a special tool called an electrostatic discharge wrist strap. One end of the wrist strap attaches to you, and the other end clips to the metal case of the computer. Using the strap prevents you from shocking the computer and possibly causing irreversible damage.

1. Turn the power off and disconnect the power cord from the case.
2. Open the case.
3. Make sure that the card that you are trying to install is the proper type for an open expansion slot.
4. Insert the card and fasten it down.
5. Close the case.
6. Turn the power back on.

expansion card
An add-on device, such as a sound or video card, that is installed directly into an expansion slot built into a motherboard. The card must be of the same bus architecture as the slot on the motherboard.

network interface card
A device that connects a computer to the physical cable media and produces signals for transferring data.

Bus Types

Many types of buses have been introduced since the creation of the personal computer. Some, such as Industry Standard Architecture (ISA), have had long histories. Others, such as IBM's MicroChannel, were never widely adopted for one reason or another. The most widely used bus today is PCI (described earlier in the section, "The Next Generations: The Pentium Family"). Not long ago, PCI was seen as adding better performance to emerging high-speed computers. Now, even the once-sought-after PCI is considered sluggish. Accelerated Graphics Port (AGP) is one bus technology that may hold some solutions.

IBM PC

The original IBM PC supported 8-bit expansion cards that ran at the same speed as its Intel 8088 processor, 4.77MHz.

IBM PC-AT, or Industry Standard Architecture (ISA)

The IBM PC-AT introduced two major enhancements: The data path was increased (by use of a second connector) to 16 bits, and the speed of the expansion cards, usually fixed at 8.33MHz, was made independent of the processor speed.

IBM MicroChannel Architecture (MCA)

IBM's third version of a motherboard expansion bus increased the width of the bus (to 32 bits) and increased the speed. However, unlike the two original bus designs, IBM didn't freely allow all the other hardware vendors to build cards that were compatible with the MCA specifications.

Enhanced Industry Standard Architecture (EISA)

In response to IBM's proprietary MCA bus, the other major hardware vendors (led primarily by Compaq) developed this enhanced bus design.

Video Electronics Standards Association (VESA) Local Bus (VL-Bus)

The VESA Local Bus is not a replacement for the other bus types, but is instead usually used as an auxiliary bus. The primary devices that support the VL-Bus are, as might be expected by its name, video cards. However, some high-performance disk controllers were released that use this standard. Using VL-Bus technology, especially over the long term, has limitations. Major limitations of the VL-Bus include a restriction in the number of VL-Bus devices, a maximum 32-bit data path (preventing expansion to the new Intel Pentium 64-bit systems), and a clock-speed limit of only 33MHz.

megabytes per second (MBps)
A measurement of the transfer speed of a device in terms of millions of bytes per second.

Peripheral Component Interconnect (PCI)

The PCI architecture is a 32-bit wide local bus design running at 33MHz. As a local bus design, PCI devices have direct access to the CPU local bus. The PCI local bus is connected to the CPU local bus and system memory bus via a PCI-Host bridge. This is a caching device providing the interface between the CPU, memory, and PCI local bus. The cache enables the CPU to hand off executions to the PCI bus to finish freeing valuable CPU resources. The CPU can continue to fetch information from the caching bridge while the cache controller provides an expansion device access to system memory.

More than one communication on more than one bus can occur at the same time. This concurrent bus operation could not happen with previous architectures (such as VESA). Additionally, PCI expansion devices are fully independent of the CPU local bus; there is no CPU dependency at all. This design enables the CPU to be upgraded without requiring new designs for devices on the CPU or expansion busses.

Accelerated Graphics Port (AGP)

AGP was developed as a replacement for PCI. AGP uses the Intel two-chip 440LX AGP set. This set of chips sits directly on the motherboard and provides similar functionality to PCI. The new chips are responsible for handling the transfer of data between memory, the processor, and the ISA cards all at the same time. Transfer of data to and from PCI cards still occurs at 132 **megabytes per second (MBps)** at 33MHz. The significant change from PCI is in the speed of transfers to RAM and to the accelerated graphics port. Both have transfer speeds of 528MBps each. This fourfold performance increase provides a significant boost, speeding data along to high-speed CPUs and RAM.

Review Questions

1. Which processor was released in the first IBM PC?

2. How did the 8086 differ from the 8088?

3. What does *CPU speed* refer to?

4. How does SDRAM differ from EDO RAM?

5. How does real mode differ from protected mode?

6. What does *clock cycles* refer to?

7. What is Virtual Real Mode?

8. What does PROM stand for, and what is it?

9. What does the term *clock doubling* refer to?

10. How many transistors make up the original Pentium processor?

_____

11. How does asymmetrical multiprocessing differ from symmetrical?

_____

12. What is a math coprocessor?

_____

13. What is the difference between a Pentium II and a PII Celeron?

_____

14. What is the recommended amount of RAM for Windows 2000 Server?

_____

15. What is the primary difference between RAM and ROM?

_____

16. What performance gains does PCI have over the EISA bus architecture?

_____

Terms to Know

- ❑ bus architecture
- ❑ pipeline
- ❑ MMX
- ❑ HCL
- ❑ BIOS
- ❑ SOI
- ❑ VAX
- ❑ ASMP
- ❑ SMP
- ❑ I/O
- ❑ RAM
- ❑ ROM
- ❑ POST
- ❑ parity
- ❑ expansion card
- ❑ network interface card
- ❑ MBps

Chapter

2

Storing Your Files: Data Storage

store *v* : to place something in a location for later use

Every computer has a collection of files. This collection includes the files that run the operating system, the files needed to use applications, and the data files you create. All these files have to be saved somewhere, and that somewhere is called data storage. In this chapter, you will learn about these data storage options:

 Hard drives

 IDE and SCSI drives

 Disk partitions

 Disk drive configurations

 Offline storage, including floppy drives, removable drives, CDs, DVDs, and tapes

Keys to Data Storage

You can store data in a variety of formats. The format you choose depends on your needs. Some factors to consider when choosing media, or types of storage devices, are:

backup

The copying of all your data to a secondary storage option. If your primary storage option becomes unavailable, you can use backups to restore the operating system, application, and data files.

◆ Should the media be fixed or removable? Fixed media stays with the computer and offers the best performance. Removable media adds the benefits of being mobile for use with another computer or for **backup** purposes but is slower.

◆ What capacity do you need now and in the future? Are you storing a small amount of data or a large amount of data?

◆ How common is the storage media? If the storage media is not commonly used, it might be incompatible with other computer types. For example, if you received a 5¼-inch floppy disk, would it work on your computer? Would it work on most computers that are sold today?

◆ What is the cost of the storage media? Cost is often a primary concern and is measured in cost per megabyte. When read/write compact discs (CDs) first became available, most users considered them to be too expensive. Because prices have dropped so significantly, CDs are now a common storage media.

Here are some storage quantities and their equivalents:

1,024 kilobytes (KB)	= 1 megabyte (MB)
1,024MB	= 1 gigabyte (GB)
1,024GB	= 1 terabyte (TB)
1,024TB	= 1 petabyte (PB)
1,024PB	= 1 exabyte (EB)

NOTE

When specifying the amount of storage you need, keep in mind that a well-built system should also have a reliable backup solution. (Tape backup is discussed on pages 54 and 55.) The key point to remember is that if you are going to need 25GB of hard-drive storage, you will need an equivalent amount of storage space on something easily transportable—in this case, a tape—to copy your data.

Here is a summary of the most common storage media.

Media	Description	Fixed or Removable	Data Capacity
Hard drive	Storage device that stores large amounts of data. Uses a series of magnetically coated disks to store ones and zeros.	Usually fixed, but some are removable	New drives are in the gigabyte range.
Floppy disk	A removable plastic disk that stores small amounts of data. This is a popular media because of its low cost and wide availability.	Removable	Standard 3½-inch floppy disks can hold 1.44MB of data.
Removable disk	Removable disks come in several formats. Most removable disks have platters similar to hard drives. Models designed for mobile users have **PC cards**.	Removable	40MB for PC cards to 2GB for removable disks.
Compact disc	CDs are optical discs that store data by using lasers. Traditional CDs can be written to one time but read many times. Rewritable CDs can be written to several times.	Removable	CDs hold about 650MB of data.
Digital video disc	DVDs are a new type of optical disc that have a storage capacity many times that of CDs.	Removable	A single-sided DVD can hold 4GB of data. A double-sided version can hold more than 8GB of data.
Tape	Tape is a magnetic media that you commonly use for backup purposes. It is a slow media for accessing data, but its large capacity and low cost make it ideal for backup.	Removable	Tapes can range from 250MB to 100GB.

PC card

Small, thin device the size of a credit card. PC cards follow the PCMCIA (Personal Computer Memory Card International Association) standard and can be of three types. Type 1 supports RAM or ROM expansions for mobile computing devices. Type 2 is slightly thicker to accommodate modems and network cards. Type 3 is the thickest and was designed for mobile storage.

Understanding Hard Drive Basics

hard drive

Stores data as a series of ones and zeros on a series of magnetically coated disks. A positive charge indicates a one, and the absence of a charge indicates a zero.

A **hard drive** is a series of magnetically coated disks that store data. Just above each disk in the drive sits a read/write head that adds a positive charge to indicate a one, and removes the charge to indicate a zero.

The hard drive consists of these pieces:

◆ A series of disks, called platters, that are stacked together. Each platter has a hole in the middle, and a spindle is inserted through these holes. The platters rotate at high speeds measured in revolutions per minute.

◆ A read/write disk head sits on top of the disk surface and reads or writes to the disk as the disk rotates.

◆ An actuator arm, which is responsible for disk head movement, moves the read/write head across the platter to write or read data.

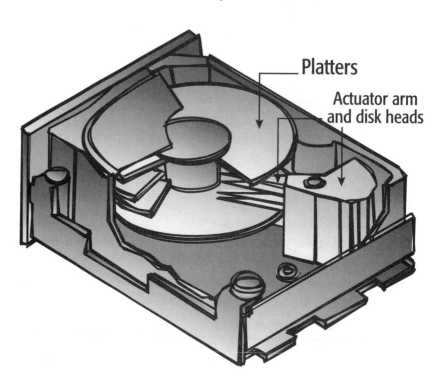

Platters

Actuator arm and disk heads

Selecting a Hard Drive

When choosing a hard drive, you should consider these options:

- ◇ Is the drive type based on a common standard such as IDE or SCSI?
- ◇ How much storage space do you need now and over the next year?
- ◇ What type of data will you be storing, and how will that affect performance?
- ◇ How critical is the data you are storing? In the event of a disk failure, how long can you afford your system to be down before the problem is fixed?
- ◇ Does the drive need any additional hardware?
- ◇ How many drives can you chain together if you need more space in the future?
- ◇ How much will everything cost?

Two of the most common drive types are IDE and SCSI. You will learn about these in more detail in the following sections.

WARNING

Because of the magnetic properties of disk drives, you should never place them near anything magnetic or near powerful electrical devices. The magnetic fields created by large power supplies can scramble data.

NOTE

Hard drives are one of the most essential forms of data storage. As with most PC components, the technology has changed significantly over the last 20 years. In the early 1980s, an average hard disk stored 10MB of data and had an average disk access time of 87 milliseconds. In addition, hard drives were extremely expensive. Now in the early 2000s, you can buy hard drives in the gigabyte range for pennies a megabyte. In addition, access time is typically 8 milliseconds or less.

Performance with IDE Drives

Integrated Drive Electronics (IDE) drives are popular because the **disk controller** and drive are integrated into a single piece of hardware. This makes IDE drives less expensive than SCSI drives (which you will learn about in the section titled "Performance with SCSI Drives"). IDE traditionally hasn't provided the same performance as SCSI—but even that has changed in recent years. New IDE standards, covered later in this section, are increasing IDE drive performance to be comparable to SCSI.

You can easily distinguish an IDE drive from a SCSI drive, because IDE uses a 40-pin connector whereas SCSI uses a 50-pin connector.

Integrated Drive Electronics (IDE)

A drive technology that integrates the drive and controller into a single piece of hardware. IDE drives are an inexpensive data-storage solution.

disk controller

Manages floppy and hard disks. It can be a separate piece of hardware, or it can be integrated with the hard drive.

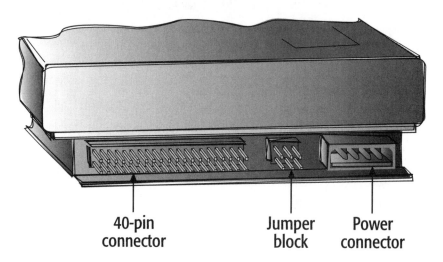

40-pin connector   Jumper block   Power connector

You can connect IDE drives to the computer in two ways:

❖ You can attach them directly to the motherboard if the IDE adapter is integrated as part of the motherboard.

❖ You can attach them to a paddleboard. The paddleboard is not a controller. It is a simple piece of hardware that facilitates the connection between the drive and the motherboard. This hardware is inexpensive, usually costing under $20.

IDE controller expansion card   Cable   Hard drive

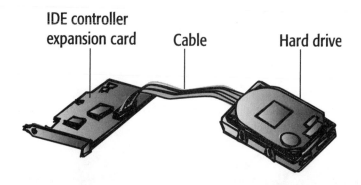

IDE technology enables you to install two drives per paddleboard. You designate one drive as the **master** drive and the second drive as a **slave** drive. **Jumpers** on the hard drive usually determine the drive designation. You should refer to the drive's documentation to see how to configure your particular drive.

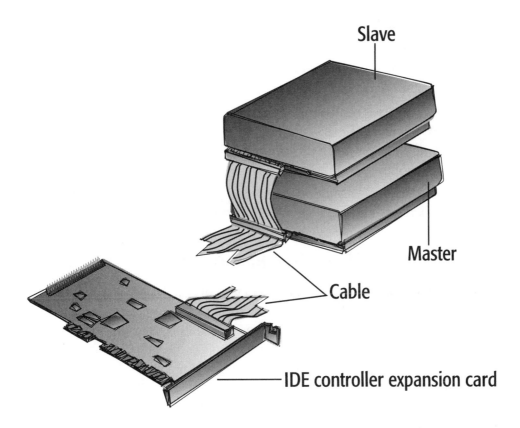

Slave

Master

Cable

IDE controller expansion card

NOTE

You can start, or boot, your computer only from the master drive.

Most IDE drives that are used today are actually **Enhanced IDE (EIDE)** drives. The original IDE specification supported drives only up to 528MB. EIDE supports drives of 27GB. IDE as the original standard specified it was limited to a maximum data transfer rate of 16.6MBps.

NOTE

In some hardware books and manuals, you will see references to RLL, MFM, and ESDI on the subject of hard drives. These standards have been obsolete for some time.

master
A device that is responsible for controlling one or more directly connected devices.

slave
A device that is controlled by another device called the master.

jumpers
Plastic-covered metal clips that are used to connect two pins on a motherboard. The connection creates a circuit that turns the setting to "on."

Enhanced IDE (EIDE)
An extended version of the IDE standard. The benefits of EIDE include the support of hard drives over 528MB, the capability to chain devices other than drives (for example, CD-ROM drives and tape drives), faster access time, and the capability to chain up to four devices.

IDE Interface Standards

IDE drives come in many formats, from 3½-inch to 5¼-inch drives, with the former being the most popular today. But physical size doesn't matter much when what really counts is the speed and accuracy of the drive. Several standards have been developed to greatly improve IDE disk-drive performance. These standards are actually protocols that the disk drive and the controller use to communicate with each another. Each protocol is made up of a set of rules that govern how communication will occur between the disk drive and the controller. Advancements in protocols can greatly improve hard disk performance. Faster communication between the hard disk and the rest of the computer means applications open more quickly and videos play more smoothly.

Several standards have been defined for IDE drives. As the standards have been released, they have typically doubled the amount of data that can be transferred. Each standard is explained below.

direct memory access (DMA)
A process wherein data moving between a device and RAM bypasses the CPU. The CPU is then free to complete other tasks.

Advanced Technology Attachment (ATA)

Advanced Technology Attachment refers to a disk standard wherein the controller responsible for moving data on and off of the disk is located in the drive. ATA is the original standard for IDE drives. ATA drives can have one or two drives connected to a single controller. As stated earlier, one of the attached drives is referred to as the master, and the second is the slave because of its dependency on the master. IDE drives slow the performance of the CPU because they must communicate directly with the CPU to access RAM. Some IDE/ATA drives have a transfer rate as high as 2MBps.

ATA-2

Someone referring to a computer with an IDE drive is more than likely talking about an Enhanced IDE drive based on the ATA-2, standard. ATA-2, or EIDE, made two significant gains over the original ATA standard. The first major advance was the capability to take advantage of the **direct memory access (DMA)** protocol. DMA improved CPU performance by accessing memory directly and avoiding the CPU whenever possible. The second enhancement was the capability of advanced BIOS to identify the type of hard drive from information on the drive itself, making installation much easier. ATA-2/EIDE has a maximum transfer rate of 16.7MBps.

Ultra-ATA

Ultra-ATA drives, like ATA-2/EIDE drives, also make use of the DMA protocol. Ultra-ATA uses a faster mode of the DMA protocol (mode 3 to be exact), which pushes transfer rates to 33MBps. As with ATA-2/EIDE, your motherboard must support Ultra-ATA.

Ultra-ATA/66 and ATA/100

The ATA/66 and the soon-to-be-released ATA/100 have been developed to complement today's larger applications and faster CPUs. With data transfer rates of 66MBps and 100MBps respectively, these two standards blur the lines between IDE and SCSI.

NOTE

The Ultra DMA/33 protocol was developed by Quantum Corporation to take advantage of faster Ultra-ATA disk drives. Ultra DMA uses **burst mode** to temporarily take control of the bus to achieve data transfer rates of 33MBps.

burst mode
The temporary increase in data transmission speeds beyond what is normal. The increase is not sustainable and usually prevents other devices from transmitting.

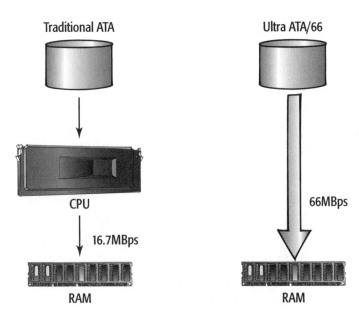

Traditional ATA

Ultra ATA/66

CPU

16.7MBps

RAM

66MBps

RAM

Performance with SCSI Drives

SCSI stands for **Small Computer System Interface** and is pronounced *scuzzy*. SCSI supports more than just drives. SCSI devices include hard disks, CD-ROM players, tape backup devices, and other hardware peripherals. Any SCSI device must communicate with the computer through a connection to a SCSI adapter. Because SCSI hard drives must be attached to an intelligent SCSI adapter, this is a more expensive disk storage solution when compared to IDE.

These are some benefits of SCSI:

◆ With a SCSI adapter, you can easily add or remove SCSI devices to or from your computer.

◆ SCSI is a high-performance storage solution with faster transfer rates and high-speed drive mechanisms.

◆ You can take advantage of new SCSI standards and adapters while maintaining compatibility with older SCSI devices.

◆ Multiple SCSI drives connected to a special adapter offer options that can greatly improve performance by enabling all the SCSI drives to work together as one, called an **array**. Arrays are important technologies for digital video editing systems.

◆ SCSI is a widely available, widely used, mature technology.

◆ SCSI drives have a long and successful history as high-performance storage solutions for high-end workstations and servers.

Small Computer System Interface (SCSI)

An interface that connects SCSI devices to the computer. This interface uses high-speed parallel technology to connect devices that include hard disks, CD-ROM players, tape backup devices, and other hardware peripherals.

array

A set of objects, all of which are the same size and type.

SCSI Standards

SCSI has been in development for nearly two decades. Since the first standard was released, SCSI has become the premier storage system for servers. Although other drive systems such as IDE have improved dramatically in performance, SCSI is still the first choice of network administrators despite its higher cost. SCSI decisions come down to the SCSI standard that will be supported on your workstations and servers. The bus speed can significantly affect performance, so select wisely.

The table below outlines the SCSI standards.

SCSI Standard	Bus Width	MBps Bus Speed	Max. Number of Supported Devices
SCSI-1	8-bit	5	8
Fast SCSI (SCSI-2)	8-bit	8	8
Fast and Wide SCSI (SCSI-2)	16-bit	20	16
Ultra SCSI	8-bit	20	8–16
Ultra Wide SCSI (SCSI-3)	16-bit	40	8–16
Ultra2 SCSI	8-bit	40	8
Wide Ultra2 SCSI	16-bit	80	16
Ultra3 SCSI, or Ultra160	16-bit	160	16
Ultra320	16-bit	320	16

SCSI-1 and SCSI-2

The original SCSI-1 standard was introduced in 1986. SCSI-1 had an 8-bit bus with a 5MBps transfer speed. It wasn't until 1994 that SCSI-2 was ratified. SCSI-2 is essentially SCSI-1 with the addition of some options. The most significant options were Fast SCSI and Wide SCSI. These two options could be used with compatible devices to boost transfer speeds to 20MBps. A SCSI device connected to a SCSI-2 adapter will still function but at the lower speed of 8MBps.

SCSI-3

SCSI-3 was developed to overcome several limitations of SCSI-2. SCSI-3 increased the total number of SCSI devices connected together from 8 in SCSI-2 to 16. The next problem was much more difficult to solve. SCSI-2 had a cable distance limitation of 3 meters. The limitation was especially a problem as the data transfer speeds increased because there was no way for SCSI devices to calculate transmission delays. Keeping the signals in order was difficult. SCSI-3 improved on this design by adding timing information to the data being sent. The additional timing information would keep the order of the data intact.

Ultra3 SCSI and Ultra320

Ultra3 SCSI takes SCSI-3 technology one giant leap forward by doubling the transfer rate to 160MBps. Like SCSI-3, Ultra3 SCSI uses timing information in the signal, but it adds a second piece of timing information to push double the amount of data.

Ultra320 is a similar specification to Ultra3 SCSI with the exception that it has a 16-bit wide bus that can deliver a whopping 320MBps transfer rate.

NOTE

Be sure to check which SCSI technology your computer will support. Some older implementations are not compatible with the newer Ultra Wide SCSI or Ultra3 SCSI. Also, keep in mind that if you use an older SCSI drive on a much faster Ultra3 SCSI bus, the SCSI bus will be only as fast as the older SCSI drive. So, if your drive is Ultra SCSI, but your bus supports Ultra3, the SCSI bus will operate at a transfer rate of 20MBps rather than the 160MBps supported by Ultra3.

SCSI Termination

Traditionally, SCSI adapters enable you to **daisy chain** up to seven devices off of each controller. The controller contains **termination**. You must also terminate the last device in the SCSI chain. The termination at the beginning and the end forms the SCSI chain. Some devices use active termination, which means you don't have to do anything. Other devices require you to manually remove the termination from devices in the middle of the chain and ensure that the last device is terminated.

---

daisy chain

To connect a series of devices, one after the other. When signals are transmitted on a daisy chain, they go to the first device, then to the second, and so on, until termination is reached.

termination

The use of a terminator at both ends of a SCSI daisy chain to keep data signals from bouncing back on the SCSI bus after they reach the end. The terminator is a small plastic connector that has a resistor (ceramic-based material that absorbs electricity) inside of it.

The graphic below illustrates the daisy-chain technique used by SCSI and the locations of the termination. The ID numbers listed next to the drives are an important part of SCSI devices. Each SCSI device must have a unique address. The ID is used to address data to the correct device in the chain. Depending on the type of SCSI technology you are using, the ID can range from 0 to 15.

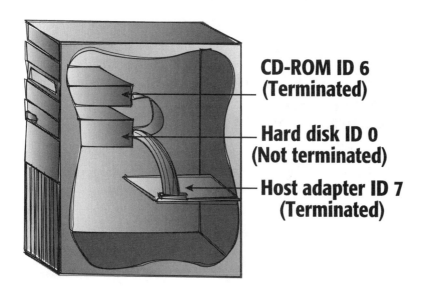

**CD-ROM ID 6
(Terminated)**

**Hard disk ID 0
(Not terminated)**

**Host adapter ID 7
(Terminated)**

NOTE

On internal SCSI cables, the terminators are built into the ends of the cables.

Organizing Disks

You can organize disk drives in several ways. One way is to use multiple hard drives. Each hard drive has an assigned drive identifier such as C, D, etc. Usually, for this type of configuration, each **physical hard drive** represents just one storage location identified with a letter.

Another alternative is to organize the disk into **volumes** on the same physical disk. This method requires the creation of partitions. Each partition that is created makes a physical change to the format of the disk. The usable space defined through partitions is considered the **logical drive.** You can define disk space however you want, regardless of the physical size of the disk. Consider these examples:

physical hard drive
The physical (or real, as opposed to conceptual) drive; for example, drive 0 or drive 1 in a two-drive configuration.

volume
A part of a physical disk that is identified by a single drive label.

logical drive
Based on how you partition your physical drive, the area of the extended partition can be organized into multiple drives. Each drive is assigned a DOS identifier from D to Z.

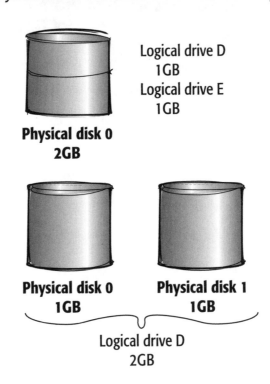

Logical drive D
1GB
Logical drive E
1GB

Physical disk 0
2GB

Physical disk 0
1GB

Physical disk 1
1GB

Logical drive D
2GB

In the first example, you have a single 2GB physical disk that is partitioned into two logical drives. Each logical drive is 1GB.

In the second example, you have two physical disks that are each 1GB. In this case, the two drives are configured as a single 2GB logical drive by using software.

NOTE

To create logical drives, you can use the DOS FDISK program, third-party utilities such as Partition Magic, Disk Administrator (if you are using Windows NT), or Disk Management (if you are using Windows 2000).

Understanding Partition Types

Before you create your partitions, you should first understand these disk concepts:

- ❖ Active and boot partitions
- ❖ Primary partition
- ❖ Extended partition

Active and Boot Partitions

When you start your computer, the start-up process looks for the partition that is marked as active. This is almost always the C drive. The **active partition** should have the system files used by your computer to load the operating system. The partition that contains the operating system files is the **boot partition**. Normally, the active partition and the boot partition are the same.

Primary Partition

Traditionally, the first partition you define is the **primary partition**. With the DOS operating system, you can have one primary partition. The primary partition is assigned all the disk space you allocate to it. For example, if you were to create the first partition as a primary partition and allocate 1GB of space, the first drive by default (the primary drive) would be the C drive and would consist of 1GB of usable space.

With the Windows 2000 operating system, you can have up to four partitions per physical disk. This can consist of four primary partitions, or three primary partitions and one **extended partition**.

Each physical partition can have only one drive letter assigned to it.

Extended Partition

An extended partition is a physical partition that cannot be used as a boot partition. Within an extended partition, you can create up to 23 logical drives. For example, you could create a single extended partition that is 1GB in size. Within the extended partition, you could then create four logical drives—D, E, F, and G—that were each 250MB.

active partition
The partition that the computer identifies as the one that will be used to boot up the computer and load the operating system.

boot partition
Synonymous with the active partition on a disk. The boot partition contains the necessary files to start the operating system on the computer.

primary partition
The first and bootable partition you create on a hard drive.

extended partition
A non-bootable partition containing DOS logical drives.

A Primer on Disk Drive Configurations

Redundant Array of Inexpensive (or Independent) Disks (RAID)

A method of using a series of hard disks as an array of drives. Some RAID implementations improve performance. Others improve performance and provide fault tolerance.

fault tolerance

The use of hardware and software to prevent the loss of data in the event of a system, hardware, or power disruption or failure.

Several disk drive configurations are available. You can create the configurations listed below by using software and hardware. Many of these types of configurations are called **Redundant Array of Inexpensive (or Independent) Disks (RAID)**. RAID storage systems require two or more disks, depending on the configuration. Each configuration has a specific level identifier that indicates the type of configuration. RAID systems are critical for servers because they provide improved performance, in some cases **fault tolerance.**

Volume Set

A volume set extends the size of a partition beyond a single physical drive. This is not a RAID configuration but is often the result of a RAID configuration. Disks that are used in a RAID configuration are physically separate from the RAID controller but appear as one large drive to software such as Windows 2000.

Disk Stripe Set—RAID Level 0

A disk stripe set combines several logical partitions of the same size into a single logical disk. Data is striped evenly over each partition. Performance is excellent in this RAID configuration, but there is no way to recover data in the event of a hard-disk failure.

RAID Level 0 is a good choice for digital-video editors and digital animators who need the storage capacity of many hard drives without sacrificing performance. Because of the improved performance inherent in RAID 0, one might consider it an option for disk-intensive applications such as databases. But keep in mind that RAID 0 provides no fault tolerance. If a disk fails, all data is lost on all drives!

NOTE

On most computers that are purchased, the operating system and other software are already installed. The hard drive is usually represented by a single letter, which typically is C. Rarely, if ever, are other configurations present, regardless of the size of the drive. But there are other configurations to consider that can add better performance or higher insurance that the data will be protected.

Mirrored Set—RAID Level 1

A mirrored set contains a primary partition and a secondary partition. Anytime data is written to the first partition, it is automatically written to the second partition. RAID Level 1 is often used to protect the drive where the operating system is located. The mirrored set provides the added fault tolerance needed for servers. It is not typically recommended that mirrored sets be created for all drives. Mirrored sets cost twice as much as any other array to implement because for each disk you want to partition you need a second disk of the exact same size.

Stripe Set with Parity Drive—RAID Level 3

A stripe set with a **parity** drive is similar to a stripe set with a parity stripe. In a stripe set with parity drive, the parity information is stored on a single drive as opposed to being striped across all drives.

Stripe Set with Parity Stripe—RAID Level 5

A stripe set with a parity stripe is similar to a stripe set, but it contains a parity stripe across all drives. This gives you the benefits of a stripe set while also offering fault tolerance. If one of the drives fails, the parity information from the other drives can be used to rebuild the data onto a new drive. RAID Level 5 is the most common configuration because of the low cost, ease of recovery of a failed disk, and performance. In cases where data availability is critical, such as databases, RAID Level 5 is the preferred choice. It adds a high level of reliability, good performance, and it is relatively reasonable in cost.

TIP

When deciding on a disk drive configuration, always consult the manufacturer of the computer first. Not only might you get some free instruction on the best type of configuration for your needs, you might even get some help implementing your new configuration.

parity
In the context of a stripe set, a series of mathematical calculations based on the data stored. If a disk fails, the stored parity information can be used to rebuild the data.

Volume Sets

A volume set extends the size of a single partition. For example, assume that you created a single partition on your 1GB physical drive. You used the partition to store a database that is approaching 1GB. You can add a second physical drive, and with the free space create a volume set.

In volume sets, the data is written sequentially, so you can extend volume sets at any time without having to back up the data, create the volume set, and then restore the data. This makes volume sets an easy way to quickly and temporarily handle a shortage of disk space until you replace your disk drive with a larger drive.

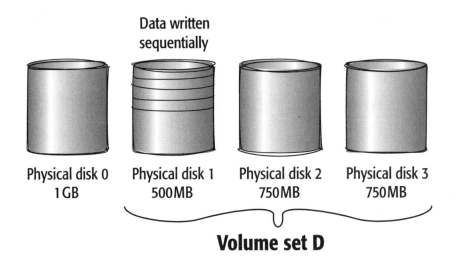

Data written
sequentially

| Physical disk 0 | Physical disk 1 | Physical disk 2 | Physical disk 3 |
| 1GB | 500MB | 750MB | 750MB |

Volume set D

Pros and Cons

Consider these factors when using volume sets:

Same-size partitions?   No. With volume sets, the partitions within the volume set do not have to be the same size.

Performance increase?   No. Volume sets write data sequentially, so there is no performance increase.

Fault tolerance?   No. Because volume sets contain no parity information, they are not fault tolerant. This means that if any physical drive within the volume set fails, the entire volume set is unusable.

NOTE

With Windows NT and Windows 2000, you can have up to 32 disks within a volume set or spanned volume respectively.

Disk Stripe Sets

In a disk stripe set, or RAID Level 0, you define logical partitions of the same size as a stripe set. There must be at least two partitions participating in a stripe set. After you create a stripe set, data is written across the set in stripes. The benefit of this disk configuration is that it enables you to take advantage of multiple disk **I/O channel**s for improved performance.

Input/Output (I/O) channel
A circuit that provides a path for an input or output device to communicate with the processor.

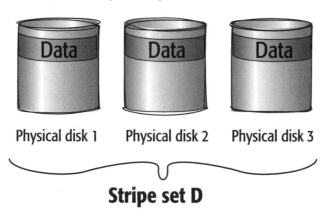

Physical disk 1   Physical disk 2   Physical disk 3

Stripe set D

Pros and Cons

Consider these factors when using stripe sets:

Same-size partitions?	Yes. Logical partitions have to be the same size in a stripe set.
Performance increase?	Yes. If the stripe set is located on multiple I/O channels, you will see a performance increase.
Fault tolerance?	No. Because stripe sets contain no parity information, if any drive within the stripe set fails, the entire stripe set will be lost. In this case, you would restore your data from your most recent backup.

TIP

If you want fault tolerance, it is technically possible to mirror a stripe set. This feature is available only on Windows NT and Windows 2000. The stripe set must be created using special RAID hardware. When NT or 2000 boot up, the stripe set appears as a single logical drive and not multiple physical disks even though the latter is true. Using the Disk Administrator in Windows NT or Disk Management software in Windows 2000, you create a software-based mirror set of two striped sets. The problem with software-based mirrored drives is that they are much slower than hardware-based drives. Also, software-based RAID configurations are prone to errors, which could cause data loss. It is not possible to mirror two stripe sets that were created with software.

Mirrored Sets

A mirrored set, RAID Level 1, consists of a primary drive and a secondary drive. Anytime data is written to the primary drive, it is copied (or mirrored) to the secondary drive. The benefit of a mirrored set is that if a disk fails, you do not lose any data.

There are two types of mirrored sets:

Disk mirroring   Uses one controller with two disks

Disk duplexing   Uses two controllers and two disks

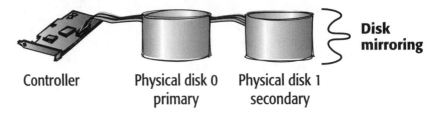

| Controller | Physical disk 0 primary | Physical disk 1 secondary | Disk mirroring |

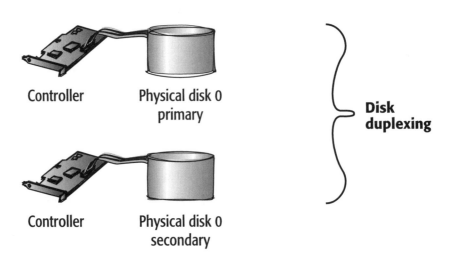

Controller   Physical disk 0 primary

Controller   Physical disk 0 secondary

Disk duplexing

Pros and Cons

Consider these factors when using mirrored sets:

Same-size partitions?	Yes. In a mirrored set, both logical partitions have to be the same size.
Performance increase?	Yes and no. With disk mirroring, performance decreases on writes, because one controller must write to both drives. With disk duplexing, you see a slight performance increase, because you are using two separate I/O channels.
Fault tolerance?	Yes. Mirrored sets are fault tolerant.

Stripe Sets with Parity Drive

A stripe set with a parity drive, RAID Level 3, arranges logical drives of equal size into a stripe set. A separate drive stores parity information. In the event that a data drive fails, the parity information and the data on the functioning drives are used in a mathematical calculation that can reconstruct the lost data.

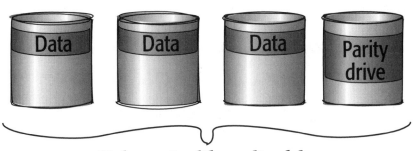

Stripe set with parity drive

Pros and Cons

Consider these factors when using stripe sets with a parity drive:

Same-size partitions?	Yes. Within any stripe set, partitions must be equal in size.
Performance increase?	Yes. Each I/O channel that the stripe set uses increases the performance of the stripe set.
Fault tolerance?	Yes and no. As long as only one drive fails (assuming that the parity drive isn't the failed drive), the stripe set with the parity drive is fault tolerant. If two or more drives fail, you must re-create the stripe set with the parity drive and then restore the data from the most recent backup.

NOTE

Although most RAID configurations are implemented using special RAID hardware, RAID 3 is not typically available as a software-based option. Windows NT and 2000, for example, only support RAID 0, 1, and 5.

Stripe Sets with Parity Stripe

A stripe set with a parity stripe, RAID 5, arranges logical drives of equal size into a stripe set. Each drive within the set has a parity stripe. As with stripe sets with a parity drive, discussed in the preceding section, the parity information and data from the functioning disks can be used to re-create a failed disk. Unlike the previous RAID examples, RAID 5 requires a minimum of 3 disks with a maximum limitation of 32 disks.

Stripe set with parity stripe

Pros and Cons

Consider these factors when using stripe sets with a parity stripe:

Same-size partitions?	Yes. Within any stripe set, partitions must be equal in size.
Performance increase?	Yes. Each I/O channel that the stripe set uses increases the performance of the stripe set.
Fault tolerance?	Yes and no. As long as only one drive fails, the stripe set with the parity stripe is fault tolerant. If two or more drives fail, you must re-create the stripe set with the parity stripe and then restore the data from the most recent backup.

NOTE

RAID 5 is not supported on Windows 2000 in the same way that it is on Windows NT. Windows 2000 distinguishes between basic disks and dynamic disks. Basic disks have the same capabilities as hard disks did in Windows NT with the exception of RAID 5. Windows 2000 introduces dynamic disks that do support RAID 5. Dynamic disks minimize the need to restart Windows 2000 when a drive change such as creating a RAID 5 volume or mirror set has occurred. The RAID 5 drive configuration is supported by Windows NT and is considered a software implementation of RAID 5. With software implementations of RAID, you can use any disk drives that are of equal size.

Types of Offline Data Storage

Hard drives are considered **online data storage**. This means that data is readily available at high speed. You do not need to do anything special to access online storage.

Another type of storage is called **offline storage**. Offline storage means that the data is not readily available without some type of user intervention. Offline storage is useful for transferring data between computers, storing large amounts of data, or providing a means of backup.

Offline storage has become a major market for manufacturers as people take information and devices on the road. The mobile workforce demands that information be readily accessible on desktop computers, laptops, and in handheld devices. Many products are available that offer incredible performance, reliability, and capacity. Some common forms of offline storage are floppy disks, **compact discs**, and tapes.

Recently, removable disks with storage capacities from 40MB to 2GB have revolutionized computing. In addition to removable disks, **digital video disc, or digital versatile disc, (DVD)** technology is also changing the way computer applications, audio, and high-quality digital video are stored and distributed.

NOTE

Near-line storage accessibility is somewhere between online and offline storage. For example, a magneto-optical drive that uses a jukebox to store data is not as readily available as a hard drive but can access data without user intervention.

Distribution Media for Applications

In the not so recent past, almost all applications were distributed on floppy disks. Now the most common distribution media is CD. If you don't have a CD player (which you should upgrade to) and you buy an application that comes on a CD, look for a card that enables you to order the application on disk. You can usually do so for a minimal fee.

Note that not all applications have this option. For example, an application with 100,000 pieces of clip art that comes on four CDs would be impractical to distribute on floppy disks.

online data storage
Holds data that is immediately available and can be quickly accessed, as is the case with hard disks.

offline storage
Holds data that is currently unavailable. You use offline storage to store large amounts of infrequently accessed data or to store computer backups.

compact disc (CD)
A plastic or optical disk that can be read using lasers. All compact discs have a maximum storage capacity of 650MB.

digital video disc or digital versatile disc (DVD)
Based on the same technology as CD-ROM, DVD uses a much smaller laser and is able to copy many times more the amount of data. DVDs can hold at least 4.7GB of data and as much as 8.5GB.

Floppy Drives

Floppy drives, which use floppy disks, provide a convenient way of transferring small amounts of data from one computer to another. Traditionally floppy disks came in two sizes: 3½-inch format and 5¼-inch format.

High-density 3½-inch floppy disks can hold up to 1.44MB of data, and high-density 5¼-inch floppy disks can hold up to 720KB of data. For the most part, 5¼-inch floppy disks are obsolete. There is also a standard for low-density disks, but these disks are also obsolete.

For transferring small amounts of data, the floppy disk is still an extremely popular option. Floppy disks are inexpensive. The standard is mature, and the media is fault tolerant. Not that anyone recommends it, but some Information Services (IS) professionals toss them about like Frisbees, without any damage to the disk or data.

High-Capacity Floppy Drives

The 3½-inch floppy drive has a long history that is about to come to an end. New floppy standards outperform the 1.44MB capacity of the floppy drive in every aspect. The Imation SuperDisk LS120 and Sony HiFD both offer larger storage capacities and transfer rates five to eight times faster than regular floppies. The SuperDisk LS120 provides 120MB of storage on a single disk, is inexpensive, and has had great success as a replacement to floppy drives in computers from almost all leading manufacturers. The Sony HiFD supports transfer rates up to 1MBps on a 200MB disk. The key feature of both these drives is that they are backward compatible with 1.44MB floppy disks. Most removable disk drives, such as the Iomega Zip, will not work with floppy disks.

Removable Disk Drives

Ten years ago, removable disk drives were the storage choice of graphic designers. When a graphic designer was ready to send artwork to a printer, the artwork would be placed on a 20MB or 40MB removable disk and sent on its way. The mobility of the original removable drives along with their storage capacity proved to be very valuable. A company could invest in an in-house graphics designer for all its original artwork needs.

Removable disks are now more valuable than ever for many more purposes than just printing. Their storage capacities and the variety of models available have made them attractive to many consumers (in addition to graphic artists).

Zip Drives

The Iomega Zip drive is a low-cost, high-volume removable disk drive solution. The Zip disk is about the same size as a floppy disk and uses a similar magnetically coated Mylar disk, called a cookie, as a floppy. Besides these two similarities, the Zip disk is different from a standard floppy. The Zip can store 100MB of data and spin the disk 10 times faster than a floppy. That translates into more data being written to and read from the Zip. Iomega has also introduced an upgraded version of the Zip at 250MB per disk. The Zip 250 does support the older Zip 100 disks.

Large Removable Drives

There are several drive options that support 1- and 2GB disks. These disk drives also support much faster transfer rates than their smaller counterparts such as the Zip and the SuperDisk and are comparable to and sometimes faster than hard drives. The Iomega Jazz is available in 2GB and 1GB drives. The Jazz 2GB drive is backward compatible with the 1GB disks. The Orb is a 2.2GB product by Castlewood that sports similar features.

NOTE

If you are in the market for a Zip drive, consider buying a USB drive. USB operates at 10MBps, which takes full advantage of the USB-based Zip 250's transfer rate of 1.2MBps. That can be a significant performance improvement over a parallel Zip drive. The parallel Zip 250 has a maximum transfer rate of 800KBps. That is a nearly 50 percent decrease in performance!

Compact Discs

The compact disc (CD) has become a popular storage media. They use an optical drive to read data. This is different from the magnetic media that standard hard disks use. This means that CDs are not susceptible to magnetism as hard drives and floppy disks are.

CDs offer several advantages:

❖ They can store up to 650MB of data.

❖ They are inexpensive to reproduce.

❖ They are lightweight.

❖ If handled properly, they are durable and can archive data for 10 years or more.

compact disc-recordable (CD-R)

A compact disc that can have data recorded onto it once using a laser and can be read many times.

CD-Recordable

Traditionally, CD devices were read-only. Now **CD-Recordable (CD-R)**, or CD read/write devices, have decreased dramatically in price and are increasing in popularity. They are considered Write Once–Read Many (WORM) devices.

CD-Rs are excellent drives for archiving data. Many companies must keep data for three or more years. Maintaining data on the hard drive of a server is impractical, as it can lead to large stores of data that are rarely if ever used. CD-Rs enable companies to write any set of data that they select to the CD and to archive that data for future use.

Writing to a CD requires the use of a strong laser. The laser in a CD-R heats the crystal material in a CD to a temperature between 900 and 1,300 degrees Fahrenheit. The heat causes the crystals to melt, creating a deformity that reflects less light. The less reflective area is called a pit and is interpreted by the computer as a one. A reflective area is called a land and is interpreted by the computer as a zero.

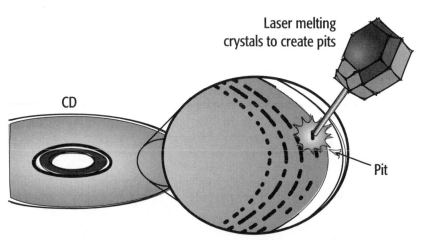

Laser melting crystals to create pits

CD

Pit

CD-Rewritable (CD-RW)

CD-Rewritable (CD-RW) discs can be written to several times. CD-RW drives are excellent because they will work not only with CD-RW discs (which cost as much as $20), but also with CD-R discs, which are less expensive. If you are considering CD-RW as an option, take into consideration that CD-RW discs are not readable on conventional CD-ROM drives. If you need to use the CD on a CD-ROM drive, you will need to use a CD-R disc.

CD-RW works the same way as CD-R at writing data to disc. Rewrites require that a second laser be used by the CD-RW drive to change the nonreflective areas (the pits) to be reflective. The laser heats the desired area to 400 degrees Fahrenheit. That is just enough heat to loosen the crystals in the disc. As the crystals cool, they assume their original structure, which reflects light.

> **compact disc-rewritable (CD-RW)**
> A compact disc that can have data rewritten to it several times using lasers. Lasers record data to the disc like a CD-R, but slightly less powerful lasers are used to erase the data. Even weaker lasers are used to read the data.

Digital Video Discs

Digital video discs have long been sought after because of their high storage capacity and diverse usage. Only recently has DVD technology become afford- able for home entertainment systems, desktop computers, and laptops.

DVD's potential is in its data storage. DVDs can store a minimum of 4.7GB to as much as 8.5GB on a double-sided DVD. Coupled with its low cost per disc, DVD is an excellent choice for digital video and audio. Movies recorded onto DVD often include additional sound tracks that will play across sophisticated stereo and surround-sound systems, giving the movie a better-than-theater experience. In addition, the picture quality of DVD can be twice that of VHS tapes. And there is still room for more. Many movies on DVD also come with additional multime- dia presentations and interactive games that can be played on a computer with a DVD drive.

DVD Platforms

DVD has many variations. Like CD-ROM technology before, DVD is versatile, meeting needs from video media to data archiving. The platforms are as follows:

> **DVD-ROM** (Read-Only Media)   Available as read-only. A typical DVD-ROM holds 4.7GB of data—enough space for a full-length movie.

DVD-Video   A standard designed for the video industry. DVD-Video is read-only, like DVD-ROM, but requires a reader that is compatible with the Content Scrambling System (CSS). CSS is used to prevent people from illegally duplicating the video.

DVD-RAM   A rewritable DVD format that will write as much as 2.6GB of data per side.

throughput
The amount of data that can be transferred in a set period of time.

NOTE

DVD is a sought-after replacement for CD technology, not only because of its storage capacity, but also because DVD drives are backward compatible with CDs. There is no loss in investment for users to migrate to DVD.

Tape Drives

Tape drives use a tape cartridge to store data. Tapes are a popular form of backup, because a single tape can hold huge amounts of data. Backups are critical for any computer, because you value your data. Any computer professional can tell you many horror stories of failed drives with outdated or no backups. The good news is, there are people who usually can recover your data. The bad news is, this method of data recovery is terribly expensive.

Although tape provides high-capacity storage, it is a slow medium to read from and write to. This is not typically a problem when backing up data, because backups are often scheduled for periods of inactivity. When choosing a tape backup device, you should consider these questions:

- ◇ How much storage space do you need?
- ◇ What **throughput** do you need for the backup?
- ◇ What is the cost of the tape device and the tapes themselves?
- ◇ What backup software is compatible with the drive you select?
- ◇ Does your computer operating system have a driver for the tape drive, and is the drive on the operating system's Hardware Compatibility List (a list that specifies what hardware can be used with the software)?

Tape Backup Strategy

Tape backups are only as good as the backup strategy in place. There are several methods of backing up data. The key to the strategies is to be able to recover data quickly and without more than a day's loss. An effective strategy requires the following components:

- ❖ Daily tape backups with a full backup at least once a week
- ❖ Regular use of a cleaning tape
- ❖ Monitoring of backup logs for failed backups
- ❖ Replacement of heavily used tapes after six months
- ❖ Offsite storage of tapes

In addition, a good backup strategy should cover at least a month's worth of data. This strategy requires at least 19 tapes. Four tapes are used for Monday through Thursday. Three tapes are used for the first, second, and third Friday of the same month. The last tape is used on the fourth Friday of the month. This tape is archived for the year. At the end of a 12-month cycle, you should have a full backup on tape for each month. This ensures that you can restore the data from any month of the past year. In addition, the latest four weeks can also be restored.

Review Questions

1. The two most common types of hard drives are:

   _____

   _____

2. True or false: IDE drives require a separate IDE adapter for installation.

   _____

3. You can easily identify an IDE hard drive because it uses a _____ -pin adapter.

4. You can easily identify a SCSI hard drive because it uses a _____ -pin adapter.

5. Which drive type typically offers better performance, IDE or SCSI?

   _____

6. What is the difference between a physical drive and a logical drive?

   _____

7. Define *volume set*.

   _____

8. List three disk drive configurations that are fault tolerant.

   _____

   _____

   _____

9. What is the difference between disk mirroring and disk duplexing?

_____

10. True or false: If two drives in a stripe set with parity fail, you can still recover the stripe set if it consists of six or more drives.

_____

11. True or false: In a drive configured as a stripe set with parity, all the partitions within the stripe set must be the same size.

_____

12. What is the difference between online and offline storage?

_____

13. How much data can be stored on a CD?

_____

14. What is the advantage of using a SuperDisk or HiFD floppy disk over a removable disk?

_____

15. Why might DVD replace CD-ROM technology?

_____

16. True or false: You should keep all floppy disks away from any magnetic field.

_____

Terms to Know
- ❏ volume
- ❏ logical drive
- ❏ active partition
- ❏ boot partition
- ❏ primary partition
- ❏ extended partition
- ❏ RAID
- ❏ fault tolerance
- ❏ parity
- ❏ I/O channel
- ❏ online data storage
- ❏ offline storage
- ❏ CD
- ❏ DVD
- ❏ CD-R
- ❏ CD-RW
- ❏ throughput

Chapter

3

Data Movement: Input/Output Devices

move·ment *n* : the act of moving something in a
particular direction

Computers process, manipulate, and send data according to instructions from a user. Each computer has input and output interfaces to enable you to connect input or output devices. The input device enables information to enter the computer, and the output device enables information to exit the computer. Without providing the capability to enter or extract information, the computer is nothing more than a box with colored lights. In this chapter, you will learn about these input/output ports and devices:

  Serial, parallel, and USB ports

  Monitors

  Keyboards

  Mouse

  Modems

  ISDN adapters

  Printers

  PC cards

Understanding Serial Ports

A serial port is either an input or output port that supports **serial communication**. Serial communication is the process of transmitting and processing data one bit at a time.

Data transmitted in a serial fashion can be sent by using one of two methods: synchronous data transmission or asynchronous data transmission.

In synchronous data transmission, a **clock signal** regulates the flow of data over a cable or wire. This transmission method is used when large amounts of data must be transferred in a short period of time.

Asynchronous data transmission uses a single information bit, referred to as the **start bit**, to tell the computer when to start transmitting data and a **stop bit** to tell it when to stop. This method is used when transferring smaller amounts of data. Both the computer sending the data and the one receiving the data must agree on the number of start and stop bits for communication to take place.

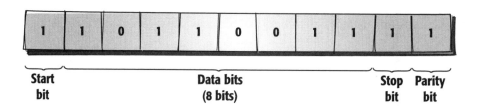

| Start bit | Data bits (8 bits) | Stop bit | Parity bit |

Most PCs are manufactured with two serial ports that are used to connect serial devices, such as a mouse, modem, or line printer, by way of a serial cable.

Serial port connectors come in two types: 9-pin and 25-pin. A 9-pin connector is referenced as DB-9 and is a common serial connector for mice and handheld devices such as the PalmPilot. DB-25 refers to 25-pin connectors and is frequently used by external modems.

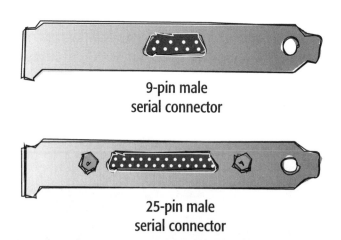

9-pin male
serial connector

25-pin male
serial connector

serial communication

The transmission of data one bit at a time.

clock signal

Controls the rate at which synchronous data is transmitted.

start bit

The bit that synchronizes the clock on the computer receiving the data. In asynchronous data transmission, the start bit is a space.

stop bit

The bit that identifies the end of the character being transmitted so that the character is clearly recognized.

Understanding Parallel Ports

A parallel port is either an input or output port that supports **parallel communication**. Parallel communication occurs when data is transmitted and processed one **byte** at a time. Eight transmission lines carry the signal. Parallel communication is typically faster than serial communication.

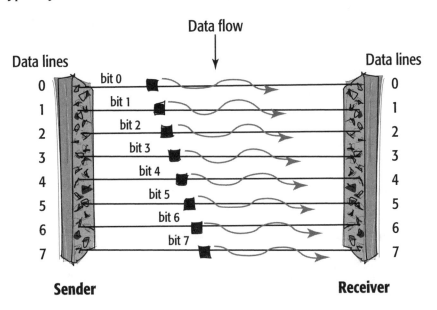

Data flow

Data lines

bit 0
bit 1
bit 2
bit 3
bit 4
bit 5
bit 6
bit 7

Data lines

Sender　　　　　　　　　　**Receiver**

Most parallel ports today are based on the **Extended Capabilities Port (ECP)** or **Enhanced Parallel Port (EPP)** standards that support data transfer speeds of more than 2MBps.

Parallel communication is often used to connect printers. Although parallel communication is not the fastest communication method, it is a cost-effective solution. Almost all computers today are built with a parallel port.

Besides printers, parallel ports can also support external storage devices (discussed in Chapter 2, "Storing Your Files: Data Storage"). External devices that communicate using the parallel port connect via a 25-pin female connector.

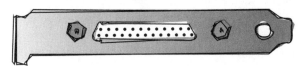

25-pin female parallel connection

NOTE

The original parallel port was designed to send information in one direction to a printer. Standards were later developed to improve the capabilities of the parallel port by allowing communication to occur in both directions and supporting multiple devices on the same port.

parallel communication
The process of transmitting and processing data one byte (eight bits) at a time.

byte
A single binary character, or eight bits.

Extended Capabilities Port (ECP)
The standard developed for parallel communication by Hewlett-Packard and Microsoft to allow for data transfer rates of more than 2MBps. In addition to the high data transfer rates, it allows for bidirectional operation.

Enhanced Parallel Port (EPP)
The standard developed for parallel communication by Intel, Xircom, and Zenith Data Systems to allow for data transfer rates of more than 2MBps. It supports bidirectional operation of attached devices and an addressing scheme.

Understanding USB Ports

Universal Serial Bus (USB) is a new external bus technology for high-speed connection of peripheral devices. The USB specification was published in 1996 through the joint work of several major computer companies. USB support has become widespread for many reasons.

USB offers support for almost every kind of external computer device known. Monitors, mice, joysticks, printers, scanners, cameras, storage devices, modems, and more can all be connected via USB. A single built-in USB controller can support up to 127 devices. The devices can be connected via additional **USB hubs**, daisy chained from one device to another, or both.

USB can transfer data at up to 12 **megabits per second (Mbps)**. That makes it an excellent choice for data-intensive applications such as video. Slower devices such as mice operate at 1.5Mbps. In addition, USB offers the following enhancements:

- ❖ Capable of self-identifying devices that are attached.
- ❖ Hot-pluggable—devices can be added or removed while the computer is running.
- ❖ Power can be supplied by the USB for devices that do not have a separate power supply.

How USB Works

Inside a computer that has USB ports, there is a USB controller. The controller is responsible for interfacing between software and hardware. Inside the controller, there is a host hub that contains two USB connectors, or ports. The cables that attach to the USB ports have four wires. One wire supplies power and another is used as an electrical ground. The two remaining wires are used for signaling.

When a USB device connects to the computer, it is automatically detected by the USB controller and is required to identify itself. After the device is recognized, the USB controller assigns it an ID. During this initial communication, the USB controller determines a device's **bandwidth** priority. Devices that require no interruption, such as video, have the highest priority. In contrast, printers, which send large amounts of data but don't care when it gets there, have the lowest priority.

USB hub

A connectivity device that provides multiple USB connections so that several USB devices can communicate with the computer.

---

megabits per second (Mbps)

A measurement of the amount of data, in the millions of bits per second, being transferred.

---

bandwidth

The capacity of a network line to carry information. Bandwidth is best thought of as a highway; four lanes support more traffic than two and have fewer slowdowns. One of the few basic rules of modern networking is that more bandwidth is always better.

NOTE

USB is not supported on all operating systems. Windows NT and the first releases of Windows 95 do not support USB. The latest release of Windows 95 had limited support for USB. Currently, Windows 98 and Windows 2000 have full support for USB.

Understanding Monitors

The monitor is the most common type of output device. It may look like a simple television, but it is not. The monitor enables the human eye to interact with the computer. Without a monitor, the computer's output capabilities would be very limited; imagine if the only output available were in printed or audible form. The monitor enables the computer to translate computer data into text and graphics and display them.

Several types of computer monitors are available, based on different technology standards. The internals of the devices are essentially the same. They all contain an **electron gun** that shoots electrically charged particles called electrons toward the back of the monitor screen. The screen is coated with a phosphorous material that glows when an electron runs into it. A beam is made up of these electrons that span across (horizontal) and down (vertical) the screen, forming an image.

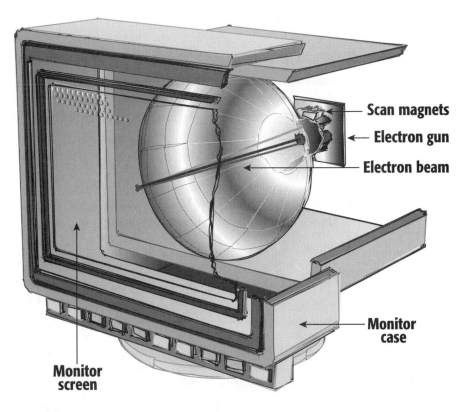

— **Scan magnets**

← **Electron gun**

— **Electron beam**

— **Monitor case**

Monitor screen

electron gun
The device that shoots electrically charged particles called electrons toward the back of the monitor screen.

refresh rate
A measurement of the number of times that an image is redrawn to the screen per second. Measured in Hertz; a higher number is better.

dot pitch
Measures the distance, in millimeters, between two dots of the same color on the monitor.

NOTE

Two ways of measuring a monitor's quality are the **refresh rate** and **dot pitch** characteristics. The refresh rate signifies the number of times the beam of electrons shot from the electron gun redraws the screen in one second. The dot pitch measures the distance between two dots of the same color on the monitor.

Video Display Adapter Standards

Video display adapters (the adapter inside your computer that connects to the monitor) have many standards. Each standard consists of specifications for the maximum supported resolution, colors supported for the maximum resolution, and connector type. Each video display adapter type has a different interface to allow for easier identification.

Resolution on the monitor is determined by the number of pixels. A **pixel** is the smallest addressable unit on a display screen. The higher the pixel resolution (the more rows and columns of pixels), the more information can be displayed.

Pixels are made up of one or more bits. The more bits you have, the greater the **bit depth**. Greater bit depth means that more shades and colors can be represented. A monochrome monitor uses one bit per pixel. On a color display, there can be 4 to 24 bits per pixel, which provides from 16 to 16 million colors.

This table defines the standards.

pixel
Short for picture element; a pixel is one dot in an image.

bit depth
A value for the number of bits that are used to make up a pixel. The higher the number of bits, the more colors that can be displayed.

Video Standard	Resolution (Pixels)	Bit Depth	Supported Colors
Monochrome Display Adapter (MDA)	80 × 25	1	Monochrome (text only)
Hercules Graphics Controller (HGC)	720 × 350	1	Mono (text and graphics)
Color Graphics Adapter (CGA)	320 × 200	2	4
	640 × 200	1	2
Enhanced Graphics Adapter (EGA)	640 × 350	4	16
Video Graphics Adapter (VGA)	640 × 480	4	16
Super VGA (SVGA)	800 × 600	24	16.7 million
	1024 × 768	24	16.7 million
	1280 × 1024	24	16.7 million
	1600 × 1200	24	16.7 million
Extended Graphics Array (XGA)	800 × 600	16	65,536
	1024 × 768	8	256
IBM 8514/A	1024 × 768	8	256

Taking advantage of the latest video technology is not exclusively a function of upgrading to Windows 98 or 2000. Software upgrades of the operating system only add support for new technologies. Your video display adapter and monitor—the hardware—must support the selected range of supported resolutions and maximum colors to function properly.

You can upgrade your video hardware to support higher resolutions and more colors. A video display adapter with additional memory will support higher-quality video. Many manufacturers include as much as 8MB of RAM on the video card. If you intend to use advanced animation or video features, you can select cards that run faster (for smoother images and motion) and have more RAM. In addition to upgrading your video card, you will also need to select a monitor that will support more colors and higher resolutions.

Liquid Crystal Display

Originally designed for watches, Liquid Crystal Displays (LCDs) quickly grew to be a direct contender with traditional tube-based computer screens. The LCD's thin profile makes it suitable for portable devices from laptops to handheld devices. LCDs are becoming so popular that they are being built for desktop use. Their sleek profile looks good in the trendy technology companies of today, and they save on space.

LCD technology is available in two types: **passive matrix** and **active matrix**. The screen of passive matrix displays looks faded because the liquid crystal cells have fewer electrodes to maintain solid colors of light. The cells begin to fade before they can be recharged. Active matrix displays have transistors located throughout the display. Each transistor keeps the liquid display cell charged, providing a much brighter and sharper image.

passive matrix
A flat-panel LCD display technology that uses horizontal and vertical wires with LCD cells at each intersection to create a video image. Passive matrix is considered inferior to active matrix but is less expensive to produce.

active matrix
Sometimes referred to as Thin Film Transistor (TFT), active matrix LCD displays offer superior clarity and color. This is due mostly to faster refresh rates and more powerful LCD cells.

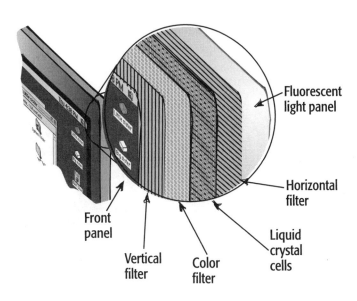

Fluorescent light panel

Horizontal filter

Liquid crystal cells

Front panel

Vertical filter

Color filter

Using a Keyboard

The keyboard is the most common type of input device. The keyboard takes in information in the form of letters and numbers. The letters and numbers are translated into instructions that the computer must perform. The computer translates literally what is entered, so any typing mistakes will result in an error.

Certain aspects of keyboards are important to consider. For example, choose a keyboard that is comfortable for you. In most cases, it is beneficial to select an ergonomically designed product. These products are designed to blend smoothly with the contour of your body.

Keyboards can connect to computers in several ways. The most common type of connection is the **DIN** 6, which is also referred to as a **PS/2** connector. The DIN 6 connector is small and looks identical to a PS/2-style mouse. It is easy to confuse these two when connecting them to the computer.

Some computers still use the older AT keyboard connector that was originally used in the IBM PCAT computers introduced in 1984. The AT was replaced by the more recent PS/2 connector described above. Like the AT-type connector that is rarely if ever specified for a new computer, the PS/2 is experiencing some competition of its own from Universal Serial Bus (discussed earlier in this chapter). The PS/2 connector won't disappear soon, but with Apple Computer shipping USB-only keyboards, don't expect the PS/2 to be around forever.

DIN

Deutsch Industrie Norm— a German standards organization.

PS/2

Also known as the mouse port and DIN 6, PS/2 was developed by IBM for connecting a mouse to the computer. PS/2 ports are supported for mice and keyboards alike.

WARNING

Don't unplug the keyboard or mouse while the computer is on. You might damage your computer with a static charge. Also, some computers may need to be rebooted to recognize the reconnected devices.

Using a Mouse

The mouse is the second most common type of input device. You use the mouse for navigating, selecting, or drawing. The mouse movements are translated into computer instructions in the form of motion and button selection. To start a mouse operation, simply move the mouse pointer on the screen until it is in the correct position and click one of the mouse buttons.

Many people use a mouse pad to provide a non-slick surface to roll the mouse on. The mouse pad serves two other important functions. First, the pad represents a finite physical space for moving the mouse. If you move off the pad, you sense the change and, given practice, move your mouse back onto the pad. Second, the pad offers a clean space that should be kept free of debris. Dust, hair, and food crumbs can degrade or damage the internal mechanical components found in most mice.

The graphic below illustrates the mechanical components found in a mouse. The ball in the center touches the pad and rolls as you move the mouse. The ball moves two rollers that are connected to mechanical sensors. The movements of both rollers are interpreted into movements of the mouse pointer on the screen.

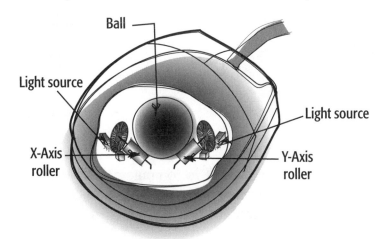

A mouse can connect to a computer using several different connector types. The DB-9 connector, the oldest, has been replaced by the DIN-type connectors. USB is the most recent connector type available.

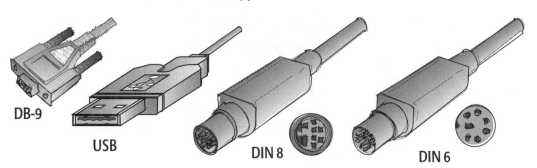

Making Remote Connections

So far, this chapter has discussed input and output in relation to a single computer. Input and output also can occur between two computers in different locations. Special devices called modems enable computers to connect to one another over the public telephone network. Through the use of modems, digital signals from the computer are sent over regular phone lines or, in some cases, over television cable.

Accessing the Internet through a traditional modem requires several steps. First, there must be a phone connection to the **central office (CO)** of the telephone company. The physical line between the central office and the commercial location is called the **local loop**. The local loop is terminated at both ends. At the commercial office end, the phone is plugged into a wall jack. At the telephone company, the cable terminates and is plugged into a telephone switch. Incoming calls to the switch are then forwarded to the appropriate location.

central office

A building in a given neighborhood where all local phone lines in that neighborhood are terminated.

local loop

The two-wire copper telephone cable that runs from a home or office to the central office of the telephone company.

bits per second (bps)

The number of bits, or ones and zeros, transmitted each second.

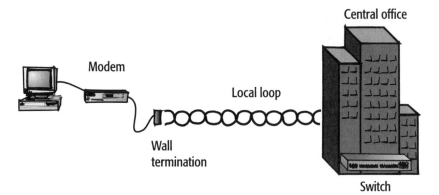

When data is transmitted between two computers, the transmission speed is measured in terms of **bits per second (bps)** and not bytes per second. This table shows the difference between the two.

Bits	Transmission Speed
1 bit	1 bit per second (bps)
1,024 bits	1 Kilobit per second (Kbps)
1,024,000 bits	1Megabit per second (Mbps)
1,024,000,000 bits	1 Gigabit per second (Gbps)

There are several communication technologies that enable computers in different locations to share data. Each uses a different signaling format, medium, or both, which yields varying levels of performance. In the next subsections, you will learn about these technologies.

Analog Modems

Modems function as input and output devices. They enable computers to communicate with one another over great distances. The word *modem* comes from the merging of the two words **modulate** and **demodulate**. Modems that send data convert digital signals from a computer into analog audible tone signals that can be transmitted over phone lines, and modems that receive data do the reverse.

Digital signals are made up of discrete values. The values represent an on or off state, which are the ones and zeros of computer language. Discrete voltages represent the on or off conditions. An on condition is represented by +5 volts, and an off condition by −5 volts or a zero value. The values do not change over time; they change instantaneously from one state to another.

Analog signals are constantly changing values. The values represent fluctuations in voltage or sound. An analog signal can consist of an infinite number of possible values.

Modulation/Demodulation

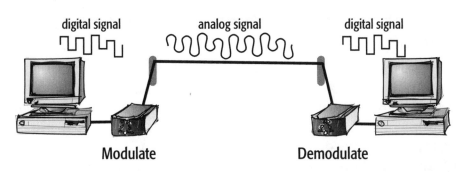

Modulate   Demodulate

Modems can communicate at speeds from 300bps to more than 56,000bps. Modems are backward compatible and slow their transmission speed to communicate with slower modems.

Modems come in two types: internal and external. External modems require a connection to an available serial port on the back of a computer using an **RS-232** cable. Internal modems plug into an expansion slot inside a computer.

NOTE

A term often associated with modems is **baud**. Baud is the number of frequency changes made per second. This term is often used synonymously with bps. This is accurate at low speeds, such as 300 baud. At higher speeds, modems use a technique that enables multiple bits to be sent on each frequency change. So, for example, a modem operating at 9,600bps may operate at only 2,400 baud.

modulate
To convert digital data into analog signals. Modulation enables digital computer data to be transferred over standard telephone lines.

demodulate
To convert an analog signal back to digital data. This is typically done on the receiving end of a computer transmission using standard phone service.

RS-232
An interface standard for use between data communications equipment (DCE) and data terminal equipment (DTE).

baud
A measurement of the number of signals that are transmitted each second.

Digital Subscriber Line (DSL)

Digital Subscriber Line (DSL) is a relatively new and inexpensive technology offered through the local telephone company. DSL offers much promise in the residential/small office Internet access market because of its high bandwidth potential. Unlike modems, which must convert digital signals to analog to transmit over the public telephone network, DSL signals are digital from beginning to end.

The completely digital transmission vastly improves performance in several ways. First, DSL does not have the transmission limitation of 56Kbps found with traditional modems. In fact, DSL is capable of transmitting 6Mbps—nearly as fast as a network connection. Second, the DSL modem does not have to convert a signal from analog to digital, and thus slow transmission, as modems do. A DSL modem is not a modem at all; it is actually a **bridge**. Since most people are comfortable with the term *modem*, it made more sense to use modem rather than introducing a new term.

DSL modems are able to achieve high transfer rates by using a technology called **Asynchronous Transfer Mode (ATM)**. ATM uses cells to transfer data. The DSL modem is a bridge that converts ATM cells coming from your **Internet Service Provider (ISP)** into **Ethernet** frames. Most computers with the right hardware can communicate via Ethernet network technology.

DSL is available in two flavors. Asymmetric DSL (ADSL) has a different download speed, usually faster, than the upload speed. This improves download times where file transfers are the largest. Symmetric DSL (SDSL) has equal download and upload speeds. If one of these versions of DSL seems more appealing than the other, you will need to find an ISP that supports your preferred technology. Most ISPs support only one of the technologies.

NOTE

DSL is not available everywhere. Two factors stand in the way of ubiquitous access. First, the current limitation for DSL connectivity is 1,750 feet from the CO. Longer distances are not able to support the minimum quality requirements for transmitting digital signals. Second, the telephone company in your area must invest a substantial amount of money toward upgrading their main facilities to support DSL. In metropolitan areas this is not a problem, but in rural or semi-rural areas, justifying the cost is difficult.

DSL check-off list:

- ✦ Does your computer support Ethernet?
- ✦ Do you have a network card?
- ✦ Are you close enough to the CO in your area?

Sidebar definitions

Digital Subscriber Line (DSL)

A digital signaling method used to transmit data over regular phone lines at speeds up to 6Mbps. DSL uses Asynchronous Transfer Mode to pass data in fixed-size cells.

bridge

A network device that enables networks using different transmission signals to communicate with one another.

Asynchronous Transfer Mode (ATM)

A network technology that uses fixed-size cells to transfer data. The fixed-size cells enable it to provide better performance.

Internet Service Provider (ISP)

A company or organization that provides the user with access to the Internet, typically for a fee. Users may gain access by using any one of many remote connection technologies, including modems, DSL, ISDN, cable modems, and others.

Cable Modems

Cable modems allow high-speed access to the Internet over cable TV (CATV) lines. The cable modem requires two connections: one to the cable outlet and the other to the computer. Cable modems are more economical than some other technologies. DSL is as cost effective, but performance is more difficult to measure. One difficulty for DSL is that it has not had the rapid growth that cable technology has, and therefore DSL is not available everywhere. Compared to ISDN, described in the next section, cable modems offer much better performance at a fraction of the cost. There is no need to dial; the connection is always active.

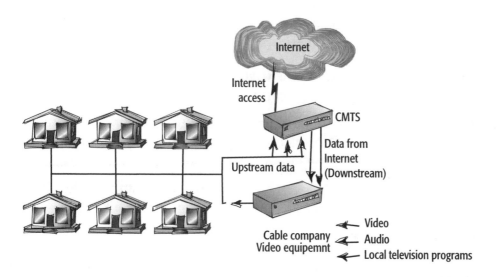

The range at which a cable modem operates varies from 200Kbps to 10Mbps. The typical range is more like 2Mbps to 10Mbps. Data that is downloaded from the Internet is transmitted at a higher rate than data that is uploaded.

In your home, the cable company will attach a splitter to the incoming cable. One connection is used for your television and the other connects to the cable modem. Your computer connects to the cable modem via a **10BASE-T** Ethernet connection to a network card installed in your computer.

When you connect your computer to a cable network, you are actually part of a large Ethernet **wide area network (WAN)**. Each house plugs into the network via the cable in the home. The other end of that cable goes into a cable hub called a **Cable Modem Termination System (CMTS) device**. The CMTS will manage where data is being sent.

CMTS devices can be two-way, meaning that they support upstream (to the Internet) and downstream (to the user) data transmission. In some locations where CMTS devices are not installed or available, a telephone connection is used for upstream data.

Ethernet

A network communication technology developed by Xerox that encloses data with a destination and source address for delivery which is called a frame. Additional information for Ethernet is also added to the frame.

10BASE-T

A signal capable of transmitting at 10Mbps over twisted-pair cable by using baseband signaling. It is the IEEE 802.3 standard for unshielded twisted-pair Ethernet.

wide area network (WAN)

A relatively low speed data connection (typically 1.546 Mbps) that uses the telephone company to connect two locations separated by a large geographical area.

Cable Modem Termination System (CMTS) device

A device used to forward user data to the Internet. Downstream data from the Internet is forwarded to the cable television equipment in that neighborhood, where it is then forwarded to the home user.

ISDN

Integrated Services Digital Network (ISDN) is a digital dial service that transmits digital data at a higher transmission rate than a standard modem. This makes ISDN more expensive than using a modem. ISDN is still cost-effective, considering that the rate for one ISDN line is less than two business lines, and it can support data, voice, and faxing capabilities.

You can connect ISDN adapters to the computer in two ways:

◆ Internal ISDN adapters plug into an available expansion slot inside a computer.

◆ External ISDN adapters connect to an available serial port on the back of a computer via a null-modem cable.

The most typical ISDN user is the **telecommuter,** who uses the high-speed service to connect with their main office from home.

ISDN adapters often link small branch offices that do not transmit large amounts of data to one another. A connection begins when data needs transmission.

You can identify the speed of an ISDN adapter by the number of signal bearer channels, or **B channel**s. An ISDN adapter configured with a single B channel can support 64Kbps, whereas a **D channel** supports only 16Kbps.

Here is a summary of available ISDN services.

ISDN Service	Channel Type	Speed
Basic Rate Interface (BRI)	2 B + 1 D channel (2 x 64K + 16K)	144 Kbps
H0	6 B channels (6 x 64K)	384 Kbps
Primary Rate Interface (PRI)	23 B (64K) + 1 D (64K) channel	1.536 Mbps

Integrated Services Digital Network (ISDN)
A technology that combines digital and voice transmission onto a single wire.

telecommuter
Someone who remotely connects to their office to work from home or a remote location.

B channel
Stands for bearer channel and is a 64Kbps circuit-switched channel. Used to carry voice and data.

D channel
Stands for delta channel and is a 16Kbps circuit-switched channel. Used to manage control signals.

Basic Rate Interface (BRI)
The basic ISDN service offered by telecommunication companies. BRI consists of two B channels and a single D channel.

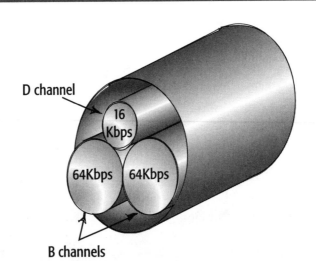

D channel — 16 Kbps

64Kbps   64Kbps

B channels

Choosing a Printer

Printers are output devices that produce a hard-copy result in the form of printed text and graphics. Printers differ from other types of devices because they not only transfer an image to paper, but they also must move the paper through the process.

Several types of printers are available based on different technology standards. Most printer types operate basically the same way. Paper is fed into the unit using a roller. The text and images are applied to the paper, and additional rollers push the paper out onto a tray.

Printers can vary in many ways, in addition to print method. For instance, print speed is a differentiating factor. This table defines printer types. *Method of imprint* refers to the method of transferring information to paper.

Printer Type	Method of Imprint
Dot matrix	Tiny pins impact an ink-filled ribbon.
Inkjet/bubble jet	Ink squirts at the paper, following a pattern to create an image.
Laser	A laser beam creates an image on a metal roller, forming an image that attracts ink from a special toner. The ink is then placed on paper, and heat bonds the ink to the paper to create a printed document.
Thermal dye transfer	Also known as dye sublimation, the process uses heat on ribbons containing dye to create photo-quality prints. The process is continuous so it creates a very high-quality output. It requires special paper.
Thermal wax transfer	Colored waxes are heated and placed on regular paper as dots. Quality is not quite photo-realistic but is less expensive and faster.

NOTE

Printers have two operating modes: text mode and graphics mode. In text mode, the computer's operating system and software look up ASCII characters, such as letters and numbers, from a character table and then produce the result in bit format to send to the printer. In graphics mode, the operating system and software work together to send instructions to the printer to control the print operation and produce a custom character or result.

H0
Another ISDN channel that includes 6 B channels. Other H channel definitions include H-10 and H-11, which are just another way of identifying the 23 B channels of the Primary Rate Interface.

Primary Rate Interface (PRI)
The high-end ISDN service offered by telecommunication companies. PRI provides 23 B channels and one D channel. This is equivalent to the 24 channels of a T1 line.

American Standard Code for Information Interchange (ASCII)
A 7-bit coding scheme that translates symbolic characters into the ones and zeros that are stored as data on a computer. Extended ASCII uses an 8-bit coding scheme.

Laser Printers: The Workhorses

If you haven't already, at some point you may likely be faced with one seemingly simple question: inkjet or laser? Many people like inkjets because of their good quality, speed, and affordability—especially for color printing. Laser printers are high-speed networkable devices. Laser printers provide the same quality output as most inkjets but at a higher initial price for the device. The additional cost of laser printers usually means that one printer will be used to serve many. Inkjets are affordable so they can be ordered for each user. So why not just go with inkjets?

In most offices, printers are heavily used devices, so they need to be selected wisely. You should consider three factors before making your decision on an inkjet or laser printer. Mean Time Between Failure (MTBF) is a measurement of how long the printer will function before a component fails. Also, monthly print volume is a figure that can be used to determine whether the printer was designed to support the usage of the user. A final indicator is cost. Inkjet printers do cost less, but printing on inkjets is much more expensive with or without color. Cartridges cost $30 and may print only a few hundred pages. Laser cartridges cost $75 and support up to 6,000 pages or more. Laser printers are the best choice for heavy, long-term use by multiple users.

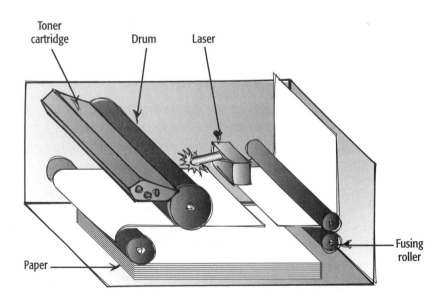

NOTE

Printers are networked to provide many users with access to a single device, thus saving the money needed to purchase a print device for every user. Modern printers include an expansion slot to plug in a network printer card or have one built in.

Choosing PC Cards

The purpose of the PC card is to enhance the capabilities of a computer. Adding a card to your computer enables you to customize it for your needs. Without this feature, the computer would not be as modular and would not allow you to add devices chosen to meet your specific needs.

Several types of PC cards exist, such as those providing sound, network, video, and input/output capabilities. Regardless of the type of PC card, they attach to the computer by plugging into an available expansion bus slot on the motherboard. The expansion bus provides a pathway that links the device with the CPU and memory inside the computer.

There are several expansion bus design standards. It is important that you identify the slot type before purchasing a new PC card. Each bus design standard has a primary connector and might have one or more extension connectors to allow for additional capabilities. Other differences include the operating speed, interface, and method of configuration.

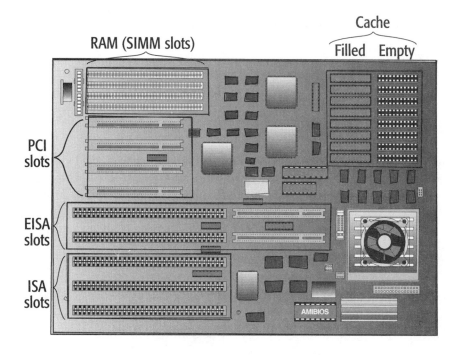

Bus Standards

When you are selecting a computer to purchase or build, you want to make sure that you are investing in the best technology to meet your needs. Most computers today will include support for the older ISA standard as well as support for the modern PCI standard. It is important that you make sure that you have selected a computer that includes enough slots for your expansion cards. The table below defines the key differences between the standards.

dual in-line package (DIP) switches
A set of tiny switches attached to a circuit board that are manually configured to alter the function of a chip for a specific computer or application.

Bus type	Interface	Speed	Configuration
ISA	8-bit or 16-bit	8–10MHz	Hardware or software
MicroChannel	16-bit or 32-bit	10–20MHz	Hardware or software
EISA	32-bit	8–10MHz	Software
VL-Bus	32-bit	40MHz	Hardware
PCI	32-bit or 64-bit	33MHz	Plug-and-Play
PCMCIA	16-bit	33MHz	Software

Plug and Play

Plug-and-Play technology was added to Windows 95 as a way to greatly simplify the installation and configuration of new hardware. Plug and Play works quite well now that most hardware manufacturers design and build their hardware to be Plug-and-Play compatible.

The technology works something like this: New hardware is installed into a Windows 98 computer. When the computer is first turned on, the BIOS checks to see what devices are attached to the motherboard or to any of the external ports. If it detects a new device, it notifies the operating system. After Windows 98 starts up, the Plug and Play Wizard loads. If the new device is recognizable by Windows 98, the software is automatically loaded from the hard drive. Also, the software is automatically configured by Windows 98. Only in rare cases does Windows 98 need assistance to configure a Plug-and-Play device. If the new device does not have software loaded into Windows 98, you will be presented with an option to insert media that contains the necessary software.

Most adapter cards in the last couple of years have been designed to the Plug-and-Play specification. Older cards that are not Plug-and-Play compatible require manual configuration through hardware, which consists of setting jumpers and **dual in-line package (DIP) switches**. This method of hardware configuration is nearly obsolete in most new hardware.

NOTE

Although Windows NT 4 does not support Plug-and-Play capability, it is a feature of Windows 2000. But Plug and Play works on Windows 2000 only for devices that are included in Microsoft's Hardware Compatibility List (HCL). Devices on the HCL have been tested and verified to be compatible with Windows 2000. If the device you are considering for use in Windows 2000 is not included on the HCL, you should seriously consider using another device that is compatible. Besides the possibility of the device not working or causing Windows 2000 errors, Microsoft may not support your installation.

Unlike DIP switches, jumpers are still found on motherboards, hard drives, CD-ROMs and some adapter cards. Jumpers are small connectors that are used to connect two pins to make a complete circuit. For example, most motherboards have a password jumper. The password jumper can be used to erase a system password used when the computer first boots up. Most systems require that you remove the jumper for a set period of time to erase the password.

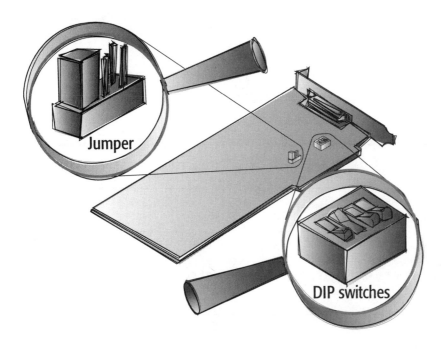

Review Questions

1. Define *serial communication*.

   _____

2. What is the difference between data that is transmitted serially and data that is transmitted in parallel?

   _____

3. True or false: The refresh rate determines how many dots of the same color are drawn on the screen.

   _____

4. Which display adapter type is the best choice to display the maximum resolution and most colors?

   _____

5. Name the four mouse interface types.

   _____

   _____

   _____

   _____

6. True or false: Digital signals represent constantly changing voltages.

   _____

7. What is the difference between a modem and a cable modem?

   _____

8. Why is performance on a DSL connection faster than with a modem?

_____

9. True or false: ISDN transmits data at a higher rate than a standard modem.

_____

10. True or false: Motherboards are manufactured to accommodate only one bus specification.

_____

11. Why are printers often attached to a network?

_____

Terms to Know
- ❑ bps
- ❑ modulate
- ❑ demodulate
- ❑ RS-232
- ❑ baud
- ❑ DSL
- ❑ bridge
- ❑ Asynchronous Transfer Mode
- ❑ ISP
- ❑ Ethernet
- ❑ 10BASE-T
- ❑ WAN
- ❑ CMTS device
- ❑ ISDN
- ❑ telecommuter
- ❑ B channel
- ❑ D channel
- ❑ BRI
- ❑ H0
- ❑ PRI
- ❑ ASCII
- ❑ DIP switches

Chapter

4

Hardware Configuration: Putting It All Together

con·fig·ure *v* : to assemble pieces so that they function as a single unit

C onfiguring your computer hardware can be an easy or difficult task to complete. Each hardware device must be configured with unique system resource settings. The resource settings enable the device to communicate with the computer's processor and memory without competing or conflicting with other devices. Most devices have the capability to accept various combinations of resource settings.

In this chapter, these hardware configuration topics are covered:

 Hardware installation

 Software drivers

 Interrupts

 Base memory

 I/O memory

 Direct memory access (DMA)

Installing Hardware

You install new hardware (for instance, a sound card or hard drive) through a multistep configuration process. The fundamental steps are to configure the device at a physical level and at one or more logical levels so that the system can communicate with the device. A device will not function properly unless it is correctly installed.

> **NOTE**
>
> Before you install any piece of hardware, take the precaution of wearing an anti-static wrist guard to protect the computer from any potential electrical shocks that might damage the circuitry.

When you install a piece of hardware, you should first properly configure it. You can determine configuration settings by reviewing the documentation that comes with the device. Traditionally, older hardware was configured through DIP switches and jumpers. Now this technology is fairly obsolete. Most hardware configuration is now done through software.

Each hardware device is unique and has its own settings that you need to configure. Common configuration settings include **interrupts**, **base memory**, **I/O memory**, and direct memory access (DMA). These items are covered in more detail in the following subsections.

Completing the physical installation of the device requires plugging it into the motherboard via a slot, cables, or both. Be sure that you have all the necessary accessories, such as screws or cables, when completing this step. If the device is a PC card, carefully plug it into an available bus slot of the same type, and secure it by screwing it into the case. It usually does not matter which slot you place the card into unless it is a Peripheral Component Interconnect (PCI), Extended Industry Standard Architecture (EISA), or MicroChannel Architecture (MCA) card; then it is identified by slot number.

After you have securely attached the device, you can begin the software configuration. In this step, you install the device drivers and set any configuration parameters that a particular operating system might need in order to communicate and interact with a device.

> **NOTE**
>
> One reason Plug-and-Play technology is so important is that it automatically configures hardware devices for you. Windows 2000 includes support for Plug and Play.

---

interrupt

A type of signal that is used to get the attention of the CPU when I/O is required. An interrupt tells the CPU that the operating system is requesting that a specific action be taken. Interrupts are prioritized; higher-numbered interrupts are serviced first.

base memory

Memory addresses that are reserved and used to store low-level control software that is required by an add-on device.

I/O memory

Memory addresses that are reserved and assigned to add-on devices. Each assignment tells the CPU about the location of a specific device.

Installing Software Drivers

Software drivers are special programs that tell the computer how to communicate with and control a hardware device. Each device has a driver that enables it to communicate with the computer. The driver is written to operate only within a certain operating system. For instance, a Windows 98 driver installed for a particular piece of hardware will not work on Windows NT.

Most software drivers are not usually generic in nature. Each piece of hardware contains unique components, and these components might not reside on a similar device, even if made by the same manufacturer. The software driver must communicate with that device to accurately interpret the instructions issued to the device from the operating system.

Some devices, such as the mouse, are generic in that most do not contain special features or chips that need customized instruction code. Therefore, changing your mouse is much easier than swapping out your sound card or replacing your printer without changing the device drivers.

When you install a device, you should have the driver disk in hand and install it when the operating system prompts you. Operating systems such as Windows 98 and 2000 use Plug and Play to auto-detect the presence of a new device and install the driver, provided they properly recognize the device. This is possible because these versions of Windows contain archives of the most common device drivers. You should install the latest device driver available for a particular operating system, because drivers are typically updated if incompatibility issues or problems are reported.

CONFIG.SYS
A DOS or OS/2 file that contains special configuration settings in the form of line statements. The file is stored in the root of the C drive and is one of the key files read when an operating system boots.

TIP

You might think of a software driver as the bridge between a piece of hardware and a specific operating system's software.

TIP

DOS-based drivers are loaded through a DEVICE= statement in the CONFIG.SYS file.

83

Handling Interrupts

Each device interacts with the computer by interrupting the processor so that it can send or retrieve data or carry out a function. A device must have a method for telling the computer's processor that it needs attention. A hardware device tells the processor that it needs attention through an **interrupt request (IRQ)** line. By using this method of interruption, the processor can function without the need to ask a device every few seconds whether it needs service.

When a device interrupts the system processor, the processor stops what it is doing and handles the interrupt request. Because each device is assigned a number when the device is configured, the system knows which device needs attention. After the processor has attended to the device, it returns to the function it was performing before the interruption.

Each device must have a unique IRQ so that the processor knows what to attend to when a service request is called. There are exceptions to this rule; for instance, serial ports (also referred to as communication, or COM, ports) can share the same IRQ, but they must be assigned another unique identifier (I/O address). If any other devices share the same interrupt and need attention from the processor, the machine will hang or immediately reboot in the confusion of determining which device requested service. Plug-and-Play devices scan the system and determine an available interrupt request to assign to a new device during installation.

interrupt request (IRQ)

The method used by a device to inform the microprocessor (CPU) that the device needs attention. Through this method of interruption, the microprocessor can function without needing to poll each device to see whether it needs service.

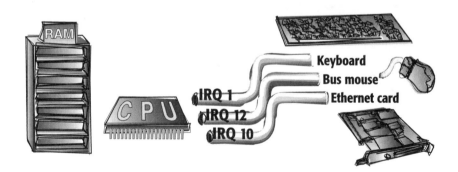

NOTE

The PCI bus standard enables devices connected to a PCI bus to communicate by using one common interrupt (IRQ 10).

The following table shows the standard interrupts that most systems use, including Windows 2000.

- ❖ *System device* refers to the device that is configured to use the specified interrupt.

- ❖ *IRQ* refers to the interrupt request line that the hardware device uses to notify the processor that it needs attention.

- ❖ IRQ numbers that are listed as *available* can be allocated to new devices that are installed in the computer.

System Device	IRQ
System timer	0
Keyboard	1
Reserved	2
COMs 2, 4	3
COMs 1, 3	4
LPT2 (usually available for other devices)	5
Floppy-disk controller	6
LPT1	7
Real-time clock	8
Redirected or cascaded to IRQ 2	9
Available (also used for PCI common interrupt)	10
Available	11
PS/2 or bus mouse port (available if not used)	12
Math coprocessor	13
Hard-disk controller	14
Available (also used for PCI secondary IDE controller)	15

Using Base Memory

Base memory refers to the reserved area in memory where devices can store data so that the processor can directly access that data. Some devices need this allocated memory range located in the system RAM. The area is typically located in the upper area of RAM memory called the **Upper Memory Area (UMA)**.

Upper Memory Area (UMA)

The area of memory between 640KB and 1MB in an IBM-compatible computer. This area of memory was originally reserved for system and video use.

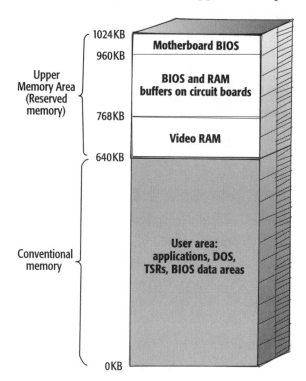

This table shows some typical base memory address assignments. When configuring address ranges, be sure that they do not overlap.

System Device	Memory Range
Video RAM	A0000–BFFFF
Available	C0000–CFFFF
Available	D0000–DFFFF
System ROM	E0000–EFFFF

TIP

When assigning a memory address range to a DOS-based device, be sure to exclude the range in the CONFIG.SYS file.

Identifying System Resources

If you run into a problem configuring the drives for your hardware or if you think there is a conflict, you may have to use the Device Manager in Windows 98 or Windows 2000 to correct the problem. The Device Manager gives you direct access to the specific settings for your hardware.

Besides being able to check what IRQ or I/O memory address is in use by a device, you can also check to see whether the driver is up-to-date. If it isn't, you can select the Update Driver option in the Properties window of the device.

If you want to check which resources are already in use on your Windows 98 computer, you can try it out on your own.

TEST IT OUT: VIEWING DEVICE RESOURCES

1. Go to the Start menu and select Settings ➤ Control Panel.
2. Open the System Control Panel by double-clicking the System icon.
3. Click the Device Manager tab at the top of the System Properties window.
4. Select the computer icon at the top of the list and click the Properties button.
5. Select the View Resources tab and click any one of the four radio buttons (as shown in the graphic below) to view the settings for your hardware.

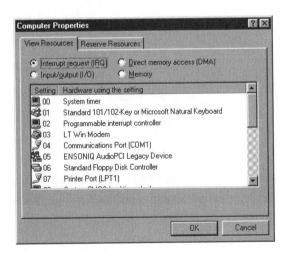

Using I/O Memory

Each device has a memory address called an I/O address. The address acts like a mailbox that the processor uses to send instructions to the device. The I/O address is also commonly called the **port address**.

port address
An address used by the computer to access devices such as expansion cards and printers.

When the CPU sends instructions to this address, the device reads the instructions and carries them out. But the device does not talk to the processor through the same mechanism. It uses the interrupt assigned to it to request service or additional instructions from the processor.

Each device must have a unique I/O address so that the correct device receives the instructions from the processor. Some older devices are coded to use only one I/O address and cannot be changed.

Most PCs are designed to support more than one I/O address for a device. This feature helps prevent a conflict between two similar devices, such as the COM ports that share the same interrupt. The two ports would have separate I/O addresses, thus preventing a clash between them.

If your device does not support an I/O address that is available (not in use by another device), you may select an address used by another device, provided you can change the other device's address to an available I/O address.

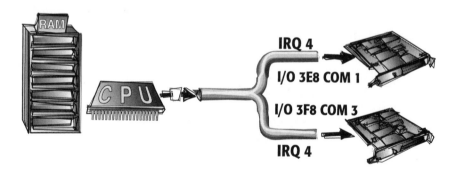

TIP

Always note the addresses your system uses, to make life easier when troubleshooting or adding a new device.

This table shows the typical I/O address assignments.

System Device	Memory Address
DMA controller	000–01F
Interrupt controller	020–03F
Timer	040–05F
Keyboard	060–06F
Real-time clock	070–07F
DMA page register	080–09F
Second interrupt controller	0A0–0BF
DMA controller 2	0C0–0DF
Math coprocessor	0F0–0FF
Primary hard-disk controller	1F0–1F8
Joystick controller	200–20F
XT expansion unit	210–217
FM synthesis interface	220–22F
CD-ROM I/O port	230–233
Bus mouse	238–23B
Plug-and-Play I/O port	274–277
LPT2 (second parallel port)	278–27F
COM 4 (serial port 4)	2E8–2EF
COM 2 (serial port 2)	2F8–2FF
Available	280–31F
XT hard-disk controller	320–32F
MIDI port	330–33F
Alternate floppy controller	370–377
LPT1 (primary printer port)	378–37F
LPT3 (third parallel port)	3BC–3BF
Color graphics adapter (CGA, EGA, VGA)	3D0–3DF
COM 3 (serial port 3)	3E8–3EF
Floppy-disk controller	3F0–3F7
COM 1 (serial port 1)	3F8–3FF

Using DMA

As stated earlier, DMA stands for direct memory access. DMA enables a device to transfer data directly to RAM without using the attention of the processor for the entire transfer period. The result is a faster and more direct method of data transfer. This method was especially useful in older PCs, enabling the DMA channel to transfer data in the background, thus freeing the processor to tend to other duties. DMA is typically used by devices such as floppy disks, hard disks, tape devices, and network cards.

This graphic shows the CPU intervening to transfer data.

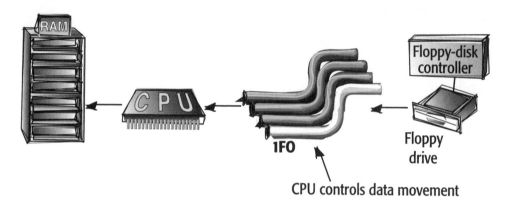

CPU controls data movement

This graphic shows the use of DMA for direct transfer of data.

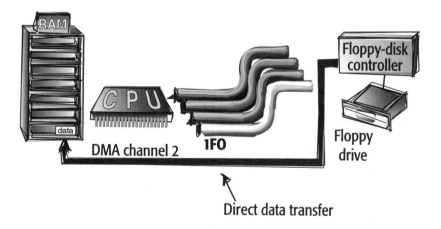

Direct data transfer

NOTE

The term *channel* is often used in describing DMA. In older PCs, a DMA controller chip handled DMA activities. The chip contained four DMA channels that were numbered 0 to 3. Technology enhancements allowed the inclusion of up to eight channels. Each type of bus standard allows a different number of DMA channels.

The following table shows the standard DMA channels that most systems use. When two devices are configured to the same DMA channel, neither device can transfer the data to memory correctly. The only available DMA channel on older PCs is DMA channel 3.

System Device	DMA Channel
Available	0
Available	1
Floppy-disk controller	2
Available	3
Not available (used for internal purposes or second DMA controller)	4
Available	5
Available	6
Available	7

TIP

If your device does not operate correctly using various combinations of DMA channel assignments, try the Disable DMA option.

TIP

If you install a piece of hardware and your computer does not work, remove the piece of hardware that you installed and restart your computer. Then, if the computer works, you know that the new piece of hardware conflicts with an existing piece of hardware.

Review Questions

Terms to Know
- ❑ interrupt
- ❑ base memory
- ❑ I/O memory
- ❑ CONFIG.SYS
- ❑ IRQ
- ❑ UMA
- ❑ port address

1. How do you accomplish the physical configuration of a hardware device?

   _____

2. What are the four hardware settings that you use to configure computer hardware?

   _____

   _____

   _____

   _____

3. How does an interrupt work?

   _____

4. Which interrupt does LPT2 typically use?

   _____

5. True or false: All devices need a reserved area of memory in which to operate (similar to Video RAM).

   _____

6. What I/O address range is typically assigned to the primary hard-disk controller?

   _____

7. How does DMA typically work?

   _____

8. Which DMA channel is typically assigned to the floppy-disk controller?

_____

9. What is a software driver?

_____

10. True or false: A software driver will work with any operating system as long as it follows the Software Driver Association guidelines.

_____

11. True or false: Two hardware devices can share the same IRQ.

_____

12. What does DMA stand for?

_____

13. What does I/O stand for?

_____

14. What does IRQ stand for?

_____

Chapter

5

Desktop Operating Systems: A Comparison

op·er·at·ing sys·tem *n* : Software that is used on an electronic device, usually a computer, to perform a set of tasks

Every computer consists of hardware and software. In the previous chapters, you learned about hardware. In this chapter, you will learn about local operating systems, which are the heart and brains of the computer's software. The local operating system manages system hardware and resources. In the past 20 years, operating systems have changed dramatically. This chapter provides an overview of common operating systems. Some of the information is provided as a historical summary to give you an idea of the evolution that has occurred in operating system development. These local operating systems and operating system concepts will be covered:

 DOS

 Windows

 Windows 95

 Windows 98

 Windows NT Workstation 4

 Windows 2000 Professional

 Unix

 Linux

 Dual-booting between operating systems

Understanding DOS

If you used a computer between 1981 and the early 1990s, chances are the computer ran some version of DOS as its operating system. DOS stands for Disk Operating System. Microsoft originally licensed DOS to IBM as an operating system to be used with IBM's personal computers. This version of DOS was called PC-DOS.

In what has become known as one of the smartest moves in the computer industry, Microsoft licensed DOS, as opposed to selling DOS, to IBM. Microsoft also retained the right to license other versions of DOS. The non-IBM version of DOS was called MS-DOS. It was used by hardware vendors who made PCs with the same Intel CPU that IBM used with its PCs. These computers were referred to as IBM clones and typically were more competitively priced than their IBM counterparts.

The following subsections describe the major features that the various evolutions of DOS offered.

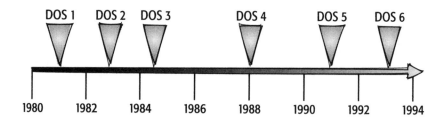

DOS 1.*x*

This version provided:

- ◇ A very limited capability to use system resources
- ◇ Support for floppy disks

DOS 2.*x*

This version provided:

- ◇ Support for 10MB hard drives
- ◇ Support for serial interfaces (for attaching peripheral devices such as a printer)
- ◇ The hierarchical tree structure used to store data within directories and subdirectories

DOS 3.x

This version provided:

- ◆ Support for larger hard drives
- ◆ Networking capabilities
- ◆ Support for two partitions on a single physical drive
- ◆ Enhancements to many utilities

DOS 4.x

This version provided:

- ◆ The **DOS shell**, which had more graphical capabilities than previous versions
- ◆ Support for a mouse

DOS 5.x

This version provided:

- ◆ The **EDIT**, **DOSKEY**, **FORMAT**, and UNDELETE programs
- ◆ The capability to load drivers into Upper Memory Area (memory beyond the 640K range)

DOS 6.x

This version provided:

- ◆ Disk utilities for tasks such as virus scanning and disk **defragmentation**, **compression** software, and backup software
- ◆ The EMM386.EXE utility, which enabled memory to be better managed

NOTE

DOS 6.22 was the last version of DOS to be released. Currently, DOS is not a commonly used operating system, primarily because it lacks a truly graphical interface but also due to its technical limitation of supporting 16-bit applications. However, many DOS commands continue to be supported under the Windows platform, and advanced users find knowing DOS commands very useful. You will learn more about DOS in Chapter 6, "DOS 101: DOS Basics Every MCSE Should Know."

DOS shell
The name that is used to describe the software that makes up the DOS user interface.

EDIT
A DOS text editor.

DOSKEY
A DOS utility that enables the user to customize settings for DOS and add key commands for DOS.

FORMAT
A DOS utility used to prepare a floppy disk or hard disk to store data.

defragmentation
The reorganization of data on a hard disk to optimize performance.

compression
A method of reducing the size of data by using a mathematical calculation.

97

Understanding Windows

Although DOS provided many functions, users wanted these functions combined with a user-friendly interface. This led to Windows, a **graphical user interface (GUI)** operating system based on top of DOS (meaning that Windows is not an operating system by itself and requires DOS to be running). The Windows platform was based on technology that supported 16-bit processing.

The first version of Windows was version 1. This version broke new ground (in the PC market) by enabling more than one application to be open at the same time. It also had windows that you could tile (meaning that you could view many windows at the same time). Windows also had full mouse support, making this operating system easier to use than DOS, which primarily used a keyboard for user input. Version 1 of Windows supported the Intel 80286 processor.

Windows 2 was the second version of Windows to be released and introduced icons to the Windows desktop. It also supported **Program Information Files (PIFs)**, which enabled users to better configure Windows. An enhanced version of Windows 2, called Windows/386, added support for the Intel 80386 processor.

The first widely accepted version of Windows was Windows 3, which introduced the File Manager and the Program Manager utilities. It changed the way memory was managed and offered the option to run Windows in 386 Enhanced Mode. In 386 Enhanced Mode, Windows runs DOS applications in their own windows and uses part of the hard drive as **virtual RAM**. This feature offers better performance, and all modern operating systems include some variation of this concept.

The next versions of Windows to be released were Windows 3.1 and 3.11. Windows 3.1 added better graphical and multimedia support. This version of Windows had better error protection and supported **object linking and embedding (OLE)**. OLE is a technology that lets applications work together and share information. Windows 3.11, also known as Windows for Workgroups, added support for networking capabilities.

graphical user interface (GUI)

An application that provides intuitive controls (such as icons, buttons, menus, and dialog boxes) for configuring, manipulating, and accessing applications and files.

Program Information Files (PIFs)

Files for a non-Windows application that include settings for running the application in Windows 3.x.

virtual RAM

A function of the operating system that is used to simulate RAM by breaking computer programs into small units of data called pages and storing the pages in a page file on the hard disk.

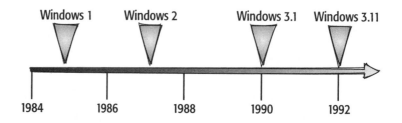

| Windows 1 | Windows 2 | Windows 3.1 | Windows 3.11 |

| 1984 | 1986 | 1988 | 1990 | 1992 |

Windows 95

Released in the fall of 1995, the Windows 95 operating system is Microsoft's 32-bit operating system that supports preemptive multitasking of applications. Preemptive multitasking is a processing method available in certain operating systems that equally allocates processor time to all tasks waiting to be completed. In this case, each application gets a share of the CPU through a series of time slices. Time slices can be adjusted so that one application has higher priority than another application, or so that all applications are processed at the same priority.

Windows 95 acts as its own operating system and does not run on top of DOS. It is compatible with DOS and Windows 16-bit applications. In addition, Windows 95 provides backward compatibility with existing hardware devices.

The key features added to Windows 95 over the Windows 3.x platform include:

- ❖ A new, more intuitive user interface
- ❖ Introduction of the Explorer utility, which makes file management easier for users
- ❖ A more dynamic configuration that does not require as much user interaction
- ❖ A more reliable and robust operating system
- ❖ Better network integration to support many types of networks
- ❖ Plug-and-Play capability, which means that hardware is much easier to install
- ❖ Support for long filenames up to 255 characters, instead of eight characters as found in DOS and Windows 3.x
- ❖ Built-in fax and electronic messaging capabilities
- ❖ Remote dial-up functionality to access the Internet
- ❖ Improved memory management
- ❖ Introduction of the Internet Explorer Web browser

object linking and embedding (OLE)
A technology that enables applications to share data. Each document is stored as an object, and one object can be embedded within another object. For example, an Excel spreadsheet can be embedded within a Word document. Because the object is linked, changes through Excel or Word will be updated through the single linked object.

TIP

With Windows 95 and Windows 98, you have the option of purchasing the Microsoft Plus! package. The Plus! pack offers additional enhancements for the Windows platform. A popular feature of the Plus! package enables you to customize your Desktop through additional sounds, mouse pointers, screen savers, color schemes, and wallpaper. Additional games also ship with the Plus! pack.

Windows 98

Released in 1998, Windows 98 followed as the next evolutionary step in desktop operating systems. The Windows 98 operating system improves the Windows 95 interface in several ways:

- ❖ The Desktop has been simplified to reduce clutter. You can access most options via the Start button.

- ❖ Windows 98 focuses on Internet integration. With Windows 98, you can use the Active Desktop, which functions as a Web page. You can view Web pages and link documents right on your Desktop. Right-clicking the Desktop turns off the View as Web Page option. Windows 98 also provides an Internet Connection Wizard to help you connect to the Internet. FrontPage Express is also bundled with Windows 98 to help you create your own Web pages.

- ❖ Windows 98 includes utilities to make your computer perform better and to optimize resources. The Tune-Up Wizard optimizes your hard drive, scans disks for errors, deletes unnecessary or unused files, and optimizes performance for applications.

- ❖ An Update Wizard checks the Microsoft Web site for system and driver updates for your computer.

- ❖ The Help system is more comprehensive—it can connect you to Microsoft's online help through the Internet.

- ❖ Windows 98 has better accessibility features for users with disabilities.

- ❖ The multimedia capabilities have been improved to take advantage of new hardware standards.

- ❖ Multiple display support is provided for users who want to view multiple monitors (connected to a single computer) simultaneously.

NOTE

The latest release for Windows 98 is Windows 98 second edition. Besides providing the latest updates, fixes, and patches, the second edition also boasts some improvements. One such enhancement is Internet Connection Sharing. Homes with multiple networked computers can share the same Internet connection at the same time.

The Business Solution: Windows NT Workstation 4

Windows NT Workstation provides the highest level of performance and security of the Microsoft desktop operating systems. It is relatively easy to use and has the same desktop interface as Windows 98. But don't make the mistake of equating Windows NT with Windows 98. The interface is the only thing that they share. Windows NT's core technologies are completely different and have been designed to support the needs of businesses. Windows 95 and 98 cannot match its performance and security.

With NT Workstation, you get these features:

◆ A 32-bit multitasking operating system.

◆ The capability to support Intel and Alpha platforms.

◆ Support for multiple processors and preemptive multitasking.

◆ Internet support as a client through Internet Explorer and support as a **server** through Peer Web Services, which enables the workstation to act as a World Wide Web (WWW) and **File Transfer Protocol (FTP)** server. With the WWW service, users can access Web documents from the Web server. With the FTP service, users can transfer files to and from the Web server.

◆ High security through mandatory logon and the NT File System (NTFS), which lets you apply security to users and groups, and view resource access through auditing. NTFS is covered in more detail in Chapter 17, "Windows 2000 Resources: File and Print Management."

◆ Support for applications written to work with DOS, 16-bit Windows, 32-bit Windows, **OS/2**, and **POSIX**.

◆ Full networking capabilities and integration with NT Server.

◆ Network services for sharing file and print resources, and support for up to 10 concurrent client connections.

◆ Support for up to 4GB of RAM and 16EB of disk space.

◆ One of the most reliable operating systems, because applications run in separate memory spaces, preventing a failed application from affecting other applications on the operating system.

NOTE

The main disadvantages of NT Workstation over Windows 95 and Windows 98 are that it has greater hardware requirements and is not as backward compatible. It also does not have Plug-and-Play capabilities.

server
A computer that provides dedicated file, print, messaging, application, or other service to client computers.

File Transfer Protocol (FTP)
An application layer protocol for transferring files between two computers. FTP involves the use of FTP client software and an FTP server.

OS/2
A 32-bit operating system originally developed by Microsoft and IBM. OS/2 can support DOS, Windows, and OS/2 applications. Since Microsoft's abandonment of the program in the late 1980s, OS/2 has been produced and sold exclusively by IBM.

POSIX
A standard originally developed for Unix that defines the interface between applications and the operating system. It is now more widely used for the development of other operating systems, including Windows 2000.

The Next Generation: Windows 2000 Professional

On the heels of the new millennium comes Microsoft's latest upgrade for Windows NT Workstation. Designed to replace Windows NT Workstation as the business desktop computer operating system, Windows 2000 Professional offers major improvements over NT. What has not changed is the stability and performance that many have come to expect from NT.

Windows 2000 Professional offers these new and enhanced features:

❖ Windows file protection in the event that an application overwrites a system file.

❖ Access to system administration tools through the Microsoft **Management Console (MMC)**.

❖ An enhanced interface.

❖ Full 32-bit OS, which improves multitasking performance.

❖ Support for gigabit networking.

❖ Plug-and-Play support.

❖ IntelliMirror function, which enables users to work on files on a server and continue working even if they disconnect from the network. Files that have changed are updated with the latest content when the user connects again with the server.

❖ Power management for laptops.

❖ Simplified installation, configuration, and removal of applications.

❖ Reduction in the number of reboots, especially when installing software.

❖ **IP Security (IPSec)** support for **virtual private networking (VPN)**.

❖ Safe mode option available during start-up that can be used to boot Windows 2000 with minimal settings.

Management Console (MMC)
A Microsoft application framework for accessing administrative tools, called consoles.

IP Security (IPSec)
A protocol standard for encrypting IP packets.

virtual private networking (VPN)
Using encrypted envelopes to securely transmit sensitive data between two points over the unsecured Internet.

Understanding Unix and Linux

Unix is another popular operating system. It is a 32-bit, multiuser, multitasking operating system. Linux is a derivative of the Unix operating system.

Unix

Unix was first developed in the late 1960s as an operating system for mainframe computers. The original development team consisted of Bell Telephone Laboratories, General Electric, and Massachusetts Institute of Technology (MIT). During the early development of Unix, many universities were able to obtain the Unix operating system by signing nondisclosure agreements that allowed them to use the software for educational purposes. Computer science students gained experience with Unix and contributed to its development.

Today two major versions of Unix exist:

- ◆ Unix System Laboratories (USL) System V UNIX
- ◆ Berkeley Software Distribution (BSD) Unix

There also are many other flavors of Unix, but most are derivatives of the versions listed above.

Different versions of Unix have been produced as commercial software, **shareware**, and **freeware**. Each variation has its own features and offers different levels of hardware and software support. Different versions of Unix are also designed to support specific hardware platforms—for example, Intel, RISC, Alpha, and PowerPC.

Because the Unix operating system was designed for engineers by engineers, it has a stigma of being difficult to use and is not as user-friendly as other operating systems. A standard for Unix called X Windows provides a graphical interface for Unix, making it easier to use.

NOTE

You may notice that Unix is referred to as both *Unix* and *UNIX*. When *Unix* is used, it specifies Unix in general. When *UNIX* is used, it specifies the Unix used by USL and is a trademark name.

shareware
Software that is generally available for trial use. If you like the software, you should pay a small licensing fee.

freeware
Software that you can use without payment.

Linux

Linux is an independent operating system that is similar in nature to Unix. The beauty of Linux is that it uses no proprietary code and is freely distributed. The code for Linux is developed and produced by the Free Software Foundation's Gnu's Not Unix (GNU) project. Linux is offered as freeware through the Web, and many applications have been written for Linux as shareware.

College student Linus Torvalds first introduced Linux to the world in 1991 as a hack operating system. By the end of the year, 100 people were using the operating system, sending feedback, and adding contributions to the code. In 1999, it was estimated that there were more than 20 million Linux users worldwide.

Linux is a popular version of Unix because it is **open-source** software and can be distributed only for free or for a minimal cost. Many of the utilities included with the distribution of Linux are also freeware or shareware. This makes Linux an attractive offer for people who want a powerful desktop operating system at little or no cost.

Linux supports all the major software that is produced for the Unix operating system. It is mostly compatible with System V, BSD, and POSIX. It is primarily designed to run on an Intel platform but has been ported to other platforms.

The advantages of Linux include the following:

- ◆ It is a true 32-bit operating system.
- ◆ It supports preemptive multitasking, which is the capability to run more than one application or task at one time.
- ◆ It offers the capability to support multiple users and includes networking capabilities.
- ◆ Security features are included, such as login/password, and directory and file permissions.
- ◆ The distribution software includes development software.

The disadvantages of Linux include the following:

- ◆ The software that ships with Linux tends to be very basic.
- ◆ Text-based versions of Linux are difficult to learn. X Windows Linux is easier to use.
- ◆ Linux accesses hardware directly, as opposed to going through a software interface, so hardware problems are more common under Linux than with Windows NT/2000 or other Unix operating systems.

open-source
Providing the source code for software free for anyone to develop to improve the application, with some licensing, authoring, and other restrictions.

Dual-Booting between OSs

With all the different operating systems out there, you may be wondering how you can test all that software without needing several computers. Fortunately, there is a way: You can run more than one operating system on one computer. The idea is especially useful in test environments where you have limited access to equipment. For example, say you have one computer at home and you want to learn Windows NT Workstation and Linux. You cannot run both operating systems concurrently, but you can load both operating systems on the same computer and, depending on how you start your computer, access one operating system or the other.

Tips for Creating a Dual-Boot Configuration

It probably shouldn't have to be said, but different operating systems don't work well together. Even Windows 98 and Windows NT Workstation can be pretty mean to each other if you don't take some initial precautions. The best way to create a **dual-boot** system is to create multiple partitions on your hard disk. If you have multiple hard disks, that will work as well. Using multiple partitions reduces the possibility of conflicts. In the case of dual-booting between Linux and Windows NT Workstation, the operating systems must exist on different partitions or disks.

Check the vendor documentation to see whether there are any recommendations for configuring the dual-boot. For example, if you will boot between DOS and NT, you should install DOS first.

Windows 98 can dual-boot with:

- ◆ MS-DOS 5.*x* or later
- ◆ Windows 3.*x*
- ◆ Windows NT
- ◆ Linux

Microsoft does not recommend dual-booting between Windows 95 and Windows 98 on the same hard disk.

Windows NT Workstation can dual-boot with:

- ◆ MS-DOS
- ◆ Windows 3.*x*
- ◆ Windows 95
- ◆ Windows 98
- ◆ Linux

dual-boot
Having two or more operating systems on your computer. At system start-up, you can select which operating system you will boot.

105

Review Questions

1. What does DOS stand for?

   _____

2. What does GUI stand for?

   _____

3. Which version of Windows 3.x first supported networking capabilities?

   _____

4. True or false: Windows 3.x acted as its own operating system and did not require DOS to be installed.

   _____

5. What is preemptive multitasking?

   _____

6. Which Microsoft operating system offers the highest performance and security options for desktop computers?

   _____

7. Which Microsoft desktop operating system first offered 32-bit processing?

   _____

8. What was the last version of DOS to be released?

   _____

9. Which Microsoft desktop operating system first offered the Active Desktop as an integrated part of the operating system?

   _____

10. What key feature found in Windows 2000 was first available in Windows 95 and makes hardware installation easier?

_____

Terms to Know

❑ FTP
❑ OS/2
❑ POSIX
❑ MMC
❑ IPSec
❑ VPN
❑ shareware
❑ freeware
❑ open-source
❑ dual-boot

11. Which Unix service offers a graphical interface?

_____

12. What are the two major versions of Unix?

_____

13. What is the popular shareware/freeware version of Unix called?

_____

14. True or false: You can dual-boot between Windows 95 and Windows 98.

_____

15. What is the standard that defines the interface between Unix applications and Unix operating systems?

_____

Chapter

6

DOS 101: DOS Basics Every MCSE Should Know

com·mand *n* : a set of instructions given to perform a task

If you are new to the computer field, you may be asking yourself why you need to know DOS. At times DOS may be the fastest and easiest way to complete a specific task. You don't need to be a DOS expert, but you should know the basics. This chapter covers the important commands and DOS concepts that every MCSE should know. Topics include:

 Organizing your disks

 Creating a directory structure

 Manipulating files

 Using DOS wildcards

 Copying and moving files

 Setting file attributes

 Changing the time and date

 Using timesaving commands

 Using DOS configuration files

Organizing Your Disks

When you purchase a computer, it is typically delivered ready to go—with software installed and configured. Just plug it in and turn it on. But as an MCSE, you will come across many situations requiring you to erase all the information on the hard drive and start from scratch. Some reasons for erasing the hard drive might include having to reinstall the operating system, remove any troublesome viruses, or reorganize the hard drive. In addition, if you want to dual-boot with multiple operating systems on the same computer (described in Chapter 5, "Desktop Operating Systems: A Comparison"), you need to organize your hard drive into separate logical spaces. This function is called **disk partitioning**. Disk partitioning is covered later in this chapter.

Three DOS commands related to disk organization are critical for you to understand: FDISK, FORMAT, and SYS. As an example of how to use these commands, first assume that you need this configuration:

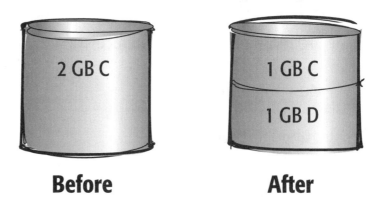

Before   **After**

Originally the drive is configured as a single 2GB partition. You need to logically divide the hard drive into two partitions, each 1GB. You can do this with the DOS commands shown below. Each is described in more detail in the subsections that follow.

Command	Purpose
FDISK	Defines the primary partition and extended partitions, deletes partitions, marks the active partition, and displays partition information.
FORMAT	Initializes a hard drive or floppy disk. Formatting a disk erases any previously stored data and prepares it as a new media on which you can store data.
SYS	Copies the DOS system files and the command interpreter, COMMAND.COM, to the floppy or hard disk that you specify. You need these files to boot DOS.

disk partitioning

The process of creating logical disks from a physical disk. You can then format the logical disks and use them to store data.

COMMAND.COM

A DOS operating system file that receives and executes commands as they are entered at the command line by the user.

Partitioning Your Hard Drive

FDISK is the command you use to configure and display information about your physical disk(s). With FDISK you can:

◆ Create and delete DOS partitions or logical drives.

◆ Set the active partition.

◆ Display partition information.

◆ Change the current fixed drive. (This option appears only if you have more than one physical drive.)

To access the FDISK program, type **FDISK** at the command prompt. Here is the main FDISK screen:

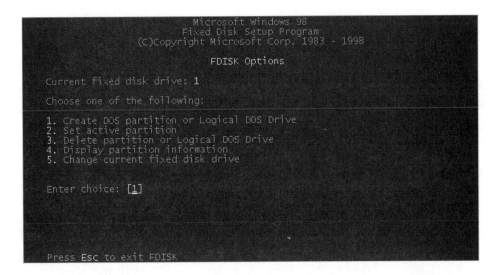

```
                    Microsoft Windows 98
                 Fixed Disk Setup Program
           (C)Copyright Microsoft Corp. 1983 - 1998

                        FDISK Options

Current fixed disk drive: 1

Choose one of the following:

1. Create DOS partition or Logical DOS Drive
2. Set active partition
3. Delete partition or Logical DOS Drive
4. Display partition information
5. Change current fixed disk drive

Enter choice: [1]




Press Esc to exit FDISK
```

NOTE

If you want to dual-boot between Windows 98 and NT, you should install Windows 98 before installing NT. You will need to use FDISK first to create at least two partitions: one for Windows 98 and one for NT. The same strategy applies in most cases when installing two operating systems on the same hard drive.

TIP

If you use FDISK to partition your disk and you use the option to make the entire physical disk the logical disk, it is automatically configured as the active partition. If you do not use the entire physical disk, you must manually specify which partition will be the active partition.

III

Formatting Your Disks

The FORMAT command prepares a floppy or hard disk for use with DOS. When you **format** a disk, you create a **File Allocation Table (FAT)** that keeps track of where data is stored on the disk. Formatting also creates the tracks and sectors on the disk that are needed to store data.

format
To initialize a floppy disk or logical drive and prepare it so that you can store data on it.

File Allocation Table (FAT)
A table stored on the outer edge of the hard drive that indicates the location and order of files on the hard drive.

TEST IT OUT: USING THE *FORMAT* COMMAND

Follow these steps to format a floppy disk:

1. Access a DOS prompt by selecting the MS-DOS shortcut in the Windows 98 Programs menu.

2. Place a floppy disk in the floppy drive.

3. From the command prompt, type A:

WARNING

You are about to erase all information on your floppy disk. Whenever you use the FORMAT command, make sure you have saved any important files to another disk.

4. At the A:\> prompt, type **FORMAT A:**

   You will see this line:

   ```
   Insert new diskette for drive A: and press ENTER when ready…
   ```

5. Press Enter. The disk will be formatted.

6. The next line prompts you for a volume label with this text:

   ```
   Volume label (11 characters, ENTER for none)?
   ```

   At this point you can type a label for the disk. Type whatever label you want to identify the disk.

7. The last question prompts

   ```
   Format another (Y/N)?
   ```

   Press N for no.

There are two important FORMAT options you should know:

FORMAT /S Copies DOS system files to the disk so that it can be bootable

FORMAT /Q Performs a quick format

Preparing a Boot Disk

A boot disk is an important resource to have available during times when your computer won't start or to run application utilities such as anti-virus programs. To make a bootable disk, you use the SYS command, which copies the DOS system files to a disk. The command copies these files:

◆ COMMAND.COM

◆ IO.SYS (This is a **hidden** file.)

◆ MSDOS.SYS (This is a hidden file.)

TEST IT OUT: USING THE *SYS* COMMAND

On the preceding page, you formatted a floppy disk. In this exercise, you will use the SYS command to copy the DOS system files to the floppy:

1. To access the floppy, type **A:**

2. From A:\>, type **DIR**

3. You will see this message (indicating that no files are on the floppy):

   File not found

4. Type **C:**

5. From C:\>, type **SYS A:**

6. You will see this message (indicating that the system files have been copied to the floppy):

   System transferred

7. Type **DIR A:**

8. You will see that COMMAND.COM is stored on the floppy disk.

IO.SYS
A DOS system file that is the first to load from disk during the boot process. This system file contains the software that facilitates interaction between attached hardware and the ROM BIOS.

---

hidden file
A file that is not viewable using the DIR command in DOS or viewable in a folder. The hidden file attribute can be set to on or off using the attribute command in DOS or by setting the file properties in Windows.

MSDOS.SYS
A DOS system file that is loaded by IO.SYS and contains the primary DOS routines.

Creating a Directory Structure

The directory structure is like a filing cabinet for your hard disk. It enables you to logically group files with similar functions. When creating your directory structure, a little planning can really pay off in terms of productivity. Think of your filing system. If you threw everything into one drawer, finding a specific document would be difficult. The same problem would occur on your computer if you put all your documents into one directory, or folder.

Consider the logic of the following sample directory structure. In this case, there are separate folders for applications and data. Each application and data folder is further divided into subdirectories to organize data even better.

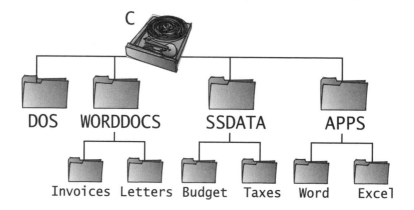

Manipulating the Directory Structure

You can use several commands to manipulate the directory structure.

This table summarizes the most useful commands for directory structure manipulation. The following subsections provide further details of these commands.

Command	Purpose	Syntax
DIR	DIRECTORY shows the directory listing, including files and subdirectories of the current directory.	C:\>**DIR**
MD	MAKE DIRECTORY creates a new directory or subdirectory.	C:\>**MD WORDDOCS**
RD	REMOVE DIRECTORY removes a directory or subdirectory.	C:\>**RD WORDDOCS**
CD	CHANGE DIRECTORY traverses the directory structure.	C:\>**CD WORDDOCS**

Listing Directories, Subdirectories, and Files

To show a list of all the files and directories on your logical drive, you use the DIR command. This is perhaps the most commonly used DOS command. After you type the DIR command, you see this information about the files and directories that are relative to (in the same folder as) the directory path that you are in:

❖ Directory name or filename and extension

❖ Date and time you created the directory or file

❖ Size of the file in bytes

❖ Total number of files and the space used by the folder as well as the remaining disk space in bytes

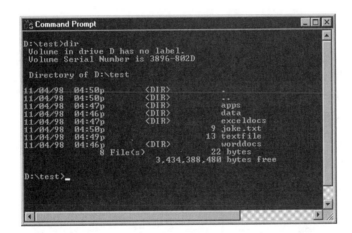

Options to use with the DIR command include the following:

DIR /P Pauses between screens—helpful when you have more than one screen of information

DIR /W Shows the list in a wide format

DIR /S Shows all the information within the subdirectories of the directory

NOTE

The use of a switch, or command option, with the DIR command can be combined with one or more other switches. For example, the command DIR /W /P will show a wide list and will pause if there is more than one page of text to display.

Creating and Deleting Directories

To define your directory structure, you use commands to create and delete directories. To create a directory, you use the MD, or MAKE DIRECTORY, command. To delete a directory, you use the RD, or REMOVE DIRECTORY, command.

TIP

Before you can remove a directory with the RD command, the directory must be empty of all files and subdirectories. To delete directories that contain files or subdirectories, you should use the DELTREE command.

TEST IT OUT: USING THE *MD* AND *RD* COMMANDS

Take these steps to practice creating and removing a directory:

1. From the C:\> prompt in a DOS screen, type **MD WORDDOCS** and then press Enter.

2. From the C:\> prompt, type **MD SSDATA** and then press Enter. This creates the directory named SSDATA.

3. From the C:\> prompt, type **MD TEST** and then press Enter. This creates the directory named TEST.

4. From the C:\> prompt, type **DIR** and then press Enter. You should see a directory listing that includes the two directories you just created.

5. From the C:\> prompt, type **RD TEST** and then press Enter. This removes the directory named TEST.

6. From the C:\> prompt, type **DIR** and then press Enter. You should see a list that still includes the directory SSDATA but not the directory TEST.

TIP

At the DOS prompt, you can type **/?** after any command for additional information and syntax options related to that command.

Changing Directories

You use the CD command to change directories. This command enables you to move fairly easily from one branch of the DOS hierarchical structure to another.

As an example of how to use the CD command, again assume you have the directory structure show earlier in the section "Creating a Directory Structure."

To move down a level—in this case, to the WORDDOCS directory—type this command at the C:\> prompt:

    CD WORDDOCS

To move back up one level of the directory structure, use the CD.. command like this:

    C:\WORDDOCS>**CD..**

If you are more than one level down the tree and want to return to the root drive (the C drive), you type **CD** like this:

    C:\WORDDOCS\LETTERS>**CD**

TEST IT OUT: USING THE *CD* COMMAND

To test directory manipulation, you will complete the directory structure shown on the preceding page. If you completed Test It Out: Using the MD and RD Commands, skip steps 1 and 2.

1. If you are not already at the C:\> prompt, type **C:** at the command prompt and press Enter.
2. From C:\> type **MD WORDDOCS** and press Enter. Type **MD SSDATA** and press Enter.
3. From C:\> type **MD DOS** and press Enter. Type **MD APPS** and press Enter.
4. Change to the WORDDOCS directory by typing **CD WORDDOCS** and then press Enter.
5. From C:\>WORDDOCS> type **MD INVOICES** and press Enter. Type **MD LETTERS** and press Enter.
6. To return to the root level of C:\, from C:\>WORDDOCS> type **CD**
7. Take the steps needed to complete the directory structure shown on the preceding page.

Manipulating Files

After you have set up your directory structure, you can then place files into directories. Most of your files will be program and application files, or data created from the application programs.

In addition, sometimes you will need to create or edit a text file. For example:

❖ You need to create a file called LOGON.BAT that specifies that ABC.EXE should run whenever the BAT file is called.

❖ You have a file called ACCT.TXT that needs to be renamed ACCT99.TXT.

❖ You have a text file that needs to be updated through editing.

The commands below are useful in file manipulation. These commands are covered in greater detail in the following subsections.

Command	Purpose
COPY CON	Lets you create a text file by capturing whatever data is written to the console (screen). This command works well for quickly creating text files.
TYPE	Displays the contents of a text file.
EDIT	Brings up a text editor that has a user-friendly interface for creating and editing text files.
DEL	The DELETE command deletes files that you no longer need.
REN	The RENAME command renames a file.

NOTE

If you are creating a small text file, COPY CON can be a time-saver. If you need to create a larger text file or edit an existing text file, use EDIT. If you are trying to create a text-only file, these commands work better than a word processor because a word processor includes formatting information within the file.

Creating a Text File from the Console

You can use the COPY CON command to quickly create a text file from the command prompt. This command is useful if you need to create a small file. The COPY CON command uses this syntax:

COPY CON *filename* [Press Enter.]

Type the text that the file will contain. [Press Enter.]

Press the Ctrl key and the Z key at the same time. This will appear on the screen as ^Z.

For example, to create a text file containing the sentence, "This is a sample text file," you type:

COPY CON TEST.TXT [Enter]

This is a sample text file.

^Z. [Enter]

The system will verify with a message saying 1 file(s) copied. The file will be created in the directory of the drive that you are currently in.

 TEST IT OUT: USING THE *COPY CON* COMMAND

In this exercise, you will create a small text file from the command prompt:

1. From the C:\WORDDOCS directory, type **COPY CON DATA.TXT** and press Enter.

2. Type any data you want.

3. Press the Ctrl key and the Z key at the same time. Press Enter.

4. You should receive the following verification:

   1 file(s) copied.

Displaying the Contents of a File

To display the contents of a text file, you can use the TYPE command. TYPE redirects the data within the file to the console screen. TYPE uses this syntax:

TYPE *drive letter:\directory\filename*

Or if the prompt is already at the correct drive and directory where the file exists, the syntax is

TYPE *filename*

NOTE

You usually use the TYPE command to see the contents of a text or **ASCII file**. The command does not produce readable information if you use it to display the contents of an executable file or a file generated by most applications.

TIP

If the text file you are trying to read contains more than a screen of information, the TYPE command can be somewhat frustrating, because it simply scrolls through the file at what seems like light speed. If this is the case, consider reading the file with the EDIT command.

ASCII file

Text file that uses the ASCII character set. ASCII is a standard for encoding letters and numbers into the ones and zeros that the computer understands.

120

Editing Text Documents

One of the easiest ways to edit and create text files is to use the EDIT command. EDIT is the user-friendly editing program in DOS.

You can call up the EDIT program and then specify which file to open for editing, or you can call up the path and filename you wish to edit when you invoke the EDIT program at the command prompt.

 TEST IT OUT: USING THE *EDIT* COMMAND

1. From the C:\> prompt, type **EDIT**. The EDIT program starts.

2. Type whatever you want the text file to say.

3. Press the Alt key and the F key together to access the File ➢ Save menu option.

4. The Save As dialog box appears. Save the file as **SAMPLE.TXT** and click the OK button.

5. Exit the EDIT program by pressing Alt+F and then select File ➢ Exit.

Deleting a File

After you no longer need a file, you can delete it with the DEL command. DEL is an easy command to use. The syntax is

DEL *drive letter:directory\filename*

Or if you are already in the directory in which the file exists, the syntax is

DEL *filename*

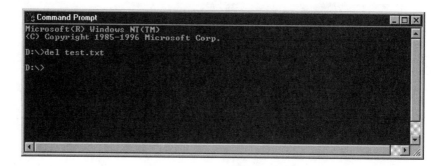

NOTE

Third-party DOS utilities—for example, Norton Utilities—can sometimes recover files that have been deleted.

TIP

If you delete a file in Windows 95/98, NT, or 2000, you can recover the deleted file from the Recycle Bin.

WARNING

Do not delete files if you are unsure of what they are. They might be program, application, or configuration files you need.

Renaming a File

Use the REN command to rename files, using this syntax:

REN *oldname newname*

For example, assume that you have a file called ACCT.TXT that you want to rename ACCT99.TXT. You would use the command shown on the screen below.

TEST IT OUT: USING THE *REN* COMMAND

In this exercise, you will create, rename, and then delete a file.

1. At the C:\ prompt, create a text file called **OLD.TXT** by using the EDIT or COPY CON command.

2. At the C:\> prompt, type **REN OLD.TXT NEW.TXT**

3. Use the DIR command to verify that your file has been renamed.

4. At the C:\> prompt, type **DEL NEW.TXT**

5. Use the DIR command to verify that your file has been deleted.

Using the DOS Wildcards

DOS uses wildcard characters to represent specific letters or numbers as a variable. This is useful when you are looking for a series of files or you want to perform an action on many files at the same time.

The asterisk (*) wildcard represents any number of characters that you are looking for.

The question mark (?) wildcard represents a single character or number. You can use multiple ? wildcards in a single query. This wildcard is not as commonly used as *.

As an example of how to use these wildcards, assume you have this directory structure:

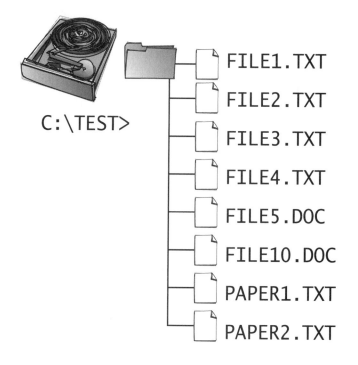

C:\TEST>

FILE1.TXT

FILE2.TXT

FILE3.TXT

FILE4.TXT

FILE5.DOC

FILE10.DOC

PAPER1.TXT

PAPER2.TXT

TEST IT OUT: USING DOS WILDCARDS

1. Create the directory structure and files shown on the preceding page. Refer to "Creating and Deleting Directories" for help on creating the DOS directory structure and to "Editing Text Documents" for help on creating the text files.

2. Access the C:\TEST directory.

3. Type **DIR *.TXT**

   You should see FILE1.TXT, FILE2.TXT, FILE3.TXT, FILE4.TXT, PAPER1.TXT, and PAPER2.TXT.

4. Type **DIR *.DOC**

   You should see FILE5.DOC and FILE10.DOC.

5. Type **DIR FILE?.***

   Notice that FILE10.DOC does not show up, because the ? wildcard indicates only a single placeholder.

6. Type **DIR P*.TXT**

   You should see PAPER1.TXT and PAPER2.TXT.

7. Type **REN F*.DOC F*.TXT**

   Type **DIR *.DOC** to see whether any DOC files remain.

8. Type **DEL P*.***

   Type **DIR P*.*** to see whether any of the files beginning with *P* remain.

NOTE

As you can see, wildcards make DOS management a lot easier and more efficient than managing files on an individual basis.

Copying and Moving Files

If you do not like the location of your files or you want to rearrange your file structure, you can use the COPY and MOVE commands.

The COPY command copies the file(s) from the source directory to the destination directory. A copy of the file then exists in both the source and destination directories.

The MOVE command moves the file(s) from the source directory to the destination directory. The file then exists only in the destination directory.

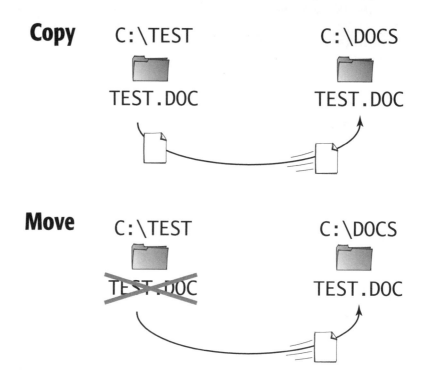

Copy   C:\TEST   C:\DOCS

TEST.DOC   TEST.DOC

Move   C:\TEST   C:\DOCS

TEST.DOC   TEST.DOC

The syntax for performing a COPY is

    COPY source path\filename destination path\filename

For example:

    COPY C:\TEST\TEST.DOC C:\DOCS\TEST.DOC

The syntax for performing a MOVE is

    MOVE source path\filename destination path\filename

For example:

    MOVE C:\TEST\TEST.DOC C:\DOCS\TEST.DOC

TEST IT OUT: USING *COPY* AND *MOVE* COMMANDS

In this exercise, you will copy and move files from one directory to another.

1. At C:\TEST, create files TEST1.DOC, TEST2.DOC, TEST3.DOC, and MOVEME.DOC. Create the directory C:\DOCS.

2. From C:\TEST, type **COPY TEST1.DOC C:\DOCS**

NOTE

When you are working with a file that is located in the current directory, there is no need to type the entire path for the file in the command.

3. Verify that the document was copied by using the DIR command at C:\TEST and C:\DOCS. Does TEST1.DOC exist in both directories?

4. Type **MOVE MOVEME.DOC C:\DOCS**

5. Verify that the document was moved by using the DIR command at C:\TEST and C:\DOCS. MOVEME.DOC should exist only in the C:\DOCS directory.

6. Type **COPY T*.DOC C:\DOCS**

Using this command, all documents in the C:\TEST directory that begin with a *T* and end with the extension DOC will all be copied to the C:\DOCS directory. Use this method to quickly move many like files all at once.

FAT32

File Allocation Table 32. A 32-bit version of the FAT file system that will recognize drives larger than 2GB. FAT32 can adjust the size of the clusters (individual cells that are used to organize the data) on a hard drive to accommodate larger-sized drives.

Working with Filenames

There are different types of file systems. You can use FAT with DOS, which restricts the names of files and folders to only eight characters with a three-character extension. With Windows 95/98 and Windows 2000, you can use **FAT32** in addition to FAT. FAT32 makes better use of disk space, supports large disk sizes greater than 2GB, and improves disk performance.

If you are using DOS, file or folder names longer than eight characters are automatically assigned an abbreviated eight-character name. Sometimes the short names are not very intuitive. For this reason, it's a good idea to try to keep your filenames fairly short.

You should also note that DOS utilities, unlike Windows 95/98/NT and 2000, do not understand spaces in filenames or long filenames. If you have a filename with spaces or a long filename, use quotation marks around the filename when using DOS utilities.

Setting File Attributes

Each DOS file has attributes that define the properties of the file. You can manipulate these attributes by using the ATTRIB command. The four DOS attributes are described below.

incremental backup
Uses the archive bit to determine which files have changed since the last incremental backup. After the incremental backup is complete, the archive bit is cleared. Incremental backups occur between each normal or full backup.

differential backup
Uses the archive bit to determine which files have changed since the last normal backup. Files that have changed are backed up. The archive bit is not reset until the next normal backup. If you have to restore data, you need only your last full backup and your last differential tape.

Attribute	Purpose
Read-only (R)	If you set the read-only attribute, you cannot modify or delete a file unless you remove the read-only attribute. This attribute safeguards a file from being accidentally modified or deleted.
Archive (A)	You use the archive attribute with backups. A file that is marked with the archive attribute indicates that it is a new file or a file that has been modified since the last backup. Use this attribute when you perform **incremental** or **differential backups**.
System (S)	The system attribute indicates that the file is a system or program file. To manipulate any of the other attributes, you must first remove the system attribute. This attribute implies that a file is read-only.
Hidden (H)	The hidden attribute keeps a file from being listed through the DIR command or from being accidentally deleted.

The syntax for the ATTRIB command is

```
ATTRIB drive letter:\directory\file [+attribute|-attribute]
```

❖ *+attribute* indicates that you are applying an attribute.

❖ *−attribute* indicates that you are removing an attribute.

❖ Note that you type only the letter abbreviation of the attribute, such as *H* for the hidden attribute.

Assume that you have a directory, D:\TEST, and that the directory contains a file called TEST.DOC.

To see the file attributes, you would type ATTRIB TEST.DOC

Note that the *A* in front of the filename indicates that the archive bit is set. This attribute is applied to all new files.

To apply the hidden attribute to the TEST.DOC file, you would type **ATTRIB TEST.DOC +H**

To remove the hidden attribute from the TEST.DOC file, you would type **ATTRIB TEST.DOC -H**

Changing the Time and Date

You can see what time your computer is set to or you can change the time with the TIME command. Use the DATE command to display or change the date.

To see the time, type **TIME** at the command prompt. To change the time, type in the time after the command at the command prompt:

> **TIME** *time*

```
Command Prompt                                          _ □ ×
D:\>time
The current time is: 17:30:27.71
Enter the new time:

D:\>
```

To see the date, type **DATE** at the command prompt. To change the date, type the date, using the syntax *mm-dd-yy*, after the command at the command prompt:

> **DATE** *date*

```
Command Prompt                                          _ □ ×
D:\>date
The current date is: Wed 11/04/1998
Enter the new date: (mm-dd-yy)

D:\>
```

Using Some Timesavers

Two options that can help you save time are the F3 key and the DOSKEY command.

The F3 key displays the last command that you typed. The F3 key can save you time when you are using the same lengthy command repeatedly and need only to change the variables slightly each time.

The DOSKEY command keeps a history of the commands that you have typed. You access it by pressing the up-arrow (↑) and down-arrow keys (↓) on the keypad. When using a set of commands repeatedly—for example, when creating and moving files—DOSKEY can save a significant amount of time that otherwise would have been spent typing.

TEST IT OUT: USING THE F3 KEY, *DOSKEY*, *TIME*, AND *DATE* COMMANDS

In this exercise, you learn how to apply new time-saving DOS commands in addition to resetting the time and date of your system. You will need to use some of the commands that you have learned in previous sections. Refer back to those sections if you forget a command.

1. From a DOS prompt, type **DOSKEY** and press Enter. You will see the message DOSKey installed displayed.

2. Type several of the commands that you have learned about in this chapter.

3. Press the F3 key to display the last command that you typed.

4. Use the up-arrow (↑) and down-arrow (↓) keys on the keypad to view the history of the commands you have issued since you invoked DOSKEY.

5. From a DOS prompt, type **TIME**. If the time is correct, press Enter. If not, type the correct time and press Enter.

6. From a DOS prompt, type **DATE**. If the date is correct, press Enter. If not, type the correct date and press Enter.

TIP

Another useful DOS command is CLS. When you type CLS at the command prompt, it clears the current screen and leaves you with a DOS prompt.

Using the DOS Configuration Files

If you boot your computer using DOS as your operating system, DOS looks for two files during start-up: CONFIG.SYS and AUTOEXEC.BAT. These files customize the configuration for your computer.

The main function of the CONFIG.SYS file is to configure system hardware and set the computer's environment parameters. The environment parameters include loading device drivers and setting the amount of memory DOS will use for applications.

The main function of the AUTOEXEC.BAT file is as a **batch file** that runs every time you start your computer. Common items in AUTOEXEC.BAT include programs that should run every time you start your computer and customization commands for your computer.

Both files are discussed further in the following subsections. In addition to these two files, a section on the BOOT.INI file has been included for anyone who will be working with a dual-boot computer.

CONFIG.SYS

CONFIG.SYS configures your computer's memory management, DOS settings, and device drivers. Here is a sample CONFIG.SYS file with commonly included items:

```
DEVICE=C:\DOS\HIMEM.SYS
DEVICE=C:\DOS\EMM386.EXE NOEMS
DOS=HIGH,UMB
FILES=20
BUFFERS=30
DEVICE=C:\FUJITSU\ATAPI.SYS /D:OEMCD001
```

The first three lines represent options for configuring how memory is managed on your computer. DOS does not use the same memory management scheme as Windows 95, Windows 98, or Windows NT. This means that without some type of memory manager, your computer can recognize only 640K of memory. For more information on memory management, you should consult a DOS manual.

The FILES=*x* option specifies how many file handles DOS can keep open at any time. *File handles* is a fancy way of saying open files. You should limit the number of open files to conserve memory.

The BUFFERS=*x* option specifies how much memory will be available to store information in RAM as opposed to disk. This is called caching. Requests that are handled through cache as opposed to disk are processed much more quickly.

The last line in the sample file represents a CD-ROM driver that is being loaded. Any other device drivers that need to be loaded would also be included.

---

batch file

A file that contains a set of commands to be executed by the operating system. AUTOEXEC.BAT is one example of a batch file that is executed during the final stages of the boot process. All batch files end in BAT.

AUTOEXEC.BAT

The AUTOEXEC.BAT file is a special batch file that loads or configures, without user input, any options that should be configured each time you start the computer or any programs that should be run. Here is a sample AUTOEXEC.BAT file:

```
PATH=C:\DOS;C:\WINDOWS;C:\WORD
C:\DOS\SMARTDRV
STARTNET
```

In this sample file, the first line sets up the path the computer will use. PATH tells the computer where it should look for executable files. For example, if you were in the C:\DOCS folder and you tried to execute WORD.EXE, the system would look in memory, then in the current folder, then in the folders listed in the PATH statement.

The second line specifies that the SMARTDRV program should be loaded. SMARTDRV improves system performance by accessing data from a disk faster.

The final line calls another batch file, STARTNET, which loads network services.

BOOT.INI

The BOOT.INI text file plays an important role on computers that dual-boot between any Microsoft Windows 3.x or 9x operating systems and Windows NT and 2000: It specifies the locations of the operating systems installed, provides for a default operating system to load, and displays a menu of the operating system choices available for the user to choose.

The BOOT.INI file is located at the root of the start-up drive. The start-up drive is usually the C drive. Inside the BOOT.INI file are commands that tell the computer to display a DOS menu during the boot process. The menu lists options for the user to select that will start one of any installed operating systems.

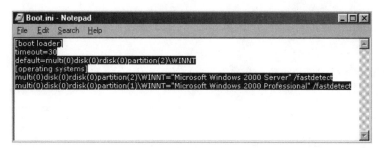

The screen shot above represents the contents of the BOOT.INI file. The first section header, [bootloader], specifies how long in seconds the menu should be displayed before the default selection is chosen. The [operating systems] section indicates the locations of the different operating systems, the text name that will appear in the menu, and the physical location of the operating system based on which partition each is installed on. When creating dual-boot systems, you might be required to manually edit the file to change any of these settings.

Review Questions

Terms to Know
- ❏ disk partitioning
- ❏ COMMAND.COM
- ❏ format
- ❏ FAT
- ❏ IO.SYS
- ❏ hidden file
- ❏ MSDOS.SYS
- ❏ ASCII file
- ❏ FAT32
- ❏ incremental backup
- ❏ differential backup
- ❏ batch file

1. Which DOS command do you use to erase data on a floppy disk or hard drive so that the media is initialized and you can store new data?

_____

2. Which DOS command do you use to copy the DOS system files and the command interpreter to the floppy disk or hard disk that you specify?

_____

3. List four options that are presented (and represent the main tasks) when you use the FDISK command.

_____

_____

_____

_____

4. Which FORMAT option performs a quick format?

_____

5. Which FORMAT option also transfers the system files as the format is performed?

_____

6. List three files that are transferred when you SYS a drive.

_____

_____

_____

7. If you were at C:\TEST\DOCS and you wanted to go to the root of C:\, which command would you use?

_____

8. Which command would you use from the C:\ prompt to delete the TEST.DOC file that is located in C:\TEST?

_____

9. What is the purpose of the COPY CON command?

_____

10. Which command do you use to change the contents of an existing text file?

   A. CHANGE

   B. EDIT

   C. COPY CON

   D. EDITOR

_____

11. True or false: You use the DISPLAY command to see the contents of a text file.

_____

12. You use the _____ command to rename a file.

13. What is the difference between the DOS * and ? wildcards?

_____

14. What is the difference between the DOS COPY and MOVE commands?

_____

15. What are the command and syntax to specify that TEST.DOC should have a hidden attribute?

_____

Chapter
7

Graphical Interface:
Windows Basics

in·ter·face *n* : a point of interaction between two systems

In this chapter, you will learn the fundamental components of the graphical interface in Windows 98. As far as the fundamentals go, Windows 98 and Windows 95 are very similar, so if you are using Windows 95, the information in this chapter still applies.

This chapter covers these topics:

 The Windows 98 Desktop

 The Start button

 My Computer

 Network Neighborhood

 The Recycle Bin

 Desktop customization

 Shortcuts

 Wizards

 Windows Explorer

 Internet Explorer

A Quick Introduction

The Windows 98 operating system was designed around many of the original goals of Windows 95. Windows 98 also added goals to take advantage of using the Internet. The goals for Windows 98 were:

command-line
The prompt in a DOS screen from which a command is executed by typing letters and characters.

- ❖ It had to be easy for people to use.
- ❖ The platform needed to be stable so that users would feel comfortable storing data on the computer.
- ❖ The interface needed to be visually pleasing and intuitive so that users would have an experience that was comfortable and productive.
- ❖ It had to provide superior integration of the latest Internet technologies, including Internet-based e-mail, Web browsing, and Internet access configuration. These features needed to have wide-reaching support for different technologies and be easy to set up.
- ❖ It needed to have support for the latest hardware.
- ❖ Performance and stability needed to improve as compared to earlier versions of Windows, including Windows 95.

Windows 98, like its predecessor, has a graphical user interface (GUI), which makes it easier to use than the old DOS **command-line** environment. Windows 98 is designed to be a *discoverable* operating system, which means that users can intuitively complete necessary tasks.

In Windows 98, using the left mouse button, sometimes called the primary mouse button, enables you to complete basic tasks, such as launching a program or opening a folder. The right, or secondary, mouse button enables you to perform more advanced tasks, such as changing a file's properties.

TIP

To introduce new users to a GUI and the mouse, let them play the game Solitaire. Playing helps them practice using a mouse. The only drawback is that most users become addicted to this game!

Brand-new users of Windows should first learn:

- ♦ To use the mouse. You do this through practice.
- ♦ To open windows so that you can easily complete common tasks. To open windows, you simply point and double-click what you want to open. To select items, you use a single click. When a window is open, you will see a screen similar to the one below.

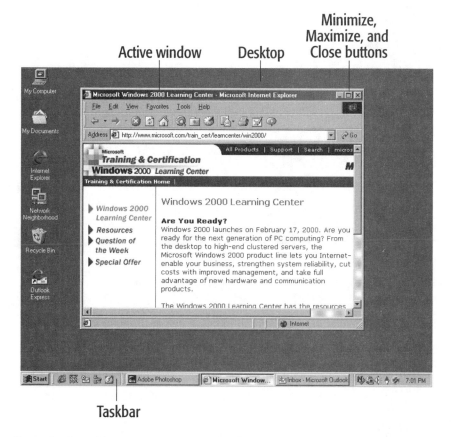

The active window (the one you are using) has three buttons in the upper-right corner:

- ♦ The ▬ button minimizes the window, making the window disappear and leaving only a button in the Taskbar to make the window reappear. The application is still running while minimized, and you can easily re-access it by clicking the item on the Taskbar.
- ♦ The ☐ button maximizes the window so that it takes up the entire screen.
- ♦ The ☒ button closes the application.

You can see which applications are running by looking at the Taskbar. By clicking an application button in the Taskbar, you specify which application will be the active window.

Introduction to the Windows 98 Desktop

When you start Windows 98, you see a screen similar to this.

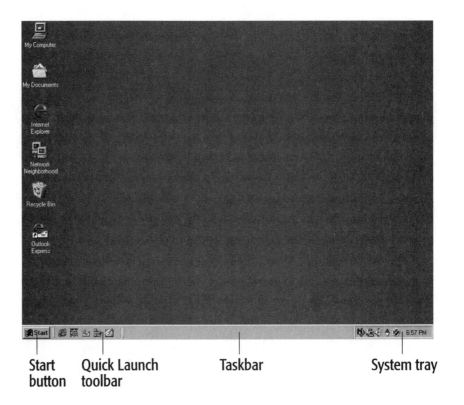

Start button   Quick Launch toolbar   Taskbar   System tray

NOTE

If your computer came with Windows 98 already installed, your Desktop might look different because of customization from the hardware manufacturer. As you use Windows 98, you can customize the Desktop to reflect your preferences.

Graphical Interface: Windows Basics

The following table provides an overview of each of the Windows 98 opening screen options. The main topics will be covered in more detail throughout this chapter.

Option	Description
The Taskbar and Start button	The bottom of the screen contains the Start button and Taskbar. From the Start button, you can run applications, access documents, configure your computer, and shut down your computer. The Taskbar shows you which applications are running and enables you to switch between applications.
System tray	The location in the Taskbar where the currently loaded system utilities are displayed. A common utility found in the system tray is antivirus software.
Quick Launch toolbar	Located in the Taskbar, shortcuts to applications can be placed here for quick access. In addition to shortcuts to **Internet Explorer** and **Outlook Express,** the Web channel icon and the Show Desktop icon (which minimizes all active windows—a great shortcut to get to the Desktop) are located here.
My Computer	My Computer shows you which disk resources your computer is using and enables you to access folders and files. You can also access the Control Panel, Printers, and **Dial-Up Networking** folders through My Computer.
Network Neighborhood	If your computer is attached to a network, Network Neighborhood enables you to browse the network for computers that offer network resources.
Outlook Express	Outlook Express is the built-in messaging application by Microsoft. Use it to check your Internet e-mail, read and post information to newsgroups, or maintain your personal address book.
Recycle Bin	The Recycle Bin enables you to store files that you have deleted so that you can undelete them if necessary.
The Internet	The Internet initially calls up the Internet Connection Wizard, which helps you connect to the Internet. After your Internet connection has been configured, clicking this icon calls up the Internet Explorer program.
Active Desktop	The Active Desktop enables you to open links to the Internet and view Web pages from within the Desktop wallpaper. No browser necessary! Access the Active Desktop by using the Display control panel or by right-clicking on the Desktop and selecting Properties.

Internet Explorer
A World Wide Web browser developed by Microsoft for viewing Web pages on the Internet.

Outlook Express
A free Internet e-mail client application developed by Microsoft.

Dial-Up Networking
A feature of Windows 95 and 98 that guides the user through setting up a network connection by using a modem, a phone line, and the pre-installed Microsoft software.

Using the Start Button

You can do almost anything from the Windows 98 Start button. When you click the Start button, you see a menu with the following options:

- ◊ Programs
- ◊ Documents
- ◊ Settings
- ◊ Find
- ◊ Help
- ◊ Run
- ◊ Log Off
- ◊ Shut Down

Each of these options is covered in more detail in the following subsections.

Programs

When you point to the Programs menu from within the Start menu, you see all the programs that have been installed on your computer.

Within the Programs menu, the top icons displayed are folder icons with an arrow to the right of each folder. This arrow indicates that you can access a cascading menu of options for each folder. The bottom icons without folders and arrows represent applications that can be opened directly by clicking the icons. This screen shows an example of the Programs menu.

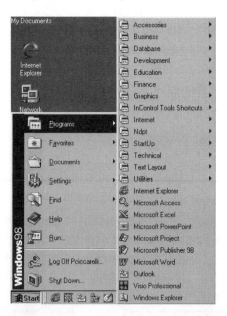

Documents

The Documents menu enables you to quickly access up to the last 15 documents that you worked with, as well as any documents that you have stored in the My Documents folder. Double-click a document filename to open it.

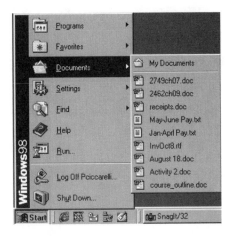

Settings

Through the Settings menu, you can configure the Control Panel, printers, the Taskbar and the Start menu, folder options, and the Active Desktop. You can also access Windows Update.

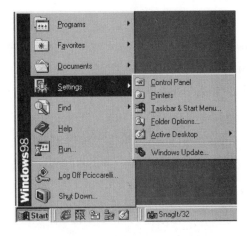

NOTE

Windows Update is a new feature with Windows 98. Using an Internet connection, Windows Update will access Microsoft on the Internet and download any necessary file updates that Windows 98 needs.

Control Panel

Through Control Panel, you configure most options for your computer. These include hardware, software, and network settings, among other items. Simply double-click an icon to access the options it represents.

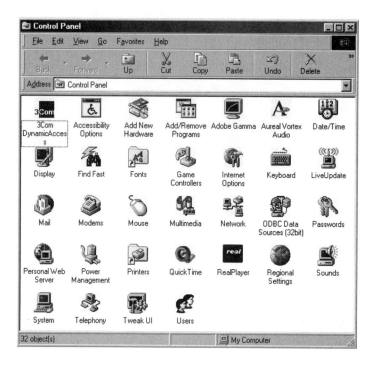

Printers

You can use the Printers folder to create, delete, and manage printers. Double-click a particular printer icon to access that printer or double-click Add Printer to add and configure a new printer.

Taskbar and Start Menu

You click Start ➢ Settings ➢ Taskbar & Start Menu to reach the Taskbar Properties dialog box. Here you can configure how Windows displays the Taskbar, and you can add, remove, or configure which items appear on the Start menu.

Find

The Start menu's Find option enables you to search files and folders based on name, location, or the time that the file was created or modified. If you use Find for advanced searches, you can search for files based on file type, text within the file, and the size of the file.

If your computer has been added to a network, you can also search for names of computers within the network.

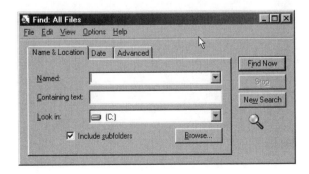

Help

Help provides online help for Windows 98. Help is arranged so that you can read it like a book by using the Contents tab, or you can use the Index and Find tabs to search for information on a specific topic.

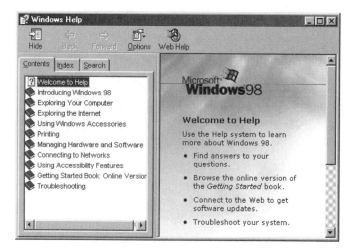

 TEST IT OUT: ACCESSING THE LEARNING WINDOWS 98 TUTORIAL

If you are not familiar with Windows 98, the Welcome to Windows 98 tutorial can help get you up and running. Follow these steps to access the tutorial:

1. Select Start ➢ Programs ➢ Accessories ➢ System Tools ➢ Welcome to Windows.

2. Click the Discover Windows 98 option to learn more about how to take advantage of all Windows 98 has to offer.

3. After the tour loads, just follow the instructions.

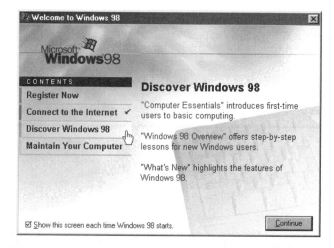

Run

The Run option enables you to run command-line utilities or to launch applications. Within Run, you can browse for files by using the Browse button. Using Run can be a faster way of launching programs or a way to launch programs that are not defined as part of the Start menu.

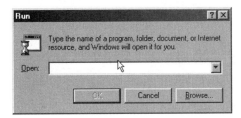

Log Off

The Log Off feature disconnects any network connections and closes all your programs so that another user can log on.

Shut Down

The Shut Down menu offers four choices, as defined in this table.

Shut Down Option	Purpose
Standby	If your computer hardware supports the Standby option, this enables you to suspend operation or put your computer in sleep mode, which conserves power. When you return your computer to a running state, you should be able to continue your work from where you left off.
Shut Down the Computer	Saves any changes that you have made and prepares the computer to be turned off.
Restart the Computer	Saves any changes that you have made and restarts your computer. Many changes to your computer require you to restart the computer for the changes to take effect.
Restart the Computer in MS-DOS Mode	Enables you to restart the computer in DOS mode, which might be needed to run specific DOS applications.

Accessing the My Computer Window

The My Computer icon on the Desktop contains information about your computer's installed drives and enables you to configure your computer. From My Computer, you see icons that represent the following:

- ◇ Floppy drives
- ◇ Logical drives (the logical disk partitions you have created, such as C)
- ◇ CD-ROM drives
- ◇ Control Panel folder
- ◇ Printers folder
- ◇ Dial-Up Networking folder
- ◇ Web folder

The contents of the My Computer window depend on your computer's configuration. Here is a sample screen.

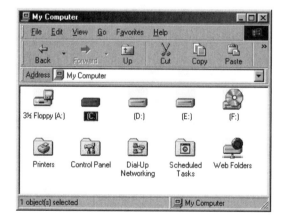

NOTE

The Control Panel and Printers folders are the same items you see under Start ≻ Settings. They also exist in other locations. Providing several ways to access these items makes finding them easier for the user.

By left-clicking an item within My Computer, you can obtain more information about that item. For example, if you click a floppy drive, logical drive, or CD-ROM drive, you see the contents of those drives, such as folders and files. Below you can see the contents of a sample C drive.

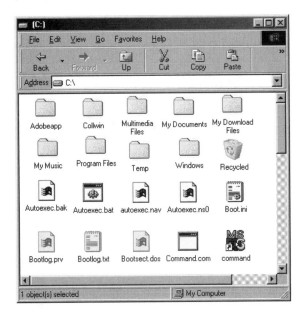

By right-clicking an item within My Computer, you access a menu that enables you to open the item, find information within the item, scan for viruses, format the drive, create a shortcut for the item, and use the Properties option.

If you choose to see Properties, you can get detailed information about capacity and use tools—such as error checking, backup, and defragmentation—that manage disk drives. The screen below shows general information about drive C.

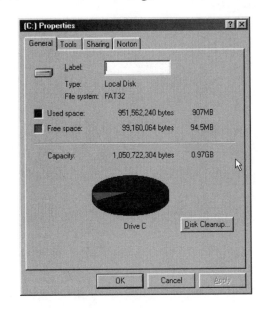

Accessing Network Neighborhood

network drive

A mapping to a network path that appears to the user as a drive letter. You access it the same way that you access a local drive.

You typically use Network Neighborhood only if your computer is connected to a network. By clicking the Network Neighborhood option with the left mouse button, you can see all the network resources. They are arranged hierarchically by network and computer name.

If you right-click the Network Neighborhood icon, you can:

- ❖ Find computers on the network
- ❖ Map **network drives**
- ❖ Disconnect network drives
- ❖ Create a new shortcut
- ❖ Rename the icon
- ❖ See network properties, which brings up Control Panel ➢ Network

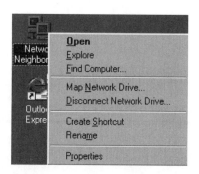

Using the Recycle Bin

If you've ever thrown anything away and then pulled it out of the trash, you already know how the Recycle Bin works. When you delete files, they are placed in the Recycle Bin. You recover the files by removing them from the Recycle Bin and specifying the destination of the files.

When you open the Recycle Bin, you see:

- The name of the files that you deleted
- The original path the files existed in
- The date and time you deleted the files
- The type of the files
- The size of the files

If you click the File menu within the Recycle Bin, you can restore files, empty the Recycle Bin (at which point, you cannot recover those files), delete specific files, and see file properties.

WARNING

When moving files from another networked computer to your Recycle Bin, the files are deleted instead of placed into the Recycle Bin. You will be prompted to confirm that you want to permanently delete the files.

Customizing Your Desktop

Having the capability to customize your Desktop means that you can personalize it to suit your needs and personality. This section shows you how to change the appearance of items on your Desktop. You can:

◆ Change the background colors your computer uses

◆ Choose whether to use a screen saver

◆ Configure Active Desktop settings by using the Web tab of the Display Properties dialog box

To easily change your computer's Desktop appearance, right-click an open space on the Desktop, and you will see this menu.

Choosing Properties opens a Display Properties dialog box similar to this screen (the options you see depend on the hardware and software that is installed on your computer).

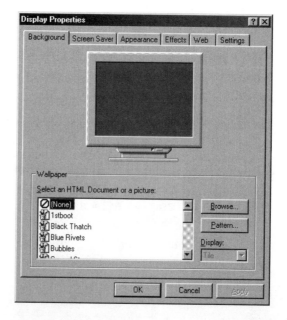

Background

The Background tab enables you to choose the wallpaper that your computer uses. Wallpaper is a predefined set of colors, patterns, and sometimes images that you apply to change the look of your Desktop. Windows 98 has many choices available. In addition, you can add your own pictures to serve as your background.

Instead of choosing wallpaper, you can choose a pattern to give your desktop color some texture.

Screen Saver

The Screen Saver tab enables you to specify that your computer should use a screen saver if there is no activity for a specified amount of time. The screen saver applies your choice of image or text to the screen in a continually changing, random order. (Beware, they can be addictive to watch!) The screen saver was created to prevent a chemical inside the computer screen from etching a permanent outline into the glass. Through this tab, you can configure the following:

- ❖ Which screen saver to use
- ❖ Whether you need a password to disable the screen saver
- ❖ The amount of time without any activity before the screen saver starts

Appearance

The Appearance tab specifies the color scheme that the Desktop, windows, and icons use. Here you can be creative and assign each item its own color, size, and font.

WARNING

The Display Properties dialog box also includes a tab called Settings. You should not modify the settings without understanding what you are doing. You should also test any changed settings before they are applied. If you configure settings incorrectly, you might not be able to see your display properly or at all.

Active Desktop

As described earlier, Active Desktop is an innovative approach to interacting with the Internet. You can add a stock market ticker tape directly to your Desktop, see automatic news updates, or turn your entire Desktop background into a Web page. You can create your own Web page and apply it to the Desktop or you can use a Web page from a site on the Internet. Use the Web tab from Display Properties, as shown below, to access the properties settings for Active Desktop.

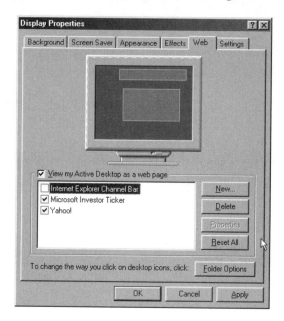

After you have selected the site you want to add, you only need to click OK to have it appear on the Desktop.

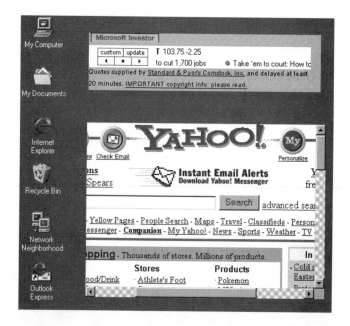

Creating Shortcuts

Shortcuts are icons that point to any Windows 98 object—applications, files, folders, disk drives, Control Panel items, and more. You can place shortcuts on the Windows Desktop or within any folder. The main advantage of shortcuts is that they enable you to quickly access resources. You can recognize a shortcut by the small arrow in the left-hand corner of the icon.

To create a shortcut, you select an object and then from the File menu choose Create Shortcut. You can also create shortcuts by right-clicking an object and choosing Create Shortcut. After you create a shortcut, you can drag and drop it anywhere you like (for example, the Desktop).

You can also create a shortcut by right-clicking the Desktop and choosing New ➤ Shortcut. This brings up the Create Shortcut dialog box.

 TEST IT OUT: CREATING A SHORTCUT

1. From an empty place on the desktop, right-click and choose New ➤ Shortcut.

2. In the Command Line box, type **Write**.

3. In the Select a Name for the Shortcut dialog box, click the Finish button to accept the name Write.

4. The shortcut will appear on your Desktop.

Using Wizards

Wizards are built into Windows 98 as an easy way for you to perform specific tasks. To install a printer, for example, you simply open the Printers folder and click Add Printer. This starts the Printer Wizard, which walks you through the installation by asking a series of questions.

In addition to the Printer Wizard, Windows 98 has Wizards to help you add new hardware, add a PC card, set up an Internet connection, and install programs.

Using Windows Explorer

Windows Explorer is an easy-to-use application that simplifies the task of accessing and managing folders, files, applications, and resources. Unlike previous file management utilities in Windows, Windows Explorer for Windows 98 integrates Internet functionality. You can open Web pages or other Internet files directly within Windows Explorer. From Explorer, you can manage:

- ◆ Floppy drives
- ◆ Logical drives
- ◆ CD-ROM drives
- ◆ The Control Panel
- ◆ The Printers folder
- ◆ The Dial-Up Networking folder
- ◆ Network Neighborhood
- ◆ The Recycle Bin

Within Explorer, the left side of the dialog box shows you a hierarchical structure of all objects. The right side of the dialog box shows you details of the object that you have highlighted on the left side of the screen.

Through Explorer, you can manage objects by adding, deleting, or manipulating properties. You can also use drag-and-drop to copy or move objects within Explorer.

If your computer is connected to a network, you can also map network drives, which enables you to access network resources in the same way that you access a local resource on your C drive. You can also disconnect network drives.

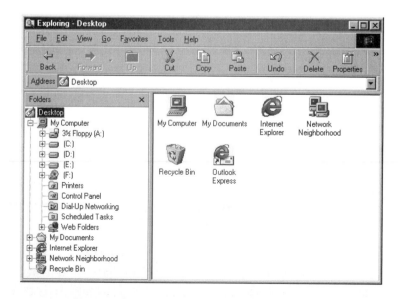

Using Internet Explorer

Internet Explorer is Microsoft's Web browser software. You can access Internet Explorer by using several methods. The Internet Explorer shortcut appears in the Quick Launch toolbar, the Desktop, and the Programs menu. To take full advantage of Internet Explorer, you should first connect to the Internet. Fortunately, Microsoft added an easy-to-use Internet connection **Wizard** for setting up your access to the Internet. After you are connected, you can take advantage of all the Internet has to offer.

The following screen shows the basic features of Microsoft's browser.

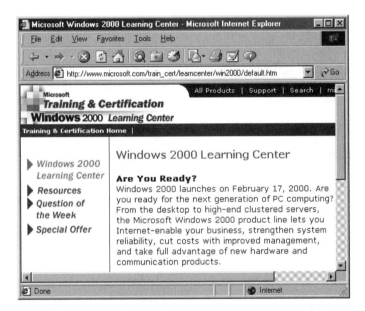

From the main screen, you can specify the **Uniform Resource Locator (URL)** that you want to access. You can also use these buttons:

Back and **Forward**   Enable you to go back and forth between pages you have already accessed

Stop   Halts the loading of a page, which is useful when you have a slow connection and the page you are trying to access is very large

Refresh   Enables you to reload the current page you are viewing

Home   Takes you back to your default home page

Search   Connects you to Internet search engines

Favorites   Enables you to bookmark your favorite sites and pages so that you can quickly access them

Print   Enables you to get a hard copy of the page you are viewing

Font   Enables you to customize font information

Mail   Enables you to compose e-mail, read e-mail, and access news services

---

Wizard
A configuration assistant that walks the user through a short series of guided steps to complete a task.

Uniform Resource Locator (URL)
The address that is used to identify and access a Web server on the Internet. www.greenpeace.org is one example.

Review Questions

Terms to Know
- ❏ command-line
- ❏ Internet Explorer
- ❏ Outlook Express
- ❏ Dial-Up Networking
- ❏ network drive
- ❏ Wizard
- ❏ URL

1. Which item on the Windows Desktop enables you to recover files that you have deleted?

   _____

2. Which item on the Windows Desktop enables you to access Internet resources?

   _____

3. Which item on the Windows Desktop enables you to access disk resources?

   _____

4. Which item on the Windows Desktop enables you to see which applications are running?

   _____

5. Which item on the Windows Desktop provides a starting point for accessing almost anything in Windows 98?

   _____

6. You go to Start ➤ _____ to see the last documents that you accessed.

7. Through Start ➤ _____, you can access Control Panel, Printers, and Taskbar Properties.

8. Through Start ➤ _____, you can access online help information.

9. What are the four Shut Down options?

_____

_____

_____

_____

10. True or false: You can access the Control Panel program from My Computer, Windows Explorer, and Start ➢ Settings.

_____

11. What is the advantage of using shortcuts?

_____

12. What is a Wizard?

_____

13. What is the difference between the Windows Explorer and the Internet Explorer?

_____

14. If you want to configure advanced properties, which mouse button do you click an object with?

_____

Chapter
8

A Communications
Framework

com·mu·ni·ca·tion *n* : the transfer of information between two or more people or devices over a medium

Communication occurs all around us in many forms. Usually, when communication happens, it is between two things that can easily understand each other. For example, two people in the same country who speak the same language can communicate with little or no problem. The same can be said for species of birds. They understand each other. But not everyone speaks the same language, and there are thousands of types of birds. Needless to say, life and work can get difficult when communication breaks down.

Communication between computers can be challenging. There are many types of computers that can communicate in any number of forms. Making them able to talk to one another and understand the information being passed is a whole other challenge. The Open Systems Interconnection (OSI) model helps make communication between devices work.

In this chapter, you will learn about:

 The need for a standard communications model

 The flow of data in the model

 The seven layers of the OSI model

Understanding OSI Model Basics

The **International Standards Organization (ISO)** began developing the OSI model in 1974 and finally adopted the model in 1977. The OSI model is not something you can buy, yet it is built into nearly all networking devices. It is a theoretical model that defines how **networks** are built and function from the ground up. By understanding the OSI model, you can develop a better understanding of networking **protocols** and **standards**. Even though networks are implemented differently, they are all based on the same or similar reference model. The OSI model defines seven layers and the function of the data flow within each layer.

The smallest unit of data begins at the Application layer. As data moves down the OSI model, more information is added at each layer to enable network communication to take place. At the receiving computer, the layers are stripped off at corresponding layers, called peer layers. The process is then reversed for the reply.

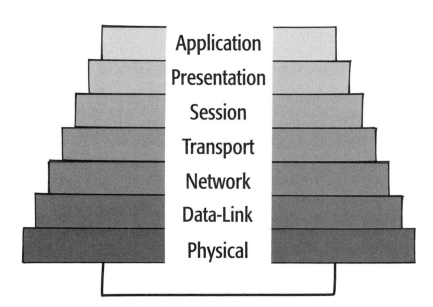

- Application
- Presentation
- Session
- Transport
- Network
- Data-Link
- Physical

Physical Connection

Using this type of model has three main advantages:

    ◊ Breaking down a large concept such as a network into smaller parts (in this case, layers) makes it easier to understand.

    ◊ Compartmentalizing network functions enables you to easily replace specific technologies without having to replace the entire network.

    ◊ Devices that are built around a common model should work together, or interoperate, regardless of the manufacturer who built the device.

International Standards Organization (ISO)
An organization dedicated to defining global communication and informational exchange standards. The American National Standards Institute (ANSI) is the American representative to the ISO.

network
Two or more computers connected for the purpose of sharing resources such as files or printers.

protocol
A set of rules for communication between two devices.

standard
An agreed upon set of rules, procedures, and functions that are widely accepted.

encryption
The process of encoding data to prevent unauthorized access.

A Communications Framework

The functions of the seven layers of the OSI model are:

OSI Layer	Function	Example of Layer Function
Application	The Application layer supports the communication of applications with the network.	Examples of Application layer services include sending and receiving messages and transferring files.
Presentation	The Presentation layer formats and translates data.	An example of a Presentation layer service is the compression or **encryption** of data.
Session	The Session layer manages communication sessions between service requesters and service providers. This layer manages communications by establishing, synchronizing, and maintaining the connection between sender and receiver.	At the Session layer, a Web server may close the session with a user after a specified period of time has elapsed without activity.
Transport	The Transport layer is usually associated with reliable end-to-end communication. It is the layer responsible for managing connections, **error control**, and **flow control** between sender and receiver.	When part of a Web page does not download due to heavy traffic, the Transport layer will resend the missing data.
Network	The Network layer is responsible for moving **packets** over an **internetwork** so that they can be routed to the correct network.	The IP address of a device is used on the Internet to determine the route that information travels to get to the correct sender and receiver.
Data-Link	The Data-Link layer includes information about the source and destination hardware addresses of the communicating devices. It also specifies lower-layer flow control and error control.	Devices that use Data-Link layer protocols are network cards and **bridge**s.
Physical	The Physical layer is responsible for the transmission of data over a physical medium.	Cables and physical connection specifications are defined at the Physical layer.

error control
A mechanism for assuring that data received is in the same condition and format that it was sent.

flow control
A feature of the Transport layer that manages the amount of data being transmitted between sender and receiver. If the receiving computer is unable to accept more data, it notifies the sending computer to pause transmission.

packet
Data that has been encapsulated with information from the Transport and Network layers of the OSI model.

internetwork
Two or more networks that are connected by using a router.

bridge
A layer 2 device that enables networks using different layer 2 protocols to communicate with one another. A bridge can also minimize traffic between two networks by passing through only those packets that are addressed to the other network.

Data Transfer in the OSI Model

When communication occurs between two computers on different networks, as in the graphic below, data is transferred across the networks through **routers**.

routers

Devices that connect two or more networks. Routers work at the Network layer of the OSI model, receiving packets and forwarding them to their correct destination.

connection-oriented

A method of communication that is considered reliable because the sender is notified when data is not received or unrecognizable.

Computer A

Router

Assume you have a file that you want to send from computer A to computer B. Many steps must occur:

1. The user on computer A creates an e-mail message using their favorite e-mail program. The e-mail program has support for specific network services that pertain to sending and receiving e-mail. The services that enable the e-mail program to communicate with e-mail servers are all part of the Application layer.

2. The next step is to translate the message into a language that is common to both computers. As humans, we see "hello," but each computer wants to see the message in a format that they can both interpret. The Presentation layer translates "hello" into ASCII code, which is internationally recognized as 96 numbers and letters and 32 nonprinting characters. The computer can then convert the ASCII code into ones and zeros.

3. At the next layer of communication, a connection, or session, is established and maintained. This connection determines when requests are made so that appropriate responses can be returned. Just like human conversations, computer communications are usually a series of requests and responses that must be answered sequentially.

4. If you want to make sure that the connection is reliable (for example, like a letter that is sent with a return receipt to confirm that it was received as opposed to a letter sent via regular mail), you might use **connection-oriented** services that guarantee reliable delivery.

5. In this example, computer A and computer B are on different networks. The Network layer routes the packets to the correct network by identifying network addresses and calculating the best route the packet should take.

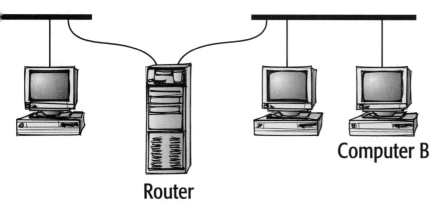

Computer B

Router

node
A connection point on a network. Nodes include computers, servers, and printers.

Media Access Control (MAC) address
A hexadecimal number that is allocated by an international organization and is burned into the network interface card by the NIC manufacturer. Media Access Control is a sublayer of the Data-Link layer.

6. After the data gets to the correct network, it must be delivered to the correct computer (sometimes called a **node**) on the network. On an Ethernet network, the packet is sent out on the network. Each computer receives the packet and reads the physical address—called the **Media Access Control (MAC) address**—to determine who the packet is intended for. The computer with the matching physical address accepts the packet and all other computers disregard the packet. Physical layer addressing occurs at the Data-Link layer of the OSI model.

7. The only physical connection that exists between the two computers is defined at the Physical layer of the OSI model. Network cables, connectors, and the hardware portion of the NIC (rather than the software) are all part of the Physical layer specification.

Here are two mnemonic devices to help you remember the seven layers.

Layer	Memory Trick Top to Bottom	Memory Trick Bottom to Top
Application	All	Away
Presentation	People	Pizza
Session	Seem	Sausage
Transport	To	Throw
Network	Need	Not
Data-Link	Data	Do
Physical	Processing	Please

Layer 1: The Physical Layer

When you get down to the nitty-gritty details of spitting the ones and zeros onto a cable, you are dealing with the Physical layer.

The Physical layer of the OSI model determines:

- ◆ The physical network structure you will use.

- ◆ The mechanical and electrical specifications of the transmission media that will be used.

- ◆ How data will be encoded and transmitted. There are all kinds of schemes used for encoding data, which specify how the ones and zeros will be transmitted. For example, Ethernet networks use a scheme called **Manchester encoding**.

The graphic below illustrates devices in the Physical layer (including the T-connector, which is used in some networks for connecting the computer to the cable).

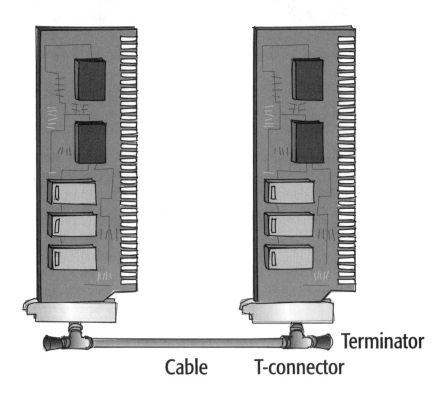

Terminator

Cable   T-connector

Manchester encoding

A method of identifying the beginning and end of a bit signal (one or zero) when it is transmitted on the network.

asynchronous communication

Begins transmission of each character with a start bit and ends transmission of each character with a stop bit. This method is not as efficient as synchronous communication but is less expensive.

synchronous communication

Transmits data by synchronizing the data signal between the sender and receiver and sending data as a continuous stream. This is the most efficient way of sending large amounts of data but requires expensive equipment.

NOTE

Topologies, Ethernet, and Token Ring are covered in greater detail in Chapter 10, "Networking the Computers."

Physical Layer Technologies

The category of technologies that the Physical layer defines include:

Connection type   Connections can be point-to-point or multipoint. Point-to-point assumes that only two devices are connected. Multipoint means that three or more devices are connected.

Physical topology   Topologies define the physical layout of the network. Common topologies include star, bus, and ring.

Type of signal   Signals can be analog or digital. Local computer networks use digital signals, and the public telephone system uses analog signals.

Type of bit synchronization   You can send data by asynchronous or synchronous means. **Asynchronous communication** requires less expensive equipment but is less efficient when transferring large blocks of data. **Synchronous communication** requires more expensive equipment but provides better efficiency.

Transmission signaling technology   You can use **baseband** technology, which is the signaling type used on Ethernet networks, or **broadband** signaling, which is used on ISDNs.

Physical Layer Hardware

Examples of Physical layer hardware are:

◇ Network interface cards

◇ Network cables

◇ **Hub**s (also referred to as concentrators)

◇ **Repeater**s

◇ Modems

◇ ISDN adapters

> **NOTE**
>
> At the Physical layer, data is referred to as *bits*.

baseband
A technology that permits a single transmission of data at a fixed frequency on a wire at any given moment.

broadband
A type of transmission that can use a single wire to transmit multiple streams of data simultaneously using different frequencies. This method is similar to the method used by radio stations all sharing the airwaves to send their signals.

hub
A Physical layer device that connects computers and other devices to make a network. A hub regenerates an incoming signal from one device and broadcasts the signal out all other ports.

repeater
A network device, similar to a hub but with only two or three ports, that can be used to extend the transmission distance of a network signal or to join two networks.

Layer 2: The Data-Link Layer

The Data-Link layer of the OSI model has three primary responsibilities:

- ❖ Establishing and maintaining the communication channel
- ❖ Identifying computers on the network by physical address
- ❖ Organizing the data into a logical group called a **frame**

Establishing and maintaining the communication channel is low-level work. At the Data-Link layer, it just means confirming that a data channel exists and that it is open. At the Session layer, there is higher-level communication management.

Each computer on the network is identified with a unique physical address, which is called the Media Access Control (MAC) address. On Ethernet and **Token Ring** cards, this is a 6-byte **hexadecimal** address that is burned into an EPROM chip on the network card. This address uniquely identifies computers when you send data from a source to a destination.

Data is logically grouped into a frame. A frame logically organizes the bits from the Physical layer. Here is an example of a frame:

Start	Destination address	Source address	LLC header	Data	CRC	End

Frame Description

In the preceding frame:

- ❖ The Start field identifies the beginning of the frame. This might be 10101010.
- ❖ The destination address is the MAC address of the computer to which the frame is being sent.
- ❖ The source address is the MAC address of the computer from which the frame is being sent.
- ❖ The **Logical Link Control (LLC)** header manages the LLC connection.
- ❖ The Data field contains the data from the upper-layer protocols.
- ❖ The **cyclic redundancy check (CRC)** is used for low-level error control. For example, is the connection valid?
- ❖ The End field indicates that this is the last field of the current frame.

---

frame
Data that has been encapsulated by the layer 2 protocol before being transmitted on the wire.

Token Ring
A layer 2 protocol developed by IBM that uses a token passing method for transmitting data. Each device on the ring takes turns using the token. The token can be used by only one device at a time.

hexadecimal
A numbering system that uses 16 instead of 10 as its base; it uses the digits 0–9 and the letters A–F to represent the decimal numbers 0–15.

Logical Link Control (LLC)
A Data-Link sublayer that establishes whether communication with another device is going to be connectionless or connection oriented.

Sublayers of Data-Link

The Data-Link layer has two sublayers:

- ◆ LLC sublayer
- ◆ MAC sublayer

The LLC sublayer provides the upper layers access to the physical hardware at the lower layers, and the MAC sublayer is used for physical addressing.

Data-Link layer	LLC (Logical Link Control)
	MAC (Media Access Control)

NOTE

Data is referred to as a *frame* at the Data-Link layer.

Data-Link Layer Devices

Examples of Data-Link layer devices are

- ◆ Bridges
- ◆ **Managed hubs**
- ◆ **Switch**
- ◆ Network interface cards

cyclic redundancy check (CRC)
A form of error detection that performs a mathematical calculation on data at both the sender's end and the receiver's end to ensure that the data is received reliably.

managed hubs
Similar to hubs but with the exception that the device can be managed using software to monitor and control network communication.

switch
The modern name used for a multi-port bridge. Like a regular bridge, each port on a switch represents a separate network. Traffic on each port is kept isolated except when the packet is destined for another device on a different port or if the packet is a broadcast. Broadcasts must be sent out all ports.

Layer 3: The Network Layer

The primary responsibility of the Network layer is to move data over an internetwork. This is called routing.

At the Data-Link layer, addressing is physical. At the Network layer, addressing is logical. Each network must have a unique network address. This address routes packets to the correct network.

The main functions of the Network layer are to:

- ◇ Logically define networks based on unique network addresses.
- ◇ Determine how packets should be delivered based on current routing information. A route, or path, to a destination network can be created in several ways. The path can be manually entered by the network administrator; the path can be learned form other routers; or the path can be a default route, which means that the router relies on the next router to determine the best path.
- ◇ Provide network-level connection services.

Sending data through the Network layer is considered to be connectionless service. This is like sending a letter through the regular mail. You drop the mail in a postal box and assume that it will reach its destination. The Network layer is similar in that you send a packet and assume that it will reach its destination.

Network Layer Example

Referring to the example network shown below, assume that you want to send a packet from computer A to computer B. These steps will occur:

1. Each router contains **route tables** that define the best path to all known networks. The first packet leaves computer A and is destined for computer B.

2. The packet first reaches the New York router. That router compares the destination address of the packet to its routing table.

3. The New York router determines that it must send the packet to the L.A. router to reach computer B. Each pass through an external router, not the New York router, is considered a **hop**.

4. The L.A. router determines the shortest path to computer B is through the Seattle router. The packet is sent on its way.

5. Seattle performs the same process as the preceding routers and sends the packet onto computer B's network, where computer B receives it.

NOTE

Data is referred to as *datagrams* or *packets* at the Network layer.

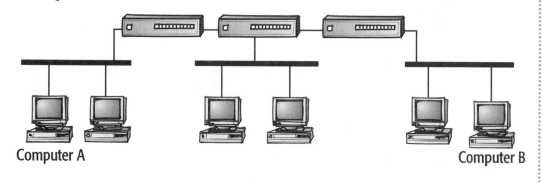

Computer A   Computer B

route table

A table created by a router that contains information on how to reach networks that are directly attached to the router and networks that are distant.

hop

The number of foreign gateways (routers other than your own) that a packet must pass through between the source and destination computers.

Layer 4: The Transport Layer

The Transport layer of the OSI model is associated with reliable delivery. With reliable delivery, the sender and receiver establish a connection, and the receiver acknowledges receipt of the data by sending an acknowledgment (ACK) packet to the sender.

Reliable delivery is a concept that can be applied to the telephone system. You place a call to a friend hoping that they answer. When they answer, you begin a conversation. If everything is going well, you will each take turns talking. But if the connection is bad, you may not hear a question that was asked. In that case, your friend, having not received an answer, would ask you again.

Most protocols have two mechanisms for sending data through the Transport layer: connection-oriented transmission and connectionless transmission.

Connection-oriented transmission:

- ❖ Is reliable
- ❖ Involves more overhead, so is slower and less efficient
- ❖ Can provide guaranteed file transfer

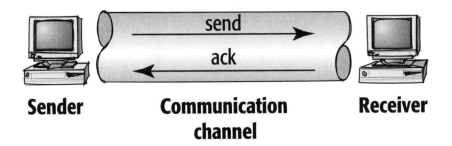

Sender   **Communication channel**   **Receiver**

Connectionless transmission:

- ❖ Is less reliable
- ❖ Involves less overhead, so is faster and more efficient
- ❖ Does not re-send packets

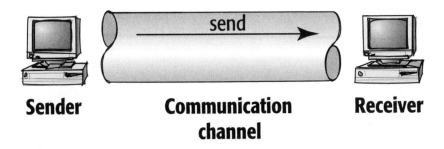

Sender   **Communication channel**   **Receiver**

Other Transport Layer Functions

Data moves down the layers of the OSI model in large chunks. After data reaches the Transport layer, it is segmented into smaller units that do not exceed the maximum packet length specified by the network in use. The Transport layer is responsible for dividing and then reassembling the data back into the original order at the receiver's end.

The Transport layer has the capability to perform some error control. If a particular unit of data does not arrive at the receiver's end, the Transport layer can request that the missing data be retransmitted.

This layer of the OSI model also performs some flow control. The sender and receiver determine how much data can be sent before an acknowledgment is required.

NOTE

Data at the Transport layer is referred to as a *datagram*, *segment*, or *packet*.

Network and Transport Layer Technologies

The Network and Transport layers of the OSI model work closely together. Many protocols function at these layers. Two are presented below:

TCP/IP   The leading industry protocol for the Internet. Transmission Control Protocol (TCP) functions at the Transport layer and Internet Protocol (IP) functions at the Network layer.

IPX/SPX   A proprietary protocol developed by Novell for their NetWare software. With Internetwork Packet Exchange/Sequenced Packet Exchange (IPX/SPX), IPX functions primarily at the Network layer, and SPX functions at the Transport layer.

Layer 5: The Session Layer

The Session layer of the OSI model is responsible for managing communications between a sender and a receiver. Some of the communication tasks performed at this layer include:

- ◆ Establishing connections
- ◆ Maintaining connections
- ◆ Synchronizing communication
- ◆ Dialog control
- ◆ Terminating connections

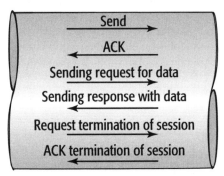

Sender   **Receiver**

Communication
channel

Creating a Connection

Creating a connection requires:

- ◆ Authenticating through a username and password that are valid on the receiving computer
- ◆ Determining which computer will be the sender, which will be the receiver, and which will send first
- ◆ Figuring out which type of communication will take place
- ◆ Specifying which lower-layer protocols will be used for transmission

Transferring Data and Using Dialog Control

Data transfer and **dialog control** consist of:

◇ The actual transfer of data

◇ Any acknowledgments that are needed

◇ Responses to requests that the sender or the receiver makes

There are three types of dialog control at the Session layer. Dialog control services include:

Simplex communication   Specifies that communication is one-way only. Simplex is more common in less complex systems for which two-way communication is not necessary.

Half-duplex communication   Specifies that communication can be two-way but only one channel can communicate at a time. Most computer networks communicate in half-duplex mode.

Full-duplex communication   Specifies that communication can be two-way simultaneously. This is a valuable function found in some recent network devices. Full-duplex should be implemented with servers for improved performance.

Terminating a Connection

After the session is complete, the connection is terminated. This enables other devices to open new sessions. Sometimes termination of the connection will come from the receiver. Other times the sender will terminate the session if it does not hear back from the receiver within a specified time.

dialog control
Manages the dialog between the sender and receiver. It consists of managing the transfer of data, determining whether an acknowledgment is required, and determining the appropriate responses to the sender.

Layer 6: The Presentation Layer

The Presentation layer of the OSI model is responsible for:

◇ Character code translation

◇ Data encryption

◇ Data compression and expansion

Extended Binary Coded Decimal Interchange Code (EBCDIC)

The 8-bit character set used by IBM mainframes.

Character Code Translation

People understand symbolic characters; for example, "hello." Computers understand data as a series of ones and zeros (binary code). In order to communicate, there must be some translation. This process occurs at the Presentation layer of the OSI model through character code translation. Examples of character codes include:

◇ ASCII

◇ **EBCDIC**

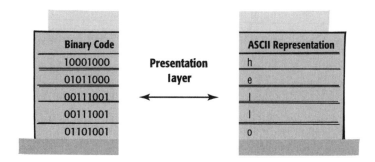

After data moves from the Application layer to the Presentation, it must be converted from its original form to a format that will be understood by the receiving device. As noted above, this format may be in ASCII or it may be in EBCDIC. The data may also need to be encrypted or compressed before being passed on to the Session layer.

Data Encryption

Data encryption is the process of encoding data so that it is protected from unauthorized access. Some of the methods used to encrypt data include:

- ◊ Transposing information within the data.
- ◊ Substituting one character for another. (Think of this as the secret code you used when you were a kid.)
- ◊ Scrambling the data with mathematical calculations that the sender and the receiver determine. This is the most secure encryption method and is the most complex. Almost all Internet sites that have security use this method.

Data Compression and Expansion

Data compression occurs at the sender's end and compacts the data so that it can be sent more efficiently.

Data expansion, or decompression, occurs at the receiver's end when the data is returned to its original format.

NOTE

There are many encryption methods that can be implemented at the Presentation layer. Some encryption methods are easily broken using available software. On the other hand, the most complex encryption methods are considered so vital to national security that the U.S. government restricts or bans exporting the technology.

Layer 7: The Application Layer

The Application layer of the OSI model supports these services:

File services   Store, move, control access to, and retrieve files

Print services   Send data to local or networked printers

Message services   Transfer text, graphics, audio, and video over a network

Application services   Process applications locally or through **distributed processing**

Database services   Use the local computer to access a network server for database storage and retrieval functions.

distributed processing
Sharing the task of processing instructions between a server and a client CPU.

NOTE

Applications such as Microsoft Word and Excel do not directly interface with the Application layer of the OSI model. However, the Application layer provides those applications with underlying services, such as file and print services.

In addition, the Application layer of the OSI model advertises any services that are being offered and determines whether requests made by the client should be serviced locally or remotely.

Service Advertisement

Service advertisement means that the computer is making its resources available over the network. For example, any NT computer running the server service automatically advertises any file or print resources that it is sharing.

Service Processing

Service processing determines whether a request should be processed locally or remotely.

Assume, as an example, that you have two computers: computer A and computer B. If computer A makes a request to its local hard drive, the I/O manager (which handles all input and output) will direct the request to be handled locally. If the computer makes a network request—in this case, computer A is using the drive letter F to represent a shared folder on computer B—the I/O manager will process the request and redirect it to the network.

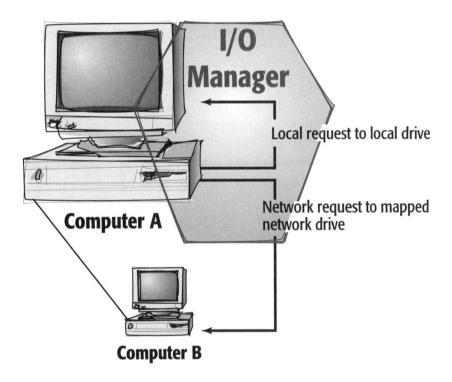

I/O Manager

Local request to local drive

Network request to mapped network drive

Computer A

Computer B

NOTE

At the Application layer of the OSI model, data is referred to as a *message* or simply *data*.

Review Questions

Terms to Know
- ❏ ISO
- ❏ network
- ❏ protocol
- ❏ standard
- ❏ encryption
- ❏ error control
- ❏ flow control
- ❏ packet
- ❏ internetwork
- ❏ bridge
- ❏ routers
- ❏ connection-oriented
- ❏ node
- ❏ MAC address
- ❏ Manchester encoding
- ❏ asynchronous communication

1. List the two main advantages of the OSI model.

2. Which layer of the OSI model is responsible for establishing, maintaining, and synchronizing the data connection?

3. Which layer of the OSI model is responsible for identifying the source and destination hardware addresses and organizing bits into frames?

4. Which layer of the OSI model is responsible for file and print services and determines whether a service request should be processed locally or routed to the network?

5. Which layer of the OSI model is responsible for moving data over an internetwork?

6. Which layer of the OSI model is responsible for moving bits over physical media?

7. Which layer of the OSI model is responsible for formatting and translating data?

8. Which layer of the OSI model is responsible for reliable delivery of data, management of connections, error control, and flow control?

_____

9. What are the two sublayers of the Data-Link layer?

_____

_____

10. Which device routes packets between two networks at the Network layer of the OSI model?

_____

11. What is the difference between connection-oriented services and connectionless services? Which is more reliable? Which is more efficient?

_____

12. What is the difference between a physical address and a network address?

_____

13. List the seven layers of the OSI model from bottom to top.

_____

_____

_____

_____

_____

_____

_____

Terms to Know

❑ synchronous communication
❑ baseband
❑ broadband
❑ hub
❑ repeater
❑ frame
❑ Token Ring
❑ hexadecimal
❑ LLC
❑ CRC
❑ managed hubs
❑ switch
❑ route table
❑ hop
❑ dialog control
❑ EBCDIC
❑ distributed processing

Chapter

9

Network Models

model *n* : a description or representation of a system

An architect who designs a building has to take into consideration the kind of structure that is needed. Designing a skyscraper, for example, reflects a very different model from a warehouse. There are different tools, systems, and uses for each design. Computer networks also have various models that are used to suit specific scenarios.

When designing a network, you can choose from several network models. Some of the considerations that go into choosing a network model include the size of the network, the number of users you will support, and the network operating system you will use. This chapter provides an overview of these common network models:

 Peer-to-peer

 Client-server, including the domain model and the directory services model

Considering Peer-to-Peer Networks

peer-to-peer network

Does not use dedicated network servers for logging in users or providing secure access to network resources. Instead, clients simply share resources, and other clients have access to whatever has been shared.

client

A computer on the network that requests network services.

You might be familiar with the following scenario. A small office has a couple of computers that are not connected to one another to form a network. Everyone has been used to using a floppy disk to transfer files, and each person has their own printer. Now, the small company isn't so small anymore; it now has 10 employees who each have a computer. The cost of supplying everyone with a printer would be expensive, and using disks to move files is slowing productivity. The company is ready for a better solution.

As you might have guessed, a **peer-to-peer network** is one solution. As a network model, peer-to-peer is an excellent choice for this budding company because it enables users to share resources on their personal computers. Resources can include files, printers, and modems. More than anything else, peer-to-peer networks offer a cost-effective solution that does not require significant expertise, management, or support.

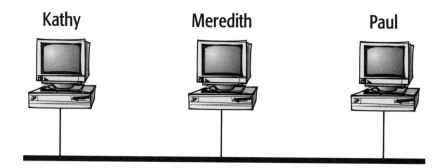

As you can see in this graphic, a peer-to-peer network does not require a dedicated computer called a server. Instead, each user can share resources on their computer. From a management standpoint, each user carries some of the responsibility for networking. If Paul needs access to a file on Meredith's computer, Meredith must share the folder that contains the file. Also, Meredith's computer will have the added responsibility of performing tasks that Paul requests, such as transferring files. This transfer could happen at the same time that Meredith is using her computer to print a document. In other words, a user sitting at a computer (called a network **client**) can share network resources while also accessing local resources (such as the hard drive) for running local applications.

When users share resources on their computers, they have the option of assigning passwords to the resources. The use of a password provides a minimum level of security. Passwords should be used anytime that the resource being shared is meant to be used only by authorized persons. In a peer-to-peer network using operating systems such as Windows 98 or 95, it is possible to assign a password to the shared resource only—not to individual users. An employee who wants to use a particular printer, for example, must have the password for that printer. This design limitation makes management of passwords confusing for users, and therefore limits the effectiveness of using passwords.

When Appropriate

Typically, you use the peer-to-peer network model in small workgroups of 10 or fewer people. Larger networks become difficult to manage and support. In addition, virtually every client operating system is limited to 12 or fewer users accessing one computer at the same time. The peer-to-peer model is well suited to organizations that need a cost-effective solution for fulfilling basic networking needs such as file and print sharing.

Here are some advantages to choosing a peer-to-peer network:

- ❖ It is easy to set up because it is designed for a small network.
- ❖ Administration is maintained by each user (so that a separate administrator is not required).
- ❖ It does not require dedicated server hardware and software.
- ❖ Peer-to-peer networking software is built into all popular operating system software.

There are also some disadvantages:

- ❖ This model does not work well if there are a large number of users.
- ❖ Security is poor because each individual is responsible for assigning and maintaining passwords to the shared resources.
- ❖ Passwords can be assigned only to resources, not users.
- ❖ Because network resources are dispersed, backup of critical data is irregular.

Common OS Examples

Examples of operating systems that are commonly used on peer-to-peer networks include:

- ❖ Windows NT Workstation and Windows 2000 Professional
- ❖ Windows 95 and Windows 98
- ❖ Windows for Workgroups 3.11
- ❖ Apple Macintosh

Configuring a Windows 98 Computer for Networking

workstation

Another name for a computer that is used by users. It is sometimes used to describe powerful computers that are used for completing complex mathematical, engineering, and animation tasks.

Windows 98 is primarily designed to act as a local operating system. These types of operating systems are covered in Chapter 5, "Desktop Operating Systems: A Comparison."

However, in addition to providing local support, Windows 98 (as well as Windows 95) also includes extensive network support. If the network consists exclusively of Windows 98 computers, the network is a peer-to-peer type. If there is a dedicated server, each of the Windows 98 computers functions as **workstation** within the client-server network. Either way, network support enables the Windows 98 computers to use network resources or provide network resources through file and print sharing.

This section details how to configure a Windows 98 computer for networking. It serves as an example of an operating system configured for a peer-to-peer network.

When you set up a Windows 98 computer, you can specify whether to install the networking components. You configure a Windows 98 computer for networking through Control Panel ➤ Network. Here you can set many options, which are detailed in the following subsections.

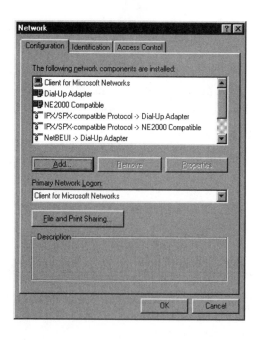

Configuration of Networking Components

To configure network components, you select Control Panel ➢ Network, click the Configuration tab, and then click the Add button. From the Select Network Component Type dialog box, you can configure the options shown in this table.

Network Component	Description	Examples
Client	This option specifies which network client software to install. The software that processes network requests is sometimes called a redirector.	Client software that comes with Windows 98 includes support for Banyan, FTP Software, Microsoft, Novell, and Sunsoft clients.
Adapter	Adapters are hardware devices that connect the computer to the network. This is covered in more detail in Chapter 10, "Networking the Computers."	The list of supported adapters is quite extensive. Some manufactures that offer adapter drivers include 3Com, SMC, Novell, and Ungerman-Bass.
Protocol	Protocols transmit data over a network. Protocols are covered in greater detail in Chapter 11, "Moving Data: Network Layer Protocols."	There is support for protocols from different manufacturers. Common protocols include TCP/IP, IPX/SPX, and NetBEUI.
Service	Services support sharing of files and printers, automating system backup, and monitoring of network resources.	Examples include File and Print Sharing for Microsoft Networks and Hewlett-Packard JetAdmin, which manages network printers.

From the Configuration tab at Control Panel ➢ Network, you can also configure:

- ◆ Primary network logon
- ◆ File and print sharing

The Primary Network Logon edit box specifies which network type you will log on to. When you specify this option, Windows 98 displays a screen at start-up that enables you to type in your username and password.

You use the File and Print Sharing button to share local file and print resources with other network users.

Identification of the Computer

The Identification tab enables you to configure the options shown in this screen.

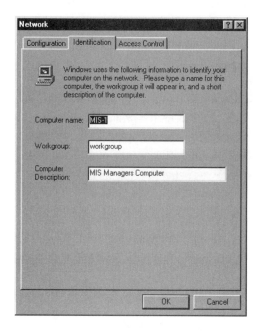

The Computer Name edit box identifies the computer on the network. Each computer on the network must have a unique name that can be up to 15 characters. It is also referred to as the computer's NetBIOS name.

The Workgroup edit box specifies which logical group your computer belongs to. This enables administrators to logically group computers.

The Computer Description edit box enables you to provide a description for informational purposes. For example, descriptions might be the department or user of the computer.

NOTE

Windows 98 offers many features that make network computing easier for everyone. But don't mistake Windows 98 for a network operating system. It's not. If you have more than 10 users, you should invest in a true NOS.

Access Control of Network Resources

The Access Control tab specifies the type of security to apply to the resources that the Windows 98 computer shares. The choices for access control are:

◊ Share-level

◊ User-level

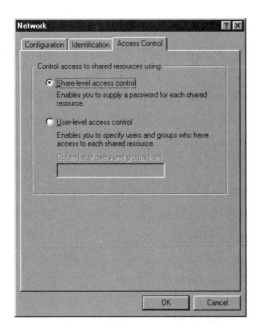

domain model
Logically groups computers, users, and groups into a domain. Users log on to the domain and have access to any resources within the domain to which their user account has permission.

Share-level access control enables you to define a password for each shared file or print resource. Users have to supply the password when they access the network resource.

User-level access control enables you to assign access based on user or group assignment. Since Windows 98 does not maintain any user database, you must specify which user database to use. In the case of an NT **domain model**, described later in this chapter, you use the NT domain database to specify which users and groups have access to the resource.

By default, Windows 98 shares no local resources. This means that even with the network options configured, files, folders, and printers on each workstation that are not defined as shared are not available on the network for others to use.

Considering Client-Server Networks

client-server network

Uses a dedicated server to centralize user and group account management. Users at a client, or workstation, log on to a server where they have user accounts and access resources on the server to which their user account has permission.

Hypertext Markup Language (HTML)

A text-based scripting language that is used in the creation of Web pages to control the presentation of text and graphics. It can also be used to add functionality to the Web page for navigation or for interfacing with other technologies like databases and multimedia.

As the number of users grows, the peer-to-peer network model loses its value and eventually becomes unfeasible. Also, large or growing companies might have different needs than a small company has. The needs might include support for hundreds of users or the creation of a centralized order processing system that can be accessed by retail stores and on the Internet. However you size it up, the needs require a powerful and flexible model.

The **client-server network** was designed specifically to meet the complex and challenging needs of larger organizations. The name *client-server* originates from a design that requires some tasks to be completed by the user's workstation and other tasks to be processed centrally on a server. As an example of a client-server model, consider a user accessing a site on the World Wide Web.

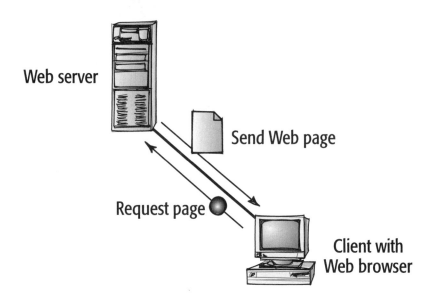

Web server

Send Web page

Request page

Client with Web browser

In the graphic above, a user at a workstation opens a Web browser. The Web browser is the client application. The user enters the URL of a Web site into the Web browser, which then makes a request to the Web server for that site. The server sends the page with all its **Hypertext Markup Language (HTML)** code. Now that the server has completed its job, the client application is responsible for converting the HTML into a Web page.

When Appropriate

Deciding between a peer-to-peer model and a client-server model is not as difficult as it may seem. First, the client-server model can be recommended to companies of all sizes and should be the first choice when there are 15 or more users. Second, you should consider potential growth. You might be a company of 10 people now, but plans might include increasing personnel to 20 or more in a short time. Planning for that growth can have a significant effect on cost savings and user productivity. Finally, certain application needs, especially those involving the Internet, require a client-server model. Common applications for centralizing resources include messaging (for example, e-mail), file and print sharing, databases, and fax/voice services.

The client-server network offers several key advantages:

- ◆ Administration is centralized.
- ◆ This model provides centralization of resources for easier backups.
- ◆ Multiple levels of network security exist through management of usernames and passwords and through controlled access to network resources.
- ◆ The network offers performance and reliability that can grow as demand grows.

However, the client-server model has some drawbacks:

- ◆ A dedicated server is normally required.
- ◆ It requires a more experienced administrator to install and manage the network than the peer-to-peer network model does.
- ◆ It needs duplicate administration if users need to access more than one server.

Common OS Examples

Common examples of software that supports the client-server model include:

- ◆ Novell NetWare versions 3, 4, and 5
- ◆ Unix
- ◆ Linux
- ◆ Windows 2000 Server and Advanced Server
- ◆ AppleShare IP 6.1
- ◆ Apple OS X Server

Considering the Domain Model

The domain model is a client-server based technology used by NT 3.x and NT 4.x. The domain model enables you to logically group resources and users into one centrally managed group called a domain.

The domain model can be compared to the administration in a school. A school has a principal and a vice-principal. The principal has the first say on who can do what in the school and how it should be done. The vice principal follows the same course of action as the principal. When the principal is away at meetings, the vice-principal is next in line to make decisions.

The Windows NT domain contains a similar backup design. A server called the **primary domain controller (PDC)** has the same role as a school principal. All decisions and responsibility regarding who can do what is maintained and controlled by the PDC. The PDC maintains a database of all the users and their security rights. The database where this information is stored is called the **Security Accounts Manager (SAM)**.

A second server, the **backup domain controller** (BDC), keeps a copy of the SAM database. Like the vice-principal in a school, the BDC can take over the **authentication** process in the event that the PDC is too busy or if the PDC fails.

The main advantage of the domain model is that all users need only one user account to log on to the domain. Users can then access any resources within the domain that they have been granted access to.

This graphic shows a sample domain:

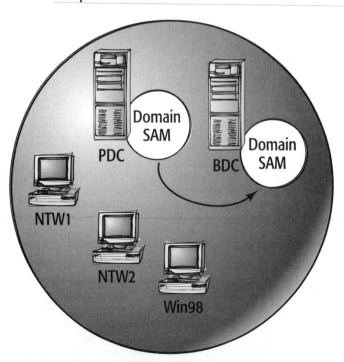

primary domain controller (PDC)

Is used in an NT domain. The PDC contains the read-write copy of the domain accounts administration database, called the Security Accounts Manager, or SAM.

Security Accounts Manager (SAM)

A database on NT servers that contains the relationship between who a user is and the level of security access that the user has to resources on the network.

backup domain controller (BDC)

Used in NT domains, it has read-only copies of the PDC accounts database. BDCs serve two primary functions: They offload logon authentication requests from the PDC, and they provide fault tolerance. If the PDC fails, the BDC can be promoted to PDC.

When Appropriate

The domain model is very **scalable** (meaning it works well with small and large networks), so you can use it in small or large organizations.

The domain model offers these benefits:

- ◆ Users need only one logon account, no matter how many servers the user needs to access.

- ◆ You can easily define and manage security.

- ◆ You can centralize account and resource management by creating the user on either the PDC or BDC and the information will be copied to all domain servers.

The model also has some drawbacks:

- ◆ This model needs a trained and experienced administrator to install and manage it.

- ◆ The domain model uses a flat structure for storing account information. You can have up to 40,000 accounts, but there is no way to hierarchically organize the users.

- ◆ Domain models do not scale as well in large national or global networks as do directory services models (explained in the next section).

Common OS Examples

Network operating systems that support the domain model are confined to Microsoft products. Although Windows 95, 98, NT Workstation, and 2000 Professional function within the domain model, they do not have domain management capabilities. The only network operating systems that allow you to build, manage, and support domains are:

- ◆ Microsoft Windows 3.1, 3.5, and 3.51 Server
- ◆ Windows NT 4 Server
- ◆ Windows 2000 Server, Advanced Server, and Datacenter Server

NOTE

Although Windows 2000 Server supports the domain model, Microsoft recommends that you migrate your network to Active Directory Services. Directory services are described in the next section.

---

authentication
A process that requires a user to enter an ID and a password and then be verified by the software to gain access to resources.

---

scalable
Capable of expanding to accommodate greater numbers of users and resources.

Considering the Directory Services Model

directory services model

Uses a hierarchical database to logically organize the network resources. This model scales well to small, medium, or large enterprise networks.

The concept of the **directory services model** grew out of a need to better manage large, complex networks found in today's organizations. The complexity was due in large part to two factors: First, applications used over the network were becoming more popular and created a greater demand; second, it was becoming more and more common to have software and hardware from different vendors in operation on the same network. Directory server provides a centralized system for managing applications, files, printers, people, and other resources in large groups or individually.

In a directory services model, a hierarchical database contains all the network resources. Conceptually, the database looks like an upside-down tree structure. The root of the tree is at the top and is used to represent the organization. Users logging on to the network are actually logging on to the directory services database. The user can access any objects within the database that they have been given access to. Objects can be users, groups, servers, printers, and so on.

The directory services database consists of a hierarchical structure of objects. You can think of objects as towns located along a river. Each town has characteristics that make it unique. Like the town, each object in directory services has properties that can be managed. Continuing with the analogy, the towns are linked together by water whether they are on the river or a tributary that connects to the river. Similar to the river that links the towns, the link between the objects is called the directory tree. The directory tree is what helps organize management of directory services. This structure enables the administrator to logically group directory service objects.

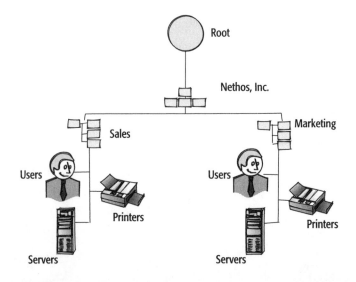

When Appropriate

For medium to large networks, this model is the wave of the future. The two main network operating systems—NetWare 4.x and 5.x, and Windows 2000—use a directory services network model.

Consider these advantages to using directory services:

- ❖ This model scales well to any size network.
- ❖ The administrator can logically group users and resources within the directory services tree.
- ❖ You can centralize or decentralize account and resource management as much as you wish. Administrative tasks can be delegated to other individuals without jeopardizing consistency in the directory services database.

You should also consider these disadvantages:

- ❖ This model is the most difficult to design and manage.
- ❖ This model requires a trained and experienced network administrator to install and manage it.
- ❖ There is added complexity when migrating from the domain model to a directory services model.

Common OS Examples

Common examples of directory services networks include:

- ❖ NetWare 4.x and 5.x
- ❖ Windows 2000

Review Questions

Terms to Know
- ❏ peer-to-peer network
- ❏ client
- ❏ workstation
- ❏ domain model
- ❏ client-server network
- ❏ HTML
- ❏ PDC
- ❏ SAM
- ❏ BDC
- ❏ authentication
- ❏ scalable
- ❏ directory services model

1. Define *peer-to-peer network model*.

2. What is the role of a PDC?

3. What are the two primary functions of BDCs?

4. Which client-server network model will Windows 2000 use?

5. True or false: The domain model is always the best network model to choose.

6. Which network model is the best choice if you have a small number of users and no dedicated server hardware?

7. What is an object in the directory services model?

8. True or false: If you have an account on one server in a client-server model, you can access resources on other servers even if you do not have a user account defined.

9. True or false: In a domain model network, you must add users and groups to the PDCs and the BDCs.

_____

10. Which network model provides the most scalability and is the best solution for large national or global networks?

_____

Chapter

10

Networking the Computers

to·pol·o·gy *n* : **the study of shapes and their spatial relationships**

Before you can even begin to install your networking software, you must have some type of hardware that connects all the computers. In this chapter, you will learn about network topologies and the two most common network communication architectures for connecting network hardware: Ethernet and Token Ring.

The following topics are covered:

 Physical and logical topologies

 Star, bus, and ring topologies

 Ethernet communication architecture

 Token Ring communication architecture

Introduction to Topologies

A topology is defined as the layout of the network. Topologies can be physical or logical:

10BASE-T

A network communication standard that uses Ethernet on unshielded twisted-pair cable in star topology at 10Mbps.

Physical topology   Describes how the network physically looks or how the network is physically designed

Logical topology   Describes how data is transmitted through the network

The concept of a topology is important because each network card is designed to work with a specific topology. Conversely, if your network cable is already installed and you want to use existing wiring, you must select your network cards based on the preexisting physical topology.

Ideally, you can design your network from scratch. Then you can choose your topology, cabling, and network cards based on what best meets your needs.

This section will review the commonly defined topologies:

- ◇ Star topology
- ◇ Bus topology
- ◇ Ring topology

Star Topology

Physically, the star topology looks like a star. The hub is at the center of the star, and all devices attach to the hub via a cable

Logically, the physical star topology operates as a logical bus topology (explained in the next section) by sending the data signal to all nodes at once. The hub at the center of the star works as a signal splitter, which means the signal is split and sent to all computers at the same time, with one exception—it is not sent back to the computer from which the signal originated. The signal is terminated at each network card, thereby preventing the signal from accidentally reentering the network. If this were to happen, data packets would travel the network endlessly—seriously slowing down network performance.

NOTE

The term *hub* is used generically to specify the central device in a star topology. In a **10BASE-T** network, the hub is technically called a concentrator. In a Token Ring network, the hub is technically called a Multi-Station Access Unit, or MAU (pronounced *mow*).

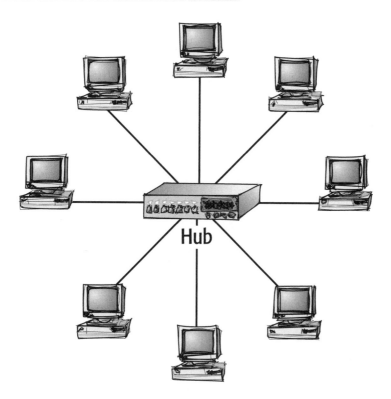

Hub

Benefits

The benefits of a star topology include the following:

◇ A star topology is more fault tolerant than other topologies, because a cable break does not bring down the entire network.

◇ Reconfiguring the network, or adding nodes, is easy because each node connects to the central hub independent of other nodes.

◇ Isolating cable failures is easy because each node connects independently to the central hub.

Drawbacks

The drawbacks of a star topology include the following:

◇ If the central hub fails, the entire network becomes unavailable.

◇ This topology is more expensive than others to install because of the additional cable and equipment involved.

Bus Topology

Physically, a bus topology uses a linear segment of cable to connect all network devices. Devices typically connect to the bus (the cable) through T-connectors. At each end of the bus are terminators. Each terminator absorbs the signal when it reaches the end of the cable. Without a terminator, a signal would bounce back and cause network errors.

Like the physical star topology, the physical bus topology uses a logical bus to transmit data on the cable in both directions. In a logical bus topology, only one transmission can occur at any given moment. Otherwise, two transmissions would collide and cause network errors. Termination ensures that the signal is removed from the cable when it reaches either end, preventing possible network errors.

Benefits

The benefits of a bus topology include the following:

◊ This is one of the least expensive topologies to install, because it uses less cable than the star topology and needs no hardware for a central device.

◊ It is an easy way to network a small number of computers.

Drawbacks

The drawbacks of a bus topology include the following:

◊ If there is a break in the cable, the entire network will fail.

◊ This topology can be difficult to troubleshoot because cabling problems often cannot be isolated to one computer.

◊ On a medium-sized to large network, reconfiguration is more difficult than the cable management of a star topology.

NOTE

In the early days of networking, the bus topology was very popular. It uses less equipment than other topologies and is therefore inexpensive to set up. But now Ethernet concentrators are inexpensive. The falling cost to build a star topology–based network, combined with its fault tolerance, has made 10BASE-T with the star topology the most popular Ethernet configuration.

Ring Topology

Physically, the ring topology is shaped in a ring. Cables pass from computer to computer until the ring is complete. When data is transmitted, each workstation receives the signal and then passes it on when they are done. Other than **Fiber Distributed Data Interface (FDDI)**, no current networks use a physical ring topology, because a break in the ring makes the entire network unavailable.

Logically, a ring topology works by passing the signal, traditionally called a **token**, from one node to another until it reaches all the way around the ring. **Token-passing** schemes use the logical ring topology.

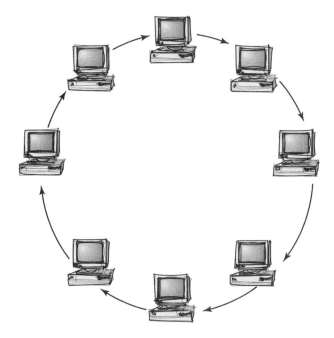

Benefits

A logical ring topology ensures access to the network without the risk of **collisions**, which can occur in logical star or bus topologies.

Drawbacks

The drawbacks of a ring topology include the following:

◊ If there is a break in the cable of a physical ring topology, the network becomes unavailable.

◊ Physical ring topologies are difficult to troubleshoot.

◊ Physical ring topologies are hard to reconfigure.

◊ There is limited support for ring networks.

◊ The costs for a ring network are significantly higher than for star or bus.

Fiber Distributed Data Interface (FDDI)
A network specification that defines a logical ring topology of fiber transmitting at 100Mbps. FDDI provides similar network connectivity as Ethernet and Token Ring, and functions at the same layers of the OSI model.

token
A special packet that signifies that a user can transmit data to a Token Ring network.

token passing
Developed by IBM, the transmission of data in a token that is passed from computer to computer on a Token Ring network. Only one token can exist on the network at once. When one computer is done using the token, the next computer in line that needs to transmit gets the token.

collisions
A problem on Ethernet networks that occurs when two computers transmit on the wire simultaneously, causing a electrical spike twice the strength than is normal for the network.

Ethernet Communication Architecture

Institute of Electrical and Electronic Engineers (IEEE)
Pronounced *I triple E*, an international organization that defines computing and telecommunications standards. The LAN standards defined by IEEE include the 802-workgroup specifications.

In the preceding section, you learned that every network has a physical and logical topology. The topology can provide important information on the capabilities of the network, from its reliability to its method of communication. The bus and star topologies are two such topologies that are used with the Ethernet standard for communication on a network.

Ethernet is one of the oldest network protocols and it is the most popular. Xerox first developed it in the 1970s. And in the 1980s, Xerox, Intel, and Digital Equipment Corporation proposed formal Ethernet specifications. It has its own standard from the **Institute of Electrical and Electronic Engineers (IEEE)**, the IEEE 802.3 standard. The Ethernet protocol is used at the Physical and Media Access Control (MAC) layers of the OSI model (see Chapter 8, "A Communications Framework").

Ethernet works with a contention scheme (a way of accessing the network) called Carrier Sense Multiple Access with Collision Detection (CSMA/CD).

CSMA/CD works by allowing any computer to transmit at any time, assuming the line is free. The steps in this process are as follows:

1. When a workstation wants to send a packet on the network, the workstation listens to see whether any other nodes are transmitting packets over the network.

2. If the network is in use, the workstation waits.

3. If the network is not in use, the workstation sends its packet.

4. If two or more workstations send packets at the same time because they both thought the line was free, a collision occurs.

5. If a collision occurs, all workstations on the network cease transmission and each implements a back-off timer that generates a random number indicating how long the workstation must wait before it retransmits.

6. After the time expires, workstations can begin transmitting again.

Two stations transmit at the same time—a collision occurs

Benefits

The benefits of Ethernet include the following:

- ◇ The protocol is fairly simple and does not have the overhead associated with Token Ring (described in the next section).

- ◇ As long as the network segment is not too busy, stations can transmit without any wait.

- ◇ Because Ethernet hardware is nonproprietary and less complicated than Token Ring hardware, Ethernet is less expensive.

Drawbacks

The drawbacks of Ethernet include the following:

- ◇ As network traffic increases, so does the probability of network collisions, which degrade network performance.

- ◇ Because all stations have equal access, there is no way to establish higher priority for nodes such as servers.

Ethernet Rules

It is estimated that about 70 percent of all networks use Ethernet. Ethernet is so popular because it is fairly easy to install and uses inexpensive hardware compared to Token Ring and FDDI. Although the latter two are well proven and reliable technologies, they are expensive.

Ethernet has the added advantage of offering higher-speed networks on the same wire. Two new Ethernet technologies, Fast Ethernet and Gigabit Ethernet, perform at 100Mbps and 1000Mbps, respectively. That is a huge performance increase. And considering that most new computers come with network interface cards that support Fast Ethernet, it should be no surprise that Fast Ethernet is the default choice on new network installations.

The most popular form of Ethernet is 10BASE-T. With 10BASE-T Ethernet, you connect to the network with **unshielded twisted-pair (UTP)** cable; a connector on the end of the cable looks similar to, but is larger than, a telephone connector. One end of the cable attaches to the network card and the other end connects to a central hub called a concentrator.

---

unshielded twisted-pair (UTP)
A type of media that can contain four, six, or eight wires. Pairs of wires are twisted together to prevent signal interference. The wires are then wrapped in a plastic cover. UTP is identified by the category nomenclature.

Ethernet Standards

Ethernet has three primary standards:

IEEE 802.3   10Mbps Ethernet

IEEE 802.3u   100Mbps Fast Ethernet

IEEE 802.3z and **IEEE 802.3ab**   1000Mbps Gigabit Ethernet

Traditionally, people think of Ethernet as a 10Mbps standard. However, with the emerging standards that require networks to support voice, video, and other high-capacity bandwidth items, Fast Ethernet is now the standard for desktop computers and servers. Gigabit Ethernet is playing an increasing role as a key technology for supporting network backbones.

Ethernet has many other characteristics in addition to speed. Depending on which Ethernet standard you choose, you will have flexibility in which physical topology and which cable type you use.

Ethernet can use the following cable types:

- ◆ Thin **coaxial** cable (RG-58AU)
- ◆ Thick coaxial cable (RG-8 or RG-11)
- ◆ Unshielded twisted-pair (UTP) cables (type depends on access speed needed)
- ◆ **Fiber-optic** cable

Ethernet Naming Conventions

The IEEE has defined naming conventions for Ethernet standards. The standards are to be named as follows:

- ◆ The first part of the name specifies the speed in megabits per second.
- ◆ The second part of the name specifies that the standard is using baseband (BASE) or broadband (BROAD) signaling.
- ◆ The last part of the name describes the type of cable being used, or an estimate of a maximum cable run for the standard.

For example, the 10BASE-T standard defines 10Mbps speed, using baseband signaling, over twisted-pair cabling.

IEEE 802.3
The IEEE standard that is also known as Carrier Sense Multiple Access with Collision Detection (CSMA/CD) and defines how most Ethernet networks function.

IEEE 802.3u
The IEEE standard for 100MBps Fast Ethernet. Defines the specifications for implementing Fast Ethernet at the Physical and Data-Link layers of the OSI model.

IEEE 802.3z
The IEEE standard for 1000MBps Gigabit Ethernet over fiber-optic cable.

IEEE 802.3ab
The IEEE standard for 1000MBps Gigabit Ethernet over unshielded twisted-pair cable (UTP).

206

Networking the Computers

This table summarizes the Ethernet standards.

Ethernet Standard	Speed in Mbps	Physical Topology	Cable Used
10BASE2	10	Bus	Thin coaxial cable RG-58AU (50-ohm cable)
10BASE5	10	Bus	Thick coaxial cable RG-8 or RG-11 (50-ohm cable)
10BASE-T	10	Star	Unshielded twisted-pair cable (category 3 or better)
10BASE-F	10	Star	Fiber-optic
100BASE-T	100	Star	Unshielded twisted-pair cable (Uses category 5 with all four pairs.)
100BASE-TX	100	Star	Unshielded twisted-pair cable
100BASE-FX	100	Star	Fiber-optic cable (Uses two strands of fiber as specified by **ANSI**.)
1000BASE-X	1000	Star	Fiber-optic and copper cable
1000BASE-T	1000	Star	Unshielded twisted-pair (UTP)

coaxial
A type of media that has a single copper wire surrounded by plastic insulation, is wrapped in metal braid or foil, and finally protected by a plastic cover.

fiber-optic
A type of media that uses glass or plastic to transmit light signals. Single-mode fiber optic contains a single fiber. Multi-mode fiber cable has two individually protected fibers.

American National Standards Institute (ANSI)
An organization that seeks to develop standardization within the computing industry. ANSI is the American representative to the ISO, or International Standards Organization.

Ethernet Hardware

Depending on which Ethernet standard you choose, you can configure Ethernet as a physical bus or a physical star topology. This section provides an example of each topology and the hardware needed to support each configuration.

Ethernet Bus Topology

In the 1980s, before 10BASE-T became standardized, the most popular way of configuring Ethernet was in a physical bus topology. You might still use the bus topology in small networks, because it does not require a concentrator as the star configuration does. However, because the cost of Ethernet hardware has dropped drastically over the last 10 years, this is often not a large concern.

The most popular configuration for the bus topology uses the 10BASE2 standard, or thin coaxial cable. In this configuration, you connect a T-connector to the network card. You attach the cables to either side of the T-connector to form a linear bus network. At the ends of the bus, you need 50-ohm terminators. You should ground one end.

Ethernet Star Topology

The Ethernet star topology is by far the most commonly implemented topology for Ethernet networks. This topology is easier to set up and configure than the bus topology. It also provides more fault tolerance because a cable break does not cause the entire segment to go down.

In the star topology, you attach all your devices to the hub, or concentrator. You can buy concentrators with whatever number of ports you require, from 4 to 48 in a single unit.

When determining the hardware that you will use, you should first decide whether you will need 10Mbps, 100Mbps, or 1000Mbps networking capabilities. This factor determines the type of hub, Ethernet card, and cabling you will need. After your hardware is in place, the star will look like the following diagram.

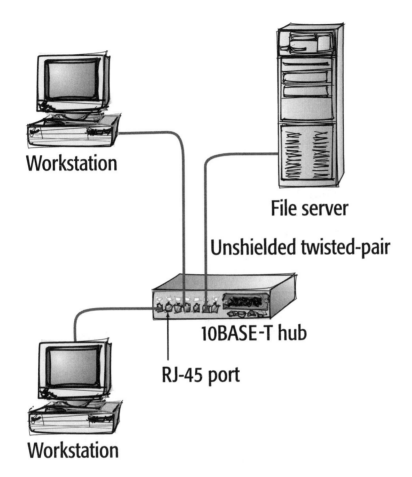

In the graphic above, both the workstations and the file server are connected to the network by using a 10BASE-T hub. In a small network of 5 to10 computers, this configuration is fine. But as the number of computers on the network grows, you will need to reconsider the design. Most network designers will select a hub that has at least a 100BASE-TX connection. The file server will connect to the 100BASE-TX to give optimum performance for multiple computers. More recently, networks are being designed with 100BASE-TX hubs to provide optimal network performance.

Token Ring Communication Architecture

IBM originally developed Token Ring as a way to connect mainframe computers with each other. Since then, IBM has also developed Token Ring for use as a network connectivity protocol. Although Token Ring was originally a proprietary protocol, the IEEE ratified the 802.5 standard for Token Ring in 1985, signifying a growing acceptance and future support for the architecture.

Physically, Token Ring looks like a star, but logically it passes data in a ring. Token Ring specifies three access speeds: 4Mbps, 16Mbps, and 100Mbps.

Token Ring works in what is called a token-passing scheme. With Token Ring, you designate one node on the network as the active monitor. The active monitor is responsible for generating a special packet called a token, and it issues only one token for the entire ring. The only time a station can transmit data is when it accesses the token. Because each network has only one token, collisions never occur.

Token-passing schemes are called deterministic because they produce predictable access, which enables you to set a priority on each computer. This capability is an advantage for large networks running mission-critical applications.

Logically, a Token Ring looks like this:

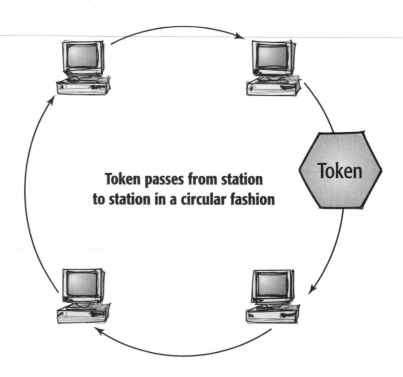

Token passes from station to station in a circular fashion

Token

Benefits

The benefits of Token Ring include the following:

◇ Token Ring eliminates the collisions associated with Ethernet.

◇ Token Ring provides connectivity to IBM mainframes and is compatible with **Systems Network Architecture (SNA)** software.

◇ Token Ring offers predictable access and load management.

◇ You can assign priorities to computers to allow faster access to mission-critical computers, such as network servers.

◇ In high-load networks, Token Ring produces better network throughput than Ethernet.

Drawbacks

The drawbacks of Token Ring include the following:

◇ Token Ring software and hardware are more complicated than Ethernet, which makes Token Ring more costly to implement.

◇ Token Ring needs more management than Ethernet, thus requiring a more experienced network administrator.

NOTE

At this point, 4Mbps Token Ring is considered obsolete and is found only in legacy networks.

NOTE

Modern Token Ring physically uses a star topology but logically passes data in a ring. This is sometimes referred to as a star-ring topology.

Systems Network Architecture (SNA)
Defined by IBM, a standard that specifies how devices can interface with IBM software.

Token Ring Hardware

Some of the original Token Ring hardware used by IBM is noticeably different from other network connectors. The early equipment, illustrated in the graphic below, used bulky cables with somewhat large black connectors. Connecting hundreds of devices together on the same network required a significant amount of equipment and space. Currently, the connectors and cables for Token Ring look identical to Ethernet hardware, which makes distinguishing the two networks from one another more difficult by visual inspection.

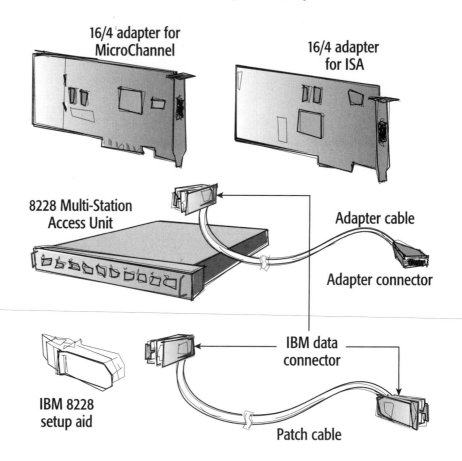

The hardware includes:

    ◇ A network interface card that supports 4, 16, or 100Mbps.

    ◇ A central device. In this case, the hub is an 8228 MAU.

    ◇ A setup aid to initialize ports on the MAU if it is a model 8228 MAU.

    ◇ Adapter cables to attach the network card to the MAU.

    ◇ Patch cables to connect MAUs or to act as an extension cable for extending the distance between a MAU and an adapter cable.

Common Token Ring Configurations

In a very small network, you might need only a single Token Ring MAU. In most cases, you will want to form a larger ring. The MAU (or whichever Token Ring hub you choose) will have two ports that are identified as Ring In and Ring Out. The Ring In and Ring Out ports form a larger ring. The Token Ring workstations attach to the data ports, as shown below.

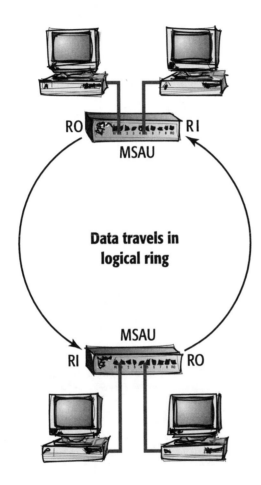

Review Questions

Terms to Know
- ❏ 10BASE-T
- ❏ FDDI
- ❏ token
- ❏ token passing
- ❏ collisions
- ❏ IEEE
- ❏ IEEE 802.3
- ❏ IEEE 802.3u
- ❏ IEEE 802.3z
- ❏ IEEE 802.3ab
- ❏ coaxial
- ❏ UTP
- ❏ fiber-optic
- ❏ ANSI
- ❏ SNA

1. List the three common topologies:

   _____

   _____

   _____

2. What is the difference between a physical topology and a logical topology?

   _____

3. What does CSMA/CD stand for?

   _____

4. What are the two access speeds at which Ethernet transmits?

   _____

   _____

5. What are the two access speeds at which Token Ring transmits?

   _____

   _____

6. Which topology offers the most fault tolerance and is the easiest to reconfigure?

   _____

7. True or false: You can use any topology with Ethernet or Token Ring.

   _____

8. Which cable does 10BASE2 Ethernet use?

    A. Thin coaxial cable

    B. Thick coaxial cable

    C. Unshielded twisted-pair cable

    D. Shielded twisted-pair cable

_____

9. Which physical topology does 10BASE-T Ethernet use?

_____

10. Token Ring uses a logical _____ topology and a physical _____ topology.

11. True or false: Token Ring offers better throughput in busier networks than Ethernet does.

_____

12. Which is more commonly implemented, Ethernet or Token Ring?

_____

13. Which IEEE standard defines Ethernet?

_____

14. Which IEEE standard defines Token Ring?

_____

Chapter

11

Moving Data: Network Layer Protocols

pro·to·col *n* : a set of rules that governs how communication should occur

In Chapter 8, "A Communications Framework," you learned about the OSI model. The two layers of this model that are responsible for moving data over an internetwork are the Network and Transport layers.

The Network layer of the OSI model determines the best route that a packet should take when it needs to be delivered over an internetwork. The Transport layer is primarily responsible for reliable data delivery.

At both layers, there must be protocols designed to fulfill the functions of packet delivery and reliability. Protocols are a set of rules that govern how communication should occur between upper and lower layers in addition to communicating with the other device. Without protocols, there would not be any agreed-upon format for how to handle data. This is especially a problem in a field with many technologies and thousands of manufacturers.

In this chapter, you will learn about the popular Network and Transport protocols that are used in modern computer networks, including:

 TCP/IP

 IPX/SPX

 NetBEUI

Using TCP/IP

One of the most popular networking protocols is Transmission Control Protocol/Internet Protocol (TCP/IP). TCP/IP was originally developed in the 1970s by the Department of Defense (DoD) as a way of connecting dissimilar networks that would be capable of withstanding a nuclear attack. Since then, TCP/IP has become a de facto industry standard. It is important to note that although TCP and IP are the cornerstone protocols, TCP/IP is actually a collection of many protocols that are generically referred to as the TCP/IP protocol suite.

The two main protocols that make up the TCP/IP suite of protocols are TCP and IP. These protocols fall into the Transport and Network layers of the OSI model, respectively.

IP functions at the Network layer of the OSI model. The primary function of IP is to provide each attached device a unique address. Each address indicates not only the individual device, but also the network to which the device belongs. The IP protocol is also responsible for routing packets over an internetwork. The IP address is used to determine the exact location of the destination network where the device exists. For example, assume that you have four subnets (independent network segments) connected through routers, and you want to send a packet from subnet A to subnet B. IP is responsible for routing the packet through the internetwork.

fully duplexed

Means that simultaneous two-way communication can take place.

virtual circuit

A logical connection between two devices that transmits and receives data.

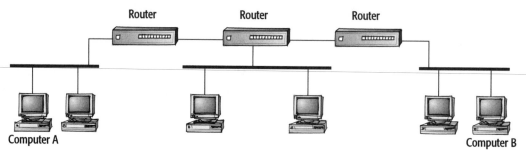

TCP is a Transport layer protocol whose primary function is to provide reliable delivery of data through a connection-oriented service. This is done by establishing a **fully duplexed**, **virtual circuit** connection. Sending data through TCP is a two-part process: The sender and receiver exchange a "handshake" to establish communication, and then acknowledgments are sent to verify that data was received. Acknowledgements are being sent throughout the transmission.

If you do not need the reliability of TCP, you can send packets through the Transport layer with a protocol called User Datagram Protocol (UDP). UDP provides connectionless service and has considerably less overhead than TCP but provides no reliability in the transmission of data. As a connectionless protocol, UDP packets are sent over the network without any confirmation from the receiver that the packets were received successfully. The packets either get there or they don't. The sender doesn't worry about it.

Transport	TCP UDP
Network	IP

OSI model layers

Benefits of TCP/IP

TCP/IP is commonly used as the Transport and Network layer protocol for these reasons:

- ◇ It is supported by almost all network operating systems. It is the required protocol for communicating over the Internet; if you want to connect to the Internet, your computer has to use TCP/IP.

- ◇ TCP/IP is scalable to small and large networks.

- ◇ The protocol is designed to be fault tolerant and is able to dynamically reroute packets if network links become unavailable (assuming alternate paths exist).

- ◇ Protocol companions such as **Dynamic Host Configuration Protocol (DHCP)** simplify IP address management.

- ◇ **Domain Name System (DNS)** is used with TCP/IP to **resolve** a **fully qualified domain name (FQDN)**, such as sybex.com, with its corresponding IP address.

Disadvantages of TCP/IP

Although TCP/IP and the Internet has been wildly successful, using this protocol has disadvantages. Of course, the disadvantages do not outweigh the advantages, but they should be taken into consideration when building your network. When you connect your network to the Internet, you will want to consider ways to avoid or minimize the following disadvantages:

- ◇ Managing IP addresses is complicated and cumbersome. IP address errors are usually due to administrative error.

- ◇ Troubleshooting TCP/IP problems on your network requires an understanding of how TCP/IP works and of the more than a dozen protocols that are included in the suite.

- ◇ Taking advantage of some of the best features of the TCP/IP suite requires considerable skill and knowledge. Depending on your type of business, mastering TCP/IP will require a significant amount of education for you or necessitate the hiring of an expert.

Dynamic Host Configuration Protocol (DHCP)
Automates the assignment of IP configuration information.

Domain Name System (DNS)
A system that resolves domain names to IP addresses by using a domain name database.

resolve
To convert from one type to another. In relationship to IP addresses and domain names, it is the conversion of an IP address to a domain name on the Internet or vice versa.

fully qualified domain name (FQDN)
The complete name registered with InterNIC that is used to identify a computer on the Internet. It includes the computer name (hostname) and the domain name. For example, mycomputer.sybex.com.

IP Addressing

A central concept of IP is addressing. The current IP version, IPv4, requires a 32-bit network address. Each **octet** consists of a number between 0 and 255 separated by a period. IP addresses must be unique for each network device that can be reached on the Internet. You should request your IP addresses from InterNIC or from an ISP. IP addresses commonly fall within three classes: Class A, Class B, and Class C. Class assignments are based on network size and the availability of IP addresses.

octet

One of four parts of an IP address. Each number in an octet is created using 8 bits.

loopback

A special function for testing a device's ability to communicate by making it communicate with itself.

broadcasts

Data transmitted to all devices on the same network segment.

NOTE

Currently, only Class C addresses are available. The supply of IP addresses has dwindled to the point that all addresses will be allocated by 2001. A new IP addressing scheme with six octets, 48 bits, is in the works. Known as IPv6, this standard will supply billions of new IP addresses.

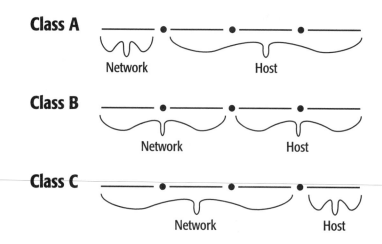

Class A — Network — Host

Class B — Network — Host

Class C — Network — Host

Network Class	Address Range of First Field	Number of Networks Supported	Number of Host Nodes Available
A	1–127	126	16,777,214
B	128–191	65,534	65,534
C	192–223	16,777,214	254

NOTE

The following addresses are reserved: 0 is not available, because it denotes that no routing is needed; 127 is a special **loopback** address used for diagnostic purposes; and 255 is used for **broadcasts**.

IP Configuration

When you configure a network device with TCP/IP, you typically need three pieces of information:

- ◇ IP address
- ◇ Subnet mask
- ◇ Default gateway, which is the IP address of a router

IP Address

As mentioned on the preceding page, each network device needs a unique IP address. The system administrator, or someone who coordinates IP address assignment and configuration, should assign this address from the pool of addresses assigned by InterNIC or your ISP.

Subnet Mask

A subnet mask defines which part of the IP address is the network address and which is the host address. By defining subnet masks, you specify which network your node belongs to. With this information and the destination address for your data, TCP/IP can determine whether source and destination nodes are on the same network segment. If they are on different segments, routing will be needed.

Default Router, or Gateway

You need a default router, or gateway, configured on your workstations if you want your packets routed over an internetwork. The default router is the IP address of the local router that you use to connect your network to the Internet. The workstation needs to have this information if it wants to send packets out to the Internet. Without it, the workstation is clueless about where to send packets destined for external networks.

NOTE

These are basic IP configuration options. Depending on the complexity of your IP network, you might also specify other configuration options, such as the DNS and **Windows Internet Naming Service (WINS)** servers that will be used.

Windows Internet Naming Service (WINS)
A Microsoft proprietary protocol that runs on a Windows NT server. The protocol is used on NT severs to resolve NetBIOS names, the workstation name on Windows computers, to IP addresses. WINS is similar in concept to DNS.

The Function of DHCP in an IP Network

Having a system administrator or other person manually configure IP addresses is inherently flawed and can potentially lead to misconfiguration, causing IP address conflicts and network errors. Fortunately, there is a TCP/IP protocol that helps automate configuration. Dynamic Host Configuration Protocol (DHCP) uses a DHCP server to automate this process.

The DHCP server contains a range of IP addresses called the scope. As requested, the DHCP server will pull available IP addresses from the scope to lease to clients. A lease option specifies how long an IP address will be assigned to a DHCP client. As long as a client keeps using the IP address, that client is allowed to keep it. If the address is not used within the lease period, it is returned to the DHCP server scope and is available for use by other DHCP clients.

DHCP uses this process to assign addresses:

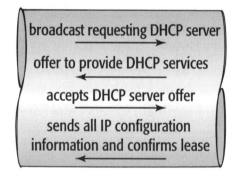

DHCP client

broadcast requesting DHCP server

offer to provide DHCP services

accepts DHCP server offer

sends all IP configuration information and confirms lease

DHCP server

DHCP Servers in an NT Environment

In an NT environment, only NT Servers can act as DHCP servers. You install the DHCP service on the server under Control Panel ➤ Network ➤ Services.

After you have installed the DHCP server, you must configure the scope and subnet mask that the DHCP clients will use. Through DHCP, you can also configure options such as the default gateway, WINS server, and DNS server.

The Function of DNS in an IP Network

The Domain Name System (DNS) is a process that allows IP addresses to be mapped to FQDNs. These are the easily remembered names that people use to access network resources, particularly Web sites. To demonstrate the usefulness of DNS, take this quiz:

1. What is the URL to access the Microsoft Web site?
2. What is the IP address of Microsoft's Web site?

If you answered microsoft.com for question 1, you are right. Most people can answer this question; however, very few people can answer the second question. This is OK, though, because this is where DNS comes into play. DNS enables you to use a name that you can remember in place of an IP address; DNS then translates the name into an address used to contact the host you wish to communicate with.

DNS uses FQDNs to logically organize resources. Domains are logically grouped by type of function into a hierarchical structure. At the top of the structure is the root. Examples of root domains include .com for business, .edu for education, and .gov for government. Domain names must be unique. InterNIC assigns and centrally manages them.

NOTE

DNS domains are different from Windows NT domains, and you should not confuse the two terms.

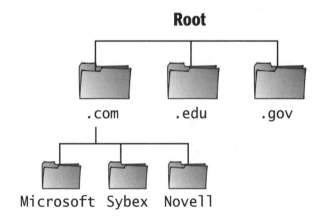

Using IPX/SPX

Internetwork Packet Exchange/Sequenced Packet Exchange (IPX/SPX) is a proprietary protocol that Novell developed for use with its **NetWare** software product. Because it is proprietary to Novell, it is not as commonly used as TCP/IP.

NetWare
A popular network operating system from Novell and a competitive product to Windows NT.

Transport	IPX SPX
Network	IPX

OSI model layers

IPX works primarily at the Network layer. Its main function is to route packets through an internetwork and to identify devices. If connection-oriented services are not needed, IPX is also used to send packets through the Transport layer.

SPX functions at the Transport layer. It provides connection-oriented, fully duplexed connections. For each packet that is sent, an acknowledgement is returned. In addition, SPX is responsible for segmenting data into packets and maintaining a sequence number for each packet. The receiving computer uses the number to reassemble the data.

Benefits of IPX/SPX

IPX/SPX shares similar benefits to TCP/IP in addition to its own, including:

- ◆ IPX addressing uses more bits per address, so there is a greater supply of addresses.
- ◆ SPX is a reliable, connection-oriented protocol.
- ◆ Upper-layer protocols can bypass SPX in some cases to improve performance.

Disadvantages of IPX/SPX

Consider these disadvantages before implementing IPX/SPX:

- ◆ IPX/SPX is considered a chatty protocol, meaning it creates a significant amount of network traffic that does not involve transferring data.
- ◆ IPX/SPX does not work on the Internet.
- ◆ IPX/SPX is proprietary, meaning that it is not a standard that other companies can use.

Using NetBEUI

NetBIOS Extended User Interface (NetBEUI) was developed in the mid-1980s to connect workgroups running IBM's OS/2 operating system and Microsoft's **LAN Manager** software. Since then, Microsoft has included NetBEUI as a default network protocol or as an option on all its operating systems. One reason for including NetBEUI is that it is simple to configure. Besides installation, no other configuration is necessary. Microsoft operating systems will communicate very well using NetBEUI.

Although NetBEUI works well with Microsoft-based operating systems, not many other operating systems are compatible with the protocol. Also, NetBEUI was not designed to work between two networks connected by a router. Software and hardware that will enable NetBEUI to work in this scenario exists, but it is complex to configure and doesn't offer good performance. If you know you are going to need to support multiple networks, it is best to select a routable network protocol.

Lan Manager
One of Microsoft's first network operating systems.

Benefits of NetBEUI

The following are NetBEUI advantages:

- ◇ It is easy to install.
- ◇ There are no configuration requirements.
- ◇ NetBEUI is an excellent choice for small, non-routed networks.
- ◇ NetBEUI has less overhead than TCP/IP and IPX/SPX; thus it offers better performance.
- ◇ NetBEUI uses less memory than TCP/IP and IPX/SPX.

Disadvantages of NetBEUI

The disadvantages of NetBEUI include the following:

- ◇ NetBEUI is not routable, so you cannot use it to transmit data between networks separated by routers.
- ◇ NetBEUI is supported only on the Windows platform.

TIP

On networks consisting of a single network segment, NetBEUI will provide the best performance because of the low overhead associated with this protocol.

Review Questions

Terms to Know
- fully duplexed
- virtual circuit
- DHCP
- DNS
- resolve
- FQDN
- octet
- loopback
- broadcasts
- WINS
- NetWare
- Lan Manager

1. What are three common IP configuration requirements?

   _____

   _____

   _____

2. Which TCP/IP protocol allows you to automate IP configuration?

   _____

3. What proprietary protocol does Novell NetWare use?

   _____

4. What is the primary purpose of IP?

   _____

5. At which layer of the OSI model does IP function?

   _____

6. NetWare uses the _____ protocol to provide connection-oriented services at the Transport layer of the OSI model.

7. Which TCP/IP address class offers the largest number of network addresses?

   _____

8. Which protocol offers the fastest service ?
   - **A.** TCP/IP
   - **B.** IPX/SPX
   - **C.** NetBEUI

   _____

9. Which protocol is most widely implemented?

    A. TCP/IP

    B. IPX/SPX

    C. NetBEUI

_____

10. True or false: NetBEUI is not a routable protocol.

_____

11. What is the primary function of DNS?

_____

12. In TCP/IP configuration, what defines which part of the address is the network address and which part is the host address?

_____

13. True or false: IPX/SPX is a proprietary protocol.

_____

14. What configuration does NetBEUI need?

_____

Chapter

12

Network Operating Systems: A Comparison

sys•tem *n* : a connection of parts designed to function together

As you learned in Chapter 10, "Networking the Computers," the client-server architecture uses a dedicated server. A server is a computer that provides a variety of services to clients. Services can include e-mail and providing access to files, databases, or other applications. The factors that determine the capabilities of the server depend on the software that is selected. The network operating system is software that runs on the server and makes centralized services, described above, possible.

In the world of networking, you have many operating systems to choose from. Some factors to consider when choosing a network operating system include price, function, interoperability, the skill set required to manage the software, existing applications, hardware and software requirements, and personal preference. In this chapter, you will learn about some of the major network operating systems, which include:

 Windows NT 4 Server

 Windows 2000 Server

 NetWare

 Unix

 Linux

Introduction to an NOS

A network operating system (NOS) is the system software designed especially for servers. You may have heard *server* used in several different ways, including in the terms **file server**, **print server**, and **database server**. Each type of server fits a particular need. In small businesses, it is not uncommon to find a single computer used as a file and print server. In large corporate networks, each server is configured to serve a specific task. More often than not, these large networks also will have multiple computers serving the same role (for example, multiple file servers).

The concept behind an NOS is that it is easier to manage a centralized network than it is to manage a network that has all its resources spread out. An example of a decentralized model (one without a server) is a peer-to-peer network. In order for centralized servers to be effective, they have to be designed to meet stringent performance and reliability demands. The design criteria include:

Reliability   If a major software error or hardware failure occurs, the server will continue to function.

Scalability   As the needs of the company grow, the NOS is able to meet the demands. This may be accomplished by supporting larger and more powerful hardware and by adding additional servers that are designed to work in tandem.

Performance   The server provides optimum performance for the task it has been configured to serve, in addition to being adapted for more demanding scenarios.

Interoperability   Now more than ever, an NOS needs to be able to integrate with other devices, systems, and software platforms. In some instances, this integration may include a single point of management for all resources on the network.

Building a system that incorporates the above criteria may seem easier than it really is. You have to remember that the NOS is only software. You still have to contend with hardware and other software (such as applications) that will be running on the system. In the case of Microsoft Windows NT, you should be able to run NT on any Intel- or Alpha-based computer. Does that mean that the system will run well or is stable? Not at all. You need to take into consideration the extent to which all of the hardware components have been tested. These include critical components such as network interface cards, tape backup drives, and special adapters (for example, SCSI cards).

file server
A computer that is dedicated to the task of centrally sharing files and folders for access by users.

print server
A centralized computer that manages printing of user documents to one or more printers. Print servers store documents temporarily when the printer is busy.

database server
A type of computer that maintains information records that can be added, deleted, changed, or searched. Database servers play a major role in most companies and on the Internet.

What to Look for in an NOS

Selecting the right network operating system for your company needs is important. Although most NOSs provide some similar features, each one has unique features that should be taken into consideration. The features available in an NOS may not be the only factors you will have to consider.

All the NOSs discussed in the later sections offer the critical features a network administrator would expect to find. These common features include the following:

Fault tolerance   Fault tolerance in a server means that it is able to recover from a hardware failure or software crash without losing any data and, ideally, without any downtime. Fault-tolerant servers support RAID storage, uninterruptible power supplies, and tape backup systems.

Multiprocessing   An NOS must be able to maintain performance under demanding loads. To accomplish a consistent level of performance on a growing network, the server will need to be able to support multiple processors. An NOS that supports multiprocessing can use two or more CPUs to process an instruction simultaneously.

Multitasking   Servers, by nature, are required to complete several tasks simultaneously. If they couldn't do that effectively, they would not be of much use on a network of a thousand users. A server capable of multitasking can juggle several actions. A powerful server can handle hundreds of tasks efficiently, and without a significant decrease in performance or stability.

Besides these features, each NOS has unique qualities that may make it a good fit for your network.

Additional features to consider include wide support for different tape backup drives, antivirus software, and RAID. Compatibility with different tape drives is critical. As your data storage needs grow, so does your demand for larger backup storage. The NOS must include support for the latest tape drive technologies. As for antivirus programs, second best doesn't cut it. With the proliferation of e-mail and Web-based viruses, a robust, networkable antivirus application needs to be supported by the NOS you select. And finally, the NOS needs to be able to support hardware- and software-based RAID options. Fortunately, this typically is not a problem because almost all NOSs, including Apple's AppleShare IP server software, will recognize a hardware RAID solution as a hard drive.

Windows NT 4 Server

Since 1993, the popularity of Windows NT has grown significantly. With the release of the 3.51 version, Windows NT has been considered a viable solution for corporate networks. But it was not until after the release of NT 4 that Windows NT Server has been widely accepted, and it is still the fastest-growing operating system for new installations.

Windows NT 4 offers adequate performance and security. It is still not comparable to Unix in these areas, but it does offer other advantages over implementing and managing Unix. First, NT 4 uses the familiar interface of Windows 95 and 98. Needless to say, the learning curve is dramatically shorter for NT than for Unix. Second, most corporations are using the Windows 95, 98, and NT desktop operating systems. Combining these desktop operating systems with NT Server creates a completely integrated network that is easier to manage and maintain.

Finally, another exciting part of NT 4 Server is the inclusion of Microsoft's domain technology, discussed in Chapter 9, "Network Models." As you have already learned, NT 4 and 3.51 servers in a domain model share a single database of users and security-access levels. This database can be maintained across multiple servers regardless of geographical location. Although a single distributed database was a unique feature in 1995, it is now a common feature of NOSs, including Novell NetWare.

When to Choose NT 4 Server

Some compelling reasons to choose NT 4 Server:

- ◇ NT 4 uses an interface that looks like Windows 95/98.
- ◇ User accounts and security are kept consistent across all servers.
- ◇ Thousands of applications are written for Windows NT.
- ◇ Version 4 includes many Internet applications, including a Web server.

Why you may not want to select NT 4:

- ◇ Configuration changes often require the server to be rebooted, resulting in downtime.
- ◇ NT 4 cannot be made as secure as Unix.
- ◇ Software conflicts are more common on NT 4 than on other NOSs.

Windows 2000 Server

As you already learned in Chapter 5, "Desktop Operating Systems: A Comparison," the Windows 2000 operating system offers many enhancements over Windows NT 4. Windows 2000 Server offers all the benefits of Windows NT 4 Server but with many improvements in Internet support, performance, and security. You'll learn more about the specific improvements in Chapter 14, "The Windows 2000 Platforms."

Beyond the major changes to the core of the software, Windows 2000 takes a different approach to network configuration. The most significant change is the introduction of Active Directory services. Unlike Windows NT 4, which uses Microsoft's domain model for managing NT servers, Windows 2000 manages resources (including other 2000 and NT computers) by using the directory services model. This model is similar in concept to Novell's NetWare Directory Services. Besides being able to manage servers, computers, printers, and users, Active Directory can maintain consistency throughout an organization, regardless of geographical location.

A much sought-after improvement to Windows 2000 is increased support for Wizards as part of configuring and managing the server. Wizards make server configuration quicker and easier.

When to Choose Windows 2000 Server

As with any new product, there are varying opinions and tests of how well a product will perform. Windows 2000 is no exception. Windows 2000 does build on the advantages of Windows NT, but what might have been a blessing may be overshadowed by the introduction of Active Directory. Because this is the first release of Active Directory, you can look forward to significant advances.

There are some clear advantages to selecting Windows 2000 Server:

- ◆ Directory services are the future in network management.
- ◆ There are fewer restarts required when adding services.
- ◆ It includes support for Windows NT domains and Active Directory.

Disadvantages to consider before adopting Windows 2000 Server:

- ◆ This is the first release of Active Directory.
- ◆ There is not wide support for Active Directory yet, which translates into limited support with other non-Windows devices on the network.
- ◆ Windows 2000 Server has tens of millions of lines of more code than Windows NT Server, which could be a problem in itself.

Novell NetWare

From the mid-1980s until the mid-1990s, Novell dominated the network operating system market. Novell still has the largest market share of existing network installations, but Microsoft has a larger share of new operating systems that are sold and installed. This section provides an overview of three of Novell's network operating systems:

- ◇ NetWare 3.*x*
- ◇ NetWare 4.*x*
- ◇ NetWare 5.1

console command
A command that is input directly from the keyboard and monitor of the server instead of remotely.

NetWare Loadable Module
Software that is added or removed to a NetWare server to provide additional functionality. Examples include adding support for Macintosh computers and print services.

NetWare 3.*x*

NetWare 3.*x* is Novell's server operating system for small networks. It supports a client-server network model, as defined in Chapter 10. Although version 3 is two versions old and considered technologically out-of-date, it is still present on many business networks. Therefore, it deserves some discussion.

In a NetWare 3.*x* network, each server contains its own database of user accounts, which are stored within three files called bindery files. These files store details about users and groups, including their security-access level. The database is local to each server and is not distributed or shared with any other servers on the network. If a user needs access to two NetWare 3 servers, two accounts must be created, one on each server.

The NetWare server is a dedicated server, which means that only the NetWare operating system can run on it. You cannot run DOS or Windows commands from the server.

From the keyboard of a NetWare server you can issue **console commands**. The console commands are used to start **NetWare Loadable Modules (NLMs)**. Each NLM is a service that can be run on the server if needed. For example, if you need to support Macintosh computers on your NetWare server, you can load the ATCONFIG module. The capability to load individual services makes NetWare a modular and flexible NOS. An important feature of NLMs is that you can load and unload them without having to restart the server.

NetWare 4.*x*

NetWare 4 radically changed NetWare architecture by introducing NetWare Directory Services (NDS). NDS uses the directory services network model, which is covered in Chapter 10.

NDS works by establishing a database of network objects. Each object in the database can represent any device, user, or group on the network. The NDS database is distributed and replicated to all NetWare servers. The advantage of NDS is that Windows NT, 2000, and Unix servers can all be centrally managed as objects. There is less of a need to have management systems for each platform. That translates into lower management costs.

NetWare 4.x also provides other key network services, including security services, file and print services, backup services, and a messaging service that you can use with compatible messaging applications to send e-mail and coordinate schedules.

The release of NetWare 4.11 (called IntraNetWare) added support for a Web server, Web client, and a new feature called the IPX/IP Gateway. The IPX/IP Gateway added support for connecting IPX-based clients to the Internet without the hassle of configuring the clients for TCP/IP.

NetWare 5.1

In the latest release of NetWare, NetWare 5.1, Novell has made many major changes. Besides expanded support and improved performance of NDS, now called NDS eDirectory, Novell has added pure IP support. Novell's proprietary protocol, IPX, is no longer used unless installed by the administrator for use with IPX-configured client computers. In addition, a growing number of Internet-based applications are included with NetWare 5.1, including DNS, DHCP, Web server, Web Search server, and a Web-based application server. Finally, NetWare 5.1 includes several new management tools, including a Web-based server administration application.

When to Choose NetWare

If you are working on a network that has existing NetWare servers, then your decision may be easier, or at least already decided. An existing NetWare network is best left NetWare. More than for management reasons, staying with NetWare-based servers and applications will result in the shortest integration time and the best performance. Always consider the learning curve required to use a new system—even if it appears easy to learn, as might be the case with Windows NT Server.

If you are looking at a new installation or migrating from an outdated system, consider these advantages and disadvantages before making your final decision.

Advantages to choosing NetWare:

- ◇ It has a large user base of NetWare users.
- ◇ It is stable and performs well.
- ◇ NetWare Directory Services has been well tested.

Before you go out and buy, consider these disadvantages:

- ◇ There are fewer new applications and tools developed for NetWare.
- ◇ It has no capability to limit user storage or to compress files on hard disks.

Unix Servers

Just like Windows NT or 2000, Unix is an operating system that can be used for workstations or servers. As a server, Unix is considered the workhorse of the Internet and is used for high-demand applications on large corporate networks. Unix has acquired this role because of its superior reliability and performance that has taken decades to develop.

Unix has had a long history. Its roots begin in the 1960s at Bell Telephone Laboratories at AT&T, where it was first developed. Since then, Unix has rapidly grown into several versions. The most notable achievement is the development of BSD Unix by students at the University of California at Berkeley. In those hallowed halls of UC Berkeley has risen an operating system that has been the basis for the development of other versions of Unix, from Sun Microsystems and Hewlett-Packard to Apple Computer.

When to Choose Unix

The list of reasons to choose Unix are as varied as the versions of Unix in existence today. The reasons for selecting Unix as your NOS include:

- It is the most stable and fastest operating system available.
- It is the best choice for supporting critical applications because of its rock-solid performance and proven reliability.
- It is the undisputed king of the Internet.
- There are hundreds, if not thousands of tools for managing your Unix server.

There are disadvantages to consider, including:

- Unix is a complex system that requires learning hundreds of archaic commands.
- Proprietary versions are expensive.
- Some proprietary versions will run only on that same company's hardware.

Linux

Linux is a version of Unix that has been written from the ground up. What makes Linux unique is that it offers comparable performance to other network operating systems, with one interesting twist: It's free!

When Linux was first released in 1991 by Linus Torvalds, a student at the University of Helsinki, it wasn't much of an operating system. In an effort to spawn rapid development of Linux, Torvalds made the source code free so that other programmers from around the world could assist him. The only condition was that anyone who developed Linux had to agree that the source code remain free as required by the **open source** license. Since those early years of the 1990s, Linux has grown into a popular operating system that has generated a lot of excitement in the computer industry.

Linux is still young; it has only a small number of installations and is only in its second version. But Linux has its place in the operating system world. As Linux matures, it will be considered more frequently than not as an option to expensive NOSs.

When to Choose Linux

With all of the excitement behind Linux, you may already be planning your download or purchase of one of the available distributions. Before you jump on board, make one final review of the following benefits and shortcomings.

Some of the benefits of Linux:

- ◆ It provides Unix performance without the cost.
- ◆ It's free.
- ◆ It runs on almost every known platform, including PCs and Macintosh.

It might fall short of your expectations in these areas:

- ◆ Like Unix, Linux can be complex to learn, with hundreds of archaic commands.
- ◆ Although popular, it has not been around that long.
- ◆ It has limited technical support from just a few companies.

---

open source
The free distribution of source code (software) for the purpose of improving the software by the programming community. Regardless of modifications or adaptations of open source software, the code is still protected by the Open Source Definition.

Review Questions

Terms to Know
- file server
- print server
- database server
- console command
- NetWare Loadable Module
- open source

1. What are two criteria for evaluating network operating system software?

2. How does multiprocessing improve NOS performance?

3. How does the domain model in Windows NT Server help to reduce server management?

4. What is one disadvantage of NT Server that results in server downtime?

5. What significant improvement did Microsoft make to Windows 2000?

6. True or False: Windows 2000 Active Directory services supports the NT domain model.

7. What type of network model does NetWare 3.x use?

8. What type of network model does NetWare 4.x use?

9. What is the current version of NetWare?

_____

10. What does NLM stand for, and what is the purpose of an NLM?

_____

11. What change was made to NetWare 5.1 that improved network performance on an IP-based network?

_____

12. Why is Unix typically the first choice for Internet servers?

_____

13. What is a disadvantage of both Unix and Linux?

_____

14. Why might Linux be a poor selection for someone new to Linux and Unix?

_____

15. What is one major reason why Linux has become so popular?

_____

Chapter

13

A Star Is Born: History of Windows 2000

or·i·gin *n* : the source from which something is derived

Windows 2000 evolved from Windows NT. The first version of NT to be released was NT 3.1, in July 1993. NT 3.5 followed in September 1994, and NT 4 was released in July 1996. The current release of Microsoft's business class workstation and server operating systems is called Windows 2000. This chapter covers each version of NT and 2000 and the differences between them. Topics include:

 Overview of NT origins

 NT 3.*x*

 NT 4

 Windows 2000

Understanding the Origins of Windows NT

During the 1980s and early 1990s, Novell cornered the network operating system market. Microsoft offered networking software—OS/2 (which was originally developed by IBM) and LAN Manager—but these operating systems never really caught on.

Microsoft decided to create a new operating system from the ground up. Designing a new operating system would eliminate the inherent limitations of older software. In late 1988, Microsoft hired Dave Cutler, a veteran of minicomputer systems architecture, from Digital Equipment Corporation, to design the new network operating system. This "New Technology" was to become Windows NT.

Before the programmers could begin creating this new operating system, the design team had to come up with the software design goals that would define what the NT operating system should do. The following subsections describe these goals.

Provide Flexibility in OS Code

The operating system code had to be written so that it could easily be modified to accommodate market demands.

In this sense, NT is fairly flexible—new software components can be added and deleted as current software and hardware standards dictate. New services and drivers can be written as standards change, and they do not affect the core operating system. Also, you can configure each server or workstation to use only the services and drivers that each unique configuration requires.

Offer High Performance

A major design goal of NT was that it had to be a high-performance operating system. Each component of NT has been optimized to provide the highest performance for individual use and on a network, including large networks with thousands of users.

Be Reliable

The operating system had to be able to handle errors in a reliable and fault-tolerant manner. This means that NT shields itself from most hardware and software errors so that the system will continue to operate.

Memory is one area where reliability is critical. NT manages memory through virtual memory. Virtual memory is the combination of physical RAM and the page file—a special file on the hard drive that is used to supplement physical RAM. Whenever you launch an application (with the exception of older Windows 16-bit applications), the memory manager in NT allocates the application its own separate memory space in RAM. The allocated portion cannot be used by any other program until the first application closes. This technique keeps a failed application from crashing or interfering with the operation of other applications or with the operating system.

The **New Technology File System (NTFS)** is also designed so that it is able to recover from many types of file errors.

New Technology File System (NTFS)
Developed by Microsoft for the NT operating systems, this feature added better file management, larger disk compatibility, and file-level security on the local computer.

Use Portable Code

As hardware standards change, NT should be able to be moved from one processor type to another. For example, NT can run on an Intel processor or an Alpha processor.

Be Compatible with Existing Standards

Another goal was that NT needed to be compatible with existing standards. This compatibility would make NT a better choice for computer networks with several types of operating systems coexisting (not just Microsoft operating systems). In addition, NT needed to be able to support existing applications that were written to run under other operating systems, particularly older Windows applications.

NT is compatible with existing network standards. For example, NT supports networking transport protocols such as TCP/IP, IPX/SPX, and NetBEUI (which are covered in Chapter 11, "Moving Data: Network Layer Protocols"). NT also is compatible with other network operating systems, such as NetWare, SNA, Unix, and AppleTalk networks.

In addition, NT supports applications by providing modular subsystems for DOS, OS/2, and POSIX applications. As new standards emerge, new subsystems can be developed. Each configuration loads only the necessary subsystems. This level of modularity means that only parts of the operating system need to be changed; the entire software code for NT does not have to be rewritten.

Understanding NT 3.x

The NT 3.x series featured three versions:

- ❖ NT 3.1
- ❖ NT 3.5
- ❖ NT 3.51

NT 3.1

The first released version of NT was NT Advanced Server 3.1 and NT Workstation 3.1. Microsoft named this version 3.1 to be consistent with Microsoft Windows 3.1, which was the current Windows software when NT was released.

The first version of NT focused on the design goals described on the previous pages. NT 3.x used the Windows 3.1 interface.

NT 3.5

The next version of NT, NT 3.5, included these changes:

- ❖ Bug fixes to 3.1 were added. (Bugs can include incompatibilities with some hardware and software, or code that causes errors in some configurations.)
- ❖ The name Advanced was dropped from Server, making the product NT Server 3.5 and NT Workstation 3.5.
- ❖ The account lockout feature was added. Account lockout specifies that if a user's attempt to log on is unsuccessful after an administratively defined number of tries, the user account will be locked. This feature provided added security to protect accounts and made it easier to monitor security threats.
- ❖ The Network Monitoring Agent was added. The Network Monitoring Agent and the Network Monitor are two tools that can be used on Windows NT to analyze traffic on a network. The Network Monitor is a valuable troubleshooting tool for diagnosing protocol and network performance problems.

---

browser service

In NT networks, broadcasts the availability of network services such as network shares or printers.

Dynamic Host Configuration Protocol (DHCP) Server

Automates the assignment of IP configurations.

Windows Internet Naming Service (WINS) Server

Maps the NetBIOS names that NT uses to identify computers with an IP address.

File Transfer Protocol (FTP) Server

Transfers files between the FTP server and FTP clients. Most Web browsers use FTP client software to download and upload files to Internet servers running the FTP service.

- Performance Monitor (which can be used to log and chart performance information about your NT computer) had counters added for the **browser**, **DHCP**, **WINS**, and **FTP** services, and for Network Monitor Statistics. These counters track performance of the different items on your computer.

- The Disk Administrator utility was enhanced so that you did not have to reboot after each configuration change.

- You could use the **Windows NT Diagnostic** utility to view information on remote computers.

- The **RDISK** utility was added so that you could create emergency repair disks, which store parts of your computer's configuration. You can use them to restore information in the event of system failure.

- Control Panel was enhanced with options for configuring your display, adding settings for your system, and creating a memory dump file that provides text-based error messages in the event that the server crashes.

- Long filename support was added, which enabled you to create filenames up to 255 characters long on a FAT partition. You could enable or disable this feature.

- Additional printer support was added for print devices such as **plotters** and for fonts using **PostScript**. The LPR (Line Printer) and Digital Print Server Monitors were added. You use these monitors with Unix and Digital print devices.

NT 3.51

NT 3.51 included bug fixes to 3.5 and added even more features:

- It could be used on PowerPC computers with the exception of the Apple Power Macintosh.

- NTFS-formatted drives could now take advantage of file compression.

- **Remote Access Service (RAS)** security was improved.

- The MS-DOS prompt could be configured through Control Panel.

NOTE

All versions of NT 3.5x used the Windows 3.1 user interface. This made the operating system easier to use for people who already had experience with the Windows operating system.

Windows NT Diagnostic

A utility in Windows NT 3.51 and 4 that displays system configuration information in a graphical format. System settings can be changed and informative reports generated from this utility.

RDISK

A critical management utility that is used to create a recovery disk that can be used in conjunction with the NT CD or disks. RDISK copies the system configuration information and the SAM database to the disk for use during the recovery process.

plotter

A special type of print device that draws high-resolution diagrams, charts, graphs, and other layouts.

PostScript

A page description language used to convert and move data from an application to a laser printer.

Remote Access Service (RAS)

Allows computers to access the network remotely; for example, through a phone, ISDN, or Internet connection.

Understanding NT 4

The most obvious change that occurred with the release of NT 4 was the adoption of the Windows 95 user interface. Although the interface had changed, administrators who were familiar with NT 3.51 quickly learned that many of the utilities had not.

NT Server 4 has two versions:

- ◆ NT Server 4 (standard)
- ◆ NT Server/E 4 (Enterprise version)

NT Server 4

Several enhancements have been made to NT 4:

- ◆ Performance improved over NT 3.51. On a single-processor computer, NT 4 runs up to 66 percent faster in file and print tests.

- ◆ More drivers are supported during installation. NT 4 increased support for more than 1,000 hardware devices beyond what NT 3.51 supported. This makes installation and setup much easier, because the driver software for network interface cards and video adapters are likely to be available through the NT installation media.

- ◆ Hardware profile support was a feature added for mobile users who use their laptops on the road and when connected to additional hardware in the office.

- ◆ Critical error messages were rewritten to provide clearer information and possible solutions.

- ◆ Administrative Wizards were added to step administrators through common configuration tasks.

- ◆ Improvements to Task Manager included the added feature of Performance Monitor, which enables you to easily and quickly view memory and resource use.

- ◆ New services, such as Internet Information Server (IIS) and Index Server, were added. Internet Information Server was Microsoft's first introduction of a World Wide Web server for NT. Index server added the capability to search directories on an NT server by using a Web browser.

- ◆ A new protocol was added for RAS. Point-to-Point Tunneling Protocol (PPTP) enables you to create encrypted communications between a Windows 95/98 or compatible client computer and an NT 4 server r-unning RAS.

clustering

Connecting two or more computers to make them appear as one system. Clustering is used to take advantage of the processing power of multiple computers.

load balancing

Distributing similar tasks (such as accessing an application or assigning an IP address) equally across multiple computers.

NT Server/E 4

This Enterprise version of NT Server adds greater support for larger networks with higher performance demands by including many features and services:

- ❖ **Clustering** services are supported for two-server clusters. These services (formerly known by the code name Wolfpack, now known as Microsoft Cluster Server, or MSCS) provide fault tolerance and **load balancing**. Clustering services are able to monitor server health and reliability, and recover applications and data in the event of system failure by using the second server in the cluster.

- ❖ The user is licensed to run more than four **symmetric processor**s without special **original equipment manufacturer (OEM)** versions of NT Server. Windows Server/E can support up to 32 Symmetric MultiProcessing (SMP) processors.

- ❖ Better memory tuning exists for applications with high memory requirements. This version can also use up to 4GB of RAM per application as opposed to previous versions of NT, which supported only 2GB of RAM.

- ❖ NT Server/E also ships with these services: Service Pack 3, Internet Information Server (IIS) 3, Microsoft Transaction Server (MTS), Microsoft Message Queue Server (MSMQ), and FrontPage 97. Each of these services addressed specific needs of large companies needing to take advantage of Enterprise's powerful features for Internet based-applications such as IIS.

NOTE

Microsoft periodically releases Service Packs for its operating system and **BackOffice** products. Service Packs typically contain fixes to known problems. NT Server Enterprise version requires that you install Service Pack 3 before you can install MSCS, MSMQ, MTS, FrontPage 97, or Internet Explorer 4. Microsoft recommends you always install the latest service pack.

WARNING

If you are currently running NT Server with Service Pack 2 or later and you wish to upgrade to NT Server Enterprise version, you should not use the WINNT32.EXE program. This upgrade method can cause severe problems for your server. Instead, you should use the WINNTUP.EXE program to upgrade to NT Server Enterprise version.

symmetric processor

Two or more processors in a computer that are each capable of completing processes simultaneously, which maximizes performance. Windows NT and 2000 Server support SMP.

original equipment manufacturer (OEM)

A term used to describe the device or software that is sold to a reseller who then passes the product on to a consumer. OEM versions of software can sometimes be altered by the reseller in an effort to make the product integrate with the reseller's hardware.

BackOffice

A suite of server applications built by Microsoft to run on the NT server platform.

Understanding Windows 2000

Just when most people thought they had NT under their belt, Microsoft announced the release of Windows 2000. Originally, Windows 2000 was named NT 5. It was supposed to ship in 1998 but was delayed. After many beta releases and an incredible level of input from the Windows community, Microsoft released Windows 2000 to manufacturers on February 17, 2000.

Windows 2000 has four **platforms**:

◆ Windows 2000 Professional is the new business desktop operating system offering the superior performance of NT workstation but with several significant enhancements.

◆ Windows 2000 Server.

◆ Windows 2000 Advanced Server replaces the Enterprise edition of NT 4 as the next generation Windows cluster server.

◆ Windows 2000 Datacenter Server is designed for the most demanding server environments found in large companies or high-demand Web sites.

All versions of Windows 2000 include several major changes over Windows NT 4:

◆ A 64-bit operating system supports Intel's 64-bit Itanium processor.

◆ Plug-and-Play capability is included. This capability enables the operating system to recognize hardware additions or changes to the system and automatically load the necessary software if available or prompt the user for the software.

◆ Microsoft Management Console (MMC) has been extended as the central management interface for all administrative tools. With MMC, administrators can customize the console they use.

◆ FAT32 disk partitions are supported. FAT32 is a way of formatting your logical drives to store data more efficiently than using FAT16. This has been supported by Windows 95/98 but not by previous versions of NT.

◆ Windows 2000 has no Alpha processor support.

platforms
The hardware or software that supports any given system. The term platform can be used, for example, to reference a Pentium III–based computer or Windows 98.

248

Many experts are questioning the rationale of changing over a completely functioning NT network to Windows 2000. There are many varying opinions, and some believe that the best way to migrate to 2000 is to scrap NT altogether and design from scratch. Although determining the better option is beyond the scope of this book, a summary comparison of the two operating systems might help you to make your decision. In the meantime, read plenty of articles and get to know the technology completely before deciding on Windows 2000.

	Windows NT 4	Windows 2000
Network Model	Domain	Directory services or domain
Plug-and-Play support	No	Yes
Management too format	Multiple	Microsoft Management Console
Performance	Minimal difference	Minimal difference
Disk formats supported	FAT, NTFS	FAT, FAT32, NTFS
Ease of use	Minimal Wizards	Improved and expanded Wizard and much improved installer
Recovery options	Use of repair disk or reinstall	Safe mode like Windows 98 and capability to repair damage
Reliability	Reboots for every device change, service installation, and some configuration changes	No reboots for device configuration, most software installations, and for configuring and starting services

Review Questions

Terms to Know
- NTFS
- browser service
- DHCP Server
- WINS Server
- FTP Server
- Windows NT Diagnostic
- RDISK
- plotter
- PostScript
- RAS
- clustering
- load balancing
- symmetric processor
- OEM
- BackOffice
- platforms

1. List the five major design goals of the NT operating system:

_____

_____

_____

_____

_____

2. Which four platforms of software will replace NT 4?

_____

_____

_____

_____

3. Which version of NT first used the Windows 95 Desktop interface?

_____

4. Which version of NT first supported long filenames?

_____

5. Which version of NT first supported NTFS file compression?

_____

6. What does MSCS stand for?

_____

7. What is the first version of NT to support 64-bit processing?

_____

8. What is the purpose of MMC?

_____

9. What is the first version of NT to support FAT32?

_____

10. What is clustering?

_____

Chapter

14

The Windows 2000 Platforms

plat·form *n* : the operating system software upon which other software runs

One of the first decisions you make for your network is what operating system you will use on the server and client machines. In the past, Microsoft has provided a number of different operating systems for you to choose from: DOS, Windows 95, and Windows NT. Each of these systems had its own specific options and capabilities, but each system needed to be learned separately. Management tools, configuration options, and support files were different depending on the OS. With Windows 2000, Microsoft has gone to a single basic operating system and provides four platforms for you to choose from based on the tasks you need the machine to accomplish.

In this chapter, you will learn about the four Windows 2000 platforms and the characteristics of each. These topics are covered:

 Reasons for choosing Windows 2000

 Windows 2000 Professional

 Windows 2000 Server

 Windows 2000 Advanced Server

 Windows 2000 Datacenter Server

Why Choose Windows 2000?

Over the past five years, Microsoft's Windows NT operating system has become an integral part of almost every major network in the world. As you saw in the preceding chapter, NT is more secure, more stable, and more efficient than Windows 3.1 or Windows 95 were. Even so, NT's domain structure and architecture limited the effective size of an NT-based organization. Managing large domains could be difficult, and managing resources (files, printers, etc.) over a large **enterprise** presented a challenge.

With Windows 2000, Microsoft has created a new network model that builds on Windows NT. Windows 2000 tightly integrates to Internet standards and provides a single operating system architecture that is flexible enough to be used as a desktop client or as an enterprise database server.

The Right OS for the Job

There are four versions of Windows 2000, each of which has different capabilities, requirements, and costs. These are:

Windows 2000 Professional   Professional is meant to be the primary desktop client in business environments. It can also be used to replace Windows 98 or NT Workstation as a high-performance home machine.

Windows 2000 Server   The Server platform is intended for network resource sharing and management on small or medium-sized networks.

Windows 2000 Advanced Server   Advanced Server is more scalable than Server and is designed for large databases or serving large networks. To this end, it supports more RAM and processors than Server, and has more features.

Windows 2000 Datacenter Server   Intended for truly massive tasks, such as real-time databases and large **data warehouses**, Datacenter Server supports even more RAM and processor power than Advanced Server.

Which platform is right for a particular job, and what are the specific features that make them different? The following pages take a closer look at Windows 2000 and each of its platforms, and will enable you to better understand its features and uses.

enterprise
A large network, generally involving thousands of users, many servers, and extensive wide area network links.

data warehouses
Through modern database technology, companies are able to store and access tremendous amounts of business data. A data warehouse is the hardware and software that provides this functionality.

An Architecture of Addition

Although Windows 2000 has four platforms, each is built on a similar model. Much as you can buy a car with few options or with many, Windows 2000 Professional is the "base" model of the line. You can consider Windows 2000 Server as simply 2000 Professional with extra options added.

That leads to the question: Why not just give everyone Server—or for that matter, Datacenter Server? Just as sunroofs, CD players, and a bigger engine add to the sticker price of your car, so do additional Windows 2000 options add to the price of your operating system. Professional is less expensive than Server, which is less expensive than Advanced Server, which is, in turn, less expensive than Datacenter Server.

Because of this architecture of addition, remember that every feature mentioned for Windows 2000 Professional is also available on the other three products. Server enhancements are therefore also available on Advanced Server and Datacenter Server, as they are higher-level products. Server features are not available on Professional.

You will more than likely find that a large network implementation will use more than one of the Windows 2000 platforms. This is exactly the way it should be. Windows 2000 Server and Advanced Server can upgrade the Windows NT machines in a company's server room even as Windows 2000 Professional is rolled out as a desktop upgrade to Windows 95/98 and Windows NT Workstation clients. Different machines will still have different roles within the company. However, a nice feature about the Windows 2000 environment is that, regardless of their role, all machines on the network run the same basic operating system, and this greatly simplifies issues of troubleshooting and maintaining the network.

NOTE

This "base model" plan is used with a number of Microsoft products, including Microsoft Office 2000, which comes in four suite options: Standard, Small Business, Professional, and Premium. As with Windows 2000, each suite is built on the standard edition, with more expensive suites providing additional software and more options.

Understanding the Features of Windows 2000 Professional

As a replacement for the Windows NT Workstation product line, all the key features of NT Workstation mentioned in the previous chapter have been retained and often improved upon. The NTFS file system is still supported, but so is Windows 95/98's FAT32. Backup using devices such as a **removable drive** or a network drive is also now possible. Mandatory logon, user profiles, and the general look and feel of the system are similar but have been updated. All versions of Windows 2000 ship with Internet Explorer 5 built in.

Professional is intended to function as a high-performance desktop OS. In this role, it leverages two crucial elements of the new Windows 2000 platform—significant advances in security and in performance.

Some of the enhancements for Windows 2000 are:

◇ More and better security options. **Kerberos** authentication, the Encrypted File System, and Internet Protocol Security (IPSec) are all supported, as are **smart cards** and other security enhancements.

◇ Better hardware detection and handling. Plug and Play was not available in Windows NT but is in Windows 2000. Other hardware enhancements include advanced power management and a new device driver model that shares drivers with Windows 98.

◇ Configuration and Setup tools. From a **disk imaging** tool to advanced virtual private networking, Windows 2000 has numerous other small enhancements.

◇ Improved printing support and printer sharing.

◇ Support for laptops/mobile users. Improved remote networking and offline folders for network shares make using your network resources when out of the office far easier and more secure.

◇ The familiar Windows 95 interface is still used, with Internet Explorer 5 built in. The interface also has been enhanced to allow further customization and personalization.

---

removable drive

Disk that can be removed from the computer and replaced. Floppy disks, rewritable CDs (CD-RW) and Zip/Jaz/Ditto drives are examples.

Kerberos

An industry-standard authentication protocol.

smart cards

A small device—about the size of a credit card—that can hold various types of personal information.

disk imaging

Disk imaging technologies enable the contents of a hard drive to be copied and then reused on other machines. This allows administrators to quickly and efficiently prepare large numbers of computers.

256

Windows 2000 Technical Requirements

This table lists the technical requirements for Windows 2000 Professional.

Component	Minimum Requirement	Recommended Requirement
Processor	Pentium 133	Pentium II or III
Memory	64MB	128MB or more
Hard disk	1GB	Depends on what will be stored

As you design a network and are looking to purchase hardware, it is crucial to remember that if employees of a company spend significant amounts of time working at a computer, slow machines not only are an annoyance to their users, but also can cause productivity to suffer. Therefore, you should always recommend that a company preparing to upgrade to Windows 2000 have machines that are well above the recommended minimum RAM and CPU levels. Although companies might think they are saving money as they get by on older equipment, this is often not the case once time lost at work watching an hourglass cursor is taken into effect.

Remember that the minimum requirements indicate the lowest hardware level on which the operating system can function. Most people will find that the performance of a P133 with 64MB running Windows 2000 is unacceptable.

NOTE

Only Windows 2000 Professional supports upgrades from Windows 95, Windows 98, and Windows NT Workstation. To find out whether your hardware will upgrade properly, check the Windows 2000 Hardware Compatibility List.

Understanding the Features of Windows 2000 Server

Active Directory
An update to the Windows NT domain structure, the Active Directory stores all information about users, computers, and the network in Windows 2000.

terminal
Terminal servers allow multiple users to access them at a single time through "thin clients" or other software. The users input information, but all processing is done on the server.

Windows 2000 Server is designed to be a powerful network server that can provide centralized file, print, application, and security functions. Designed to replace Windows NT Server 4, its primary benefits include:

◇ The **Active Directory**, which replaces NT's domain structure with a system based on Internet DNS. The Active Directory is explained in further detail in the next chapter.

◇ Microsoft's Management Console (MMC), which provides a single interface for managing server tools and applications.

◇ Scalability. NT domains could allow only about 40,000 objects (users, groups, and computers). A Windows 2000 Active Directory can have far more (millions!) of accounts.

◇ Internet Web and FTP services, indexing and **terminal** access available.

◇ Multiprotocol routing, ATM support, and Remote Access enhancements.

NOTE

You will learn more about Active Directory in Chapter 15: "Windows 2000 Active Directory."

Windows 2000 Server Technical Requirements

This table defines the technical requirements for 2000 Server.

Component	Minimum Requirement	Recommended Requirement
Processor	Pentium 133	Pentium II or III Up to four processors
Memory	128MB	256MB or higher
Hard disk	1GB	1GB plus storage space for data and applications

Windows 2000 Advanced Server

Sometimes, four processors and 4GB of RAM just isn't enough—which is why Microsoft also offers Windows 2000 Advanced Server. Advanced Server has all the features of Professional and Server, but supports even more hardware and adds new features.

Hardware limits are increased, with up to eight processors using Symmetrical Multiprocessing (SMP) and an 8GB limit on RAM. NT 4's memory model allowed only 4GB.

Advanced Server also allows for Windows clustering. Clustering means connecting several large servers so that they run as a single system. This can be important on systems that can tolerate no downtime, as a hardware or software failure detected on one machine can be worked around by having another server in the cluster take over those duties. An administrator can then repair the malfunctioning machine and return it to the cluster.

Besides redundancy, Windows clustering can also be used to allow for faster response times to clients, by using load balancing to ensure that a heavily used application can be served by any member of the cluster, rather than by only one machine.

As you may have guessed, with the cost of software and hardware that is needed for this sort of process, Windows clustering and Advanced Server are not for everyone. Large firms with time-sensitive data and a need for nearly continuous service will find that the cost is well worth it, but you probably don't need to be running Advanced Server clusters at home—although that would probably make a *very* nice Quake server.

NOTE

You may have noticed that there has been no mention of primary domain controllers (PDCs) or backup domain controllers (BDCs). The new Active Directory does not make these distinctions between servers.

Windows 2000 Datacenter Server

For the highest capacity tasks, Microsoft's Datacenter Server adds even more hardware options. Windows 2000 Datacenter supports up to 32 processors and increases the memory (RAM) limit to 64GB. Datacenter Server, as its name implies, is intended for use as a database and application server in a large enterprise network. It would also be at home as a server on a high-volume Internet site. Two possible applications are Online Transaction Processing (OLTP) and Application Service Provider (ASP) functionality. Online Transaction Processing involves high-volume, real-time commerce or business transactions, and Application Service Providers allow users to rent applications and run them over the Internet or a dedicated link. The ASP provider maintains and upgrades the hardware, and the users pay a monthly fee for the service. An ASP may have dozens or hundreds of people using a single application, and response times and availability are crucial.

You might find that your company has no need for a Datacenter server, and in fact only a small number of firms are large enough to make a business case for a server with 32 processors and 64GB of RAM. For most companies, Server or Advanced Server will provide more than enough horsepower and all the needed features.

NOTE

Microsoft will not be releasing the Datacenter platform with the other three, and its final specifications have not yet been set. Be sure to check the Microsoft Web site, www.microsoft.com, for additional information when Datacenter is released.

Comparing the Windows 2000 Platforms

In the following table, the major features of Windows 2000 are summarized by platform. For more information, a number of excellent white papers are available at Microsoft's Windows 2000 site.

Windows 2000	Professional	Server	Adv. Server	Datacenter
Target audience	Business desktops and notebooks	File, print, intranet, and networking	Large businesses, e-commerce	Large critical applications, data warehouses, OLTP, ASPs and ISPs
Processors	2	4	8	32
RAM min (max)	64 (4GB)	128 (4GB)	256 (8GB)	To be announced
Drive space	1GB free	1GB free	1GB free	To be announced
Alpha support	No	No	No	No
Kerberos authentication	Yes	Yes	Yes	Yes
Plug and Play	Yes	Yes	Yes	Yes
Active Directory		Yes	Yes	Yes
Management Console	Yes	Yes	Yes	Yes
Internet Server	No	Yes	Yes	Yes
Clustering	No	No	Yes	Yes
Load balancing	No	No	Yes	Yes

NOTE

A 1GB drive is in practice nearly impossible to find, because it is simply too small. Most modern servers have total disk capacity in the area of 20 to 100GB, with terabytes of storage (1000GB) not unusual.

Review Questions

Terms to Know
❏ enterprise
❏ data warehouses
❏ removable drive
❏ Kerberos
❏ smart cards
❏ disk imaging
❏ Active Directory
❏ terminal

1. You have been using Windows NT 4 Workstation at your office and are looking to upgrade to Windows 2000. Which platform of 2000 supports upgrades from NT Workstation?

_____

2. You have purchased a four-processor computer to use with a database you are setting up in the enterprise. Which Windows 2000 platform(s) can you use?

_____

_____

_____

3. True or False: All platforms of Windows 2000 support Plug and Play.

_____

4. The _____ is used as a common interface to administrate Windows 2000.

5. A terabyte is _____ megabytes.

6. You are looking for a cost-effective server for your local area network. You require file and print sharing, and Active Directory administration. Which Windows 2000 platform would be best for you?

_____

7. The minimum amount of RAM needed for Windows 2000 Server is _____ .

8. You are planning a network of over 50,000 users. Your client is looking to have a single domain to centralize administration. Would you recommend Windows NT or Windows 2000 as a server platform?

_____

9. Windows 2000 Professional supports _____ folders for remote users.

10. Both _____ and _____ are security enhancements supported under all Windows 2000 platforms.

11. A 2TB database server with 32GB of RAM would require which Windows 2000 platform? Could Windows NT Server be used instead?

_____

12. All Windows 2000 platforms come standard with which Web browser version?

_____

Chapter

15

Windows 2000
Active Directory

di·rec·to·ry ser·vice *n* : the format used by an operating system to identify and organize objects on the network

O ver the last few years, Windows NT 4 became the operating system of choice in businesses of many sizes. Even so, large companies and companies with complex administrative structures found that the NT domain structure became unwieldy. NT domains do not scale particularly well, and allow no more than 40,000 total accounts—users, computers, and groups combined. Moreover, managing and administrating large multi-domain networks is difficult. Because of this, Microsoft has introduced the Active Directory in Windows 2000. The Active Directory can replace NT domains, but also can serve as an upgrade that coexists with existing NT domains.

In this chapter, you will be introduced to the following information:

 Features of the Active Directory

 Domains

 Organizational units

 Forests and trees

 Trusts

 Site Links

 Domain controllers

Features of the Active Directory

One of the major tasks of any network operating system is keeping track of users and regulating resource access. In Windows NT 4, this was done through the use of NT domains and the Security Accounts Manager (SAM) database. Although Windows 2000 still supports domains, network security has been simplified and enhanced by the addition of a directory service—the Windows 2000 Active Directory.

physical location

The actual location of a resource. Each resource must be homed on a server somewhere on the network. Windows 2000 enables you to organize resources logically, rather than physically.

NOTE

For a review of the differences between a domain model and a directory service model, refer back to Chapter 9.

share

A share is resource, such as a directory or a printer, that is made available to network users. A share can have permissions associated to it to control which users can access its resources.

In Windows 2000, the directory service provides a means of keeping track of users, machines, groups, and other network and user-related information. The Active Directory does all of this just as the NT domain structure did, but it provides these services more efficiently and with more features.

One of the most interesting differences between NT's domains and Windows 2000's Active Directory is that the location of a resource—its **physical location**—is transparent to users. In NT 4, a user could find a **share** only by browsing the server on which the share was created. In Windows 2000, shared directories and printers can be accessed just by knowing the name of the share. The Directory does the rest, finding and connecting the user to the resource they have requested.

Another interesting element of the Active Directory is that it is tightly tied to TCP/IP and the Internet Domain Name System (DNS). All Windows 2000 domain names are structured like Internet domains. If your company's NT 4 domain is FOO, your Windows 2000 domain might be foo.com. The domain name (FOO) is a NetBIOS name, which is understood only by other Microsoft-compatible machines; the domain name (foo.com) can be understood and referenced by any machine that can use the TCP/IP protocol. This is just one of many ways in which the Active Directory tightly integrates with and complies with Internet standards.

TIP

Because of this level of integration, Windows 2000's Active Directory is dependent upon the presence of the TPC/IP protocol suite. TCP/IP must be installed in order to use Windows 2000 domains.

The following table shows other Internet specifications that are supported by Active Directory. Note that each of the specifications listed below is in actuality a TCP/IP protocol. The TCP/IP protocol suite is made up of a number of "plug-in" protocols that work together to provide network functionality, and Windows 2000 supports more of these than Windows NT did. Each of the items in the list below is therefore a separate Internet protocol, with its specific function listed to the right of it.

Specification	Purpose
DHCP	IP addresses must be unique for each machine on a network, and DHCP automates the process of assigning addresses and other TCP/IP information.
SNTP	Simple Network Time Protocol provides timekeeping and time synchronization functions, which allow machines to check their internal clocks and make certain that the entire network knows the proper time.
LDAP	Lightweight Directory Access Protocol provides a way to query the Active Directory to request e-mail addresses, usernames, and other data.
LDIF	Lightweight Directory Information Format is used for directory synchronization.
Kerberos	This advanced authentication protocol provides enhanced security during logon and resource access.
X.509 certificates	Certificates are used to prove who you are (by allowing you to encrypt a signature into your messages) or allow you to secure your messages by encrypting them for transmission.

X.500

An industry-standard directory structure used by Windows 2000 to organize and name network elements. Other network operating systems, such as Novell's NetWare Directory Services, also use X.500.

Last, Windows 2000's Active Directory uses the naming structure known as **X.500**. This is an industry-standard naming structure that allows for the unique naming of millions of objects easily and logically. An X.500 username for Humphrey Bogart, a user on the foo.com network, would look like this:

```
DC=com,DC=foo,CN=Users,CN=Humphrey Bogart
```

Structure of the Active Directory

The Active Directory structure in Windows 2000 differs significantly from the directory structure in Windows NT. But because MCSEs are expected to be familiar with Windows NT, it's important to understand NT's directory structure.

In Windows NT 4, Microsoft used a **flat directory** model for its domains. The resulting structure was simple and straightforward on small- and medium-size networks, but could become confusing and difficult to manage on an enterprise scale. In NT 4, one machine—the primary domain controller (PDC)—held the only authoritative copy of the domain's directory database. This database, called the SAM, could then be replicated out to other machines functioning as backup domain controllers (BDCs).

A Windows NT 4 domain was managed as a single entity. As a result, anyone who needed administrative access on one part of the domain would automatically gain administrative access to all other machines that were authenticating to that domain. Splitting up administrative authority or adding large numbers of users required the addition of more domains in the enterprise, which were then connected by **trust**s to enable them to communicate and share resources.

With the Active Directory, Windows 2000 avoids these problems by enabling you to use a new set of options: organizational units, domains, trees, and forests are now all part of the administrative mix. Each is explained in the following sections.

flat directory

Used in many simple directory schemes, a structure that does not allow for compartmentalization of resources, users, or other accounts. It also has no hierarchical relation between directory elements.

trust

A trust is configured to allow two Windows NT domains to share user authentication information and to allow users from one domain to access resources in another domain.

TIP

If you are familiar with the Windows NT structure, think of domains as being much the same as NT domains, with organizational units (OUs) added as subdivisions of domains, and trees and forests as better ways of organizing and connecting domains.

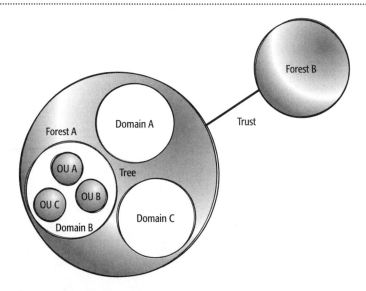

Windows 2000 Domains

The most basic Windows 2000 security structure is the domain. Domains are independent administrative units, with their own security and administrative policies. All domain controllers within a domain **replicate** their information to each other automatically. This is known as a multi-master replication model. Any domain controller can receive changes and then replicate these out to other servers in the domain.

To allow for an orderly migration from NT 4 to Windows 2000, both 2000 and the Active Directory support communication with existing NT domain structures and security. This is done through the use of a mixed-mode domain model. Then, after all your domains have been upgraded to Windows 2000, you can perform a one-time conversion to native mode. Native-mode domains have additional features that are unavailable to mixed-mode domains, but no longer support NT 4 domain controllers. Below is a Windows 2000 General configuration tab, from which you can switch modes.

replicate
The process by which a machine sends a copy of its databases to another machine. This usually occurs on a scheduled basis.

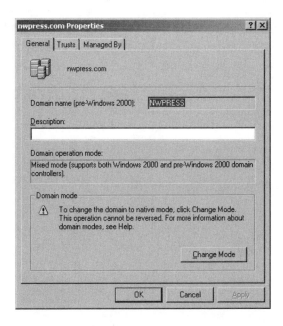

![nwpress.com Properties dialog box showing the General tab with Domain name (pre-Windows 2000): NWPRESS, a Description field, Domain operation mode: Mixed mode (supports both Windows 2000 and pre-Windows 2000 domain controllers), and a Domain mode section with a Change Mode button.]

TIP

You do not have to upgrade clients or member servers to use native mode. Windows NT 4 workstations and Windows 95/98 clients will simply have to update their network client software.

Organizational Units (OUs)

Within the Active Directory, you can categorize the objects in the domain by using **organizational units (OUs)**. This allows for administrative possibilities that were not available under Windows NT's domain model:

organizational units (OUs)

Organizational units are new with Windows 2000, and are compliant with the X.500 directory. They break the directory into subdivisions and are one of the enhancements that has added administrative depth to the previously flat domain directory structure.

Limiting administrative authority within the domain If your domain has three campuses, you can create an OU for each, and assign a different administrator access to each.

Organizing users by function OUs can be created for Sales, Accounting, Manufacturing, etc. Users and resources can then be added to these, and can be managed as a group. Below, users and resources have been arranged using organizational units.

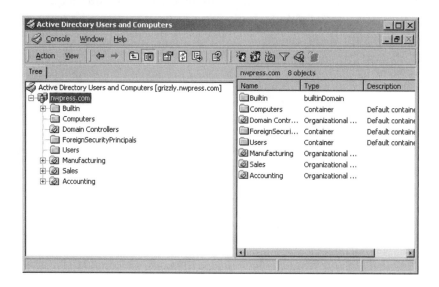

The beauty of combining Active Directory's capability to support millions of objects and its capability to subdivide domains into organizational units is that a single domain will be all that many companies ever need.

TIP

Trusts, which you will learn about later in this chapter, now exist only at the forest level, and should be needed only in cases of mergers or other cases of extreme administrative separation.

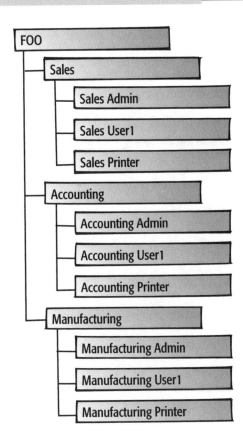

parent domain
The domain from which all other domains in a tree take their name.

namespace
The part of the naming structure occupied by a certain domain or tree. If the domain is `foo.com`, all machines and sub-domains of `foo.com` exist within its namespace: `www.foo.com`, `accounting.atlanta.foo.com`, etc.

Trees and Forests

Microsoft's use of the words *tree* and *forest* can be confusing. You do not, for instance, need a bunch of trees to make a forest. A tree is simply a set of domains that all have a similar DNS naming structure, and a forest is all the trees within a single organization.

When the first server is installed in a new domain (`foo.com`), it becomes a domain controller within that domain and also is the **parent domain** of a new tree. If you are not entering an existing forest, this tree also becomes the root tree of a new forest. Although you have installed only one server, you now have a domain, a tree, and even a forest.

The real difference between a tree and a forest is not in the numbers. Within a single tree, all the domains must fall under a contiguous **namespace**. Assume that you have created the domain called `foo.com` in your New York office, and now want to create additional geographically based domains in Hong Kong, Rome, and Fargo. If you want to allow permissions to flow without the use of trusts (which you will learn about in the next section), you need to put the new domains into the same tree. To do this, the new domains will need to incorporate the existing DNS name.

Trees

Note the two following graphics. In the graphic on the top, notice how the DNS namespaces are in different branches. These, therefore, cannot be in a single tree. In the bottom graphic, the three new domains nest under the foo.com parent domain and share its DNS namespace. They are able to incorporate into the tree.

root tree

The top domain within a newly created namespace. All other domains in the tree must fall within the root tree's namespace.

child domain

A tree created under the namespace of an existing tree.

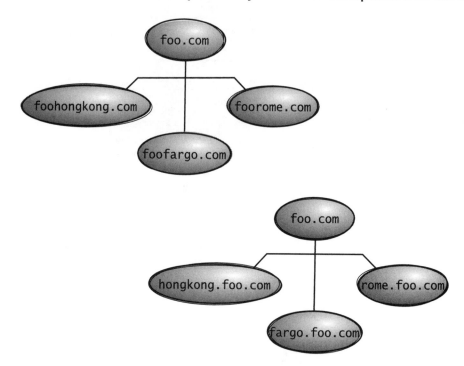

What all of this means is that if you have a company with four offices, you may want to split up network administration by using four autonomous domains in a tree. As long as the naming structure is not an issue, this is the easiest and most integrated approach to adding domains.

Forests

Forests are similar to trees, in that both are ways of connecting domains. Forests are created to connect domains whose naming conventions make them incompatible for use in a single tree, or can also be used to keep two domains more distinct from each other.

The first tree you create also becomes the **root tree** of a new forest. As new domains are added, you have three choices:

◇ Create the new domain as a **child domain** in the existing tree. If you simply create the new domain as a child domain, permissions and other configuration information automatically are shared between the domains.

❖ Create the new domain as a new tree in the existing forest. Config-uration data—the **schema** and **global catalog**—will be shared, but the domains will be separate administrative entities. To connect two trees, you must use a trust.

❖ Create the new domain as a new tree in a new forest. This provides the greatest degree of administrative separation and makes interaction between the domains more difficult. No configuration data is shared, and trusts must be set up to share resources between forests.

Users who have seen Microsoft's Exchange will be at an advantage in under-standing the Active Directory's forest, as Exchange's structure is similar to Win-dows 2000's. Both are based on the X.500 directory standard.

Even if you haven't used Exchange, though, thinking of the forest in terms of organization helps to better define it. In most cases, all trees in a single com-pany will be placed into a single forest. Trees will be created based on geo-graphic or administrative need, and additional domains can be added to trees as security or administrative circumstances dictate.

TIP

Remember that Windows 2000's Active Directory will support millions of users and other objects. You should begin your Windows 2000 planning by assuming a single domain/tree/forest is best, and only modify this based on particular requirements of your company or client. The major reasons for creating multiple domains in Windows NT 4—distributed administra-tion and scaling problems—no longer should be factors.

Windows 2000 Trusts

Like other features of Windows 2000, trusts have changed. As an MCSE, you will need to understand how trusts function in Windows NT and Windows 2000.

In both Windows NT 4 and Windows 2000, there are two types of trusts: one-way and two-way. In NT networks, though, a two-way trust was really nothing more than an administrator in domain A manually creating a trust with domain B, and an administrator in domain B then manually creating a trust back to domain A.

schema
The set of configuration elements that defines a particular directory. The schema contains infor-mation about all objects in the directory.

global catalog
A fast-access copy of the full directory that includes only those objects that are commonly used, such as usernames and logon names.

273

One-Way Trusts

Trusts in NT were difficult for a number of reasons, not the least of which was that they were not **transitive**. Because of this, if five domains all needed to trust each other—referred to as a complete trust—20 trusts needed to be created and maintained. As you might suspect, this could quickly become an administrative nightmare, as shown in the graphic below. (Note that each arrow represents a one-way trust.)

transitive

Trusts that are transitive allow a domain to act as an intermediary for two other domains. If A trusts B, and B trusts C, there is a physical path between A and C. Even with that physical link, though, directory information will pass from A to C only if B acts as a transitive link.

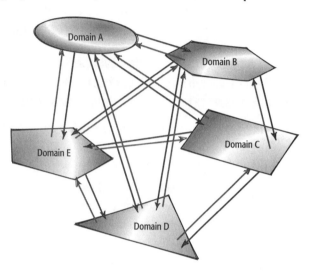

The model above is still available in Windows 2000, but is intended only for the purpose of backward compatibility or for short-term or emergency connections between otherwise separate domains. Windows 2000 one-way trusts, therefore, have similar characteristics to NT trusts. They are configured in each direction separately (if two-way trusting is needed) and the trust that is established is nontransitive. Below is the Trusts tab on a Windows 2000 server, showing two trusts that have been established with a Windows NT 4 domain. Note how the trust is configured in each direction individually.

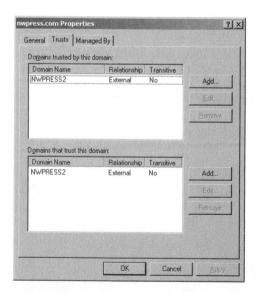

Two-Way Trusts

Looking at the preceding example, if you had created five Windows 2000 domains within a single tree and did not have any remaining Windows NT 4 domains to integrate, you would not need even a single trust to be able to share resources and administration. This saves 20 trusts and endless headaches! If you have to connect to another tree within your forest, you can do this through the Active Directory or through trusts, depending on your preference.

Trusts are necessary in Windows 2000 only when the domains that wish to share resources are not in the same forest. Moreover, in Windows 2000, most trusts are two-way and transitive. In the graphic below, the trusts established between forest A and forest B, and between forest B and forest C, also allow permission and resource flow between forest A and forest C.

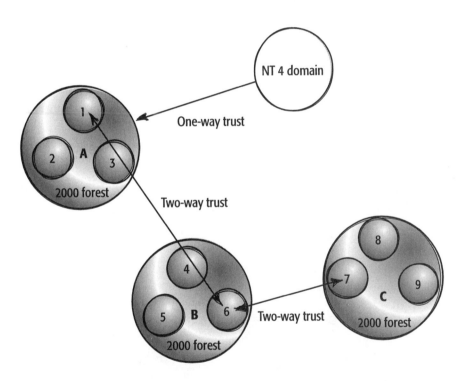

NOTE

Although the NT 4 domain is connected to a domain in forest A, the non-transitive nature of the trust relationship means that the NT domain may do no resource sharing with other forests—or with other domains in forest A!

The Physical Network

Besides the logical structure of domains, trees, and forests discussed earlier, there are also other considerations when planning a network. One of these is the layout and configuration of the actual physical network. This involves two primary considerations:

◇ Geographical placement of servers

◇ Bandwidth availability and management

Sites

A site is generally defined as a part of the network that is connected by high-speed **local area network (LAN)** links. The advantage of multiple sites is that replication traffic and other server-to-server communications can be configured to occur at certain times, or at certain frequencies, using a **Site Link**.

In the example below, your headquarters in Fargo has branch offices in Los Angeles, Atlanta, and New York. Each of the sites has a 512Kbps connection back to headquarters. To save bandwidth during the day, you may create each office as a separate site, and use Site Links to configure them to replicate information only in the evenings. Also, the central site will pass the configuration changes on to all sites, so connectors do not need to be created between Atlanta and Los Angeles, and so on.

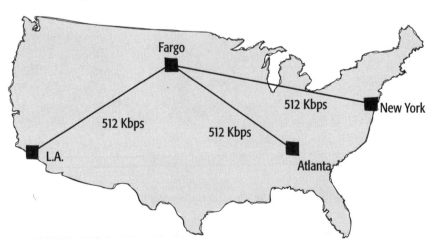

---

local area network (LAN)

A LAN is contained within a single building or campus and can operate independently of any outside connection.

Site Link

A logical connection that links two sites and controls the flow of traffic over WAN links. Just as a trust regulates the flow of permissions and resources, a site link regulates the speed and type of traffic that is allowed across the WAN. Site links therefore enable an administrator to optimize bandwidth usage.

TIP

Remember that the logical and physical structures of the network do not have to be the same. A network with a physical connection structure like the one above still can easily use a single Windows 2000 domain.

Domain Controllers

Domain controllers are servers that contain information about users and the security structure of the network. In previous versions of NT, Microsoft used a hierarchical domain controller plan centered on a PDC. Only the PDC could process changes to the security database, and replication would then transfer these changes down to one or more BDCs. Although this has advantages, it also has problems. A user wanting to change their password in Los Angeles would request a password change. The change would be made on the PDC in Fargo, but the user would find that, until the next **replication cycle**, their own BDC (in L.A.) would not register the change.

replication cycle
The means by which a group of machines synchronize their information; replication is usually done on a pre-configured schedule that can be adjusted due to network or organizational need.

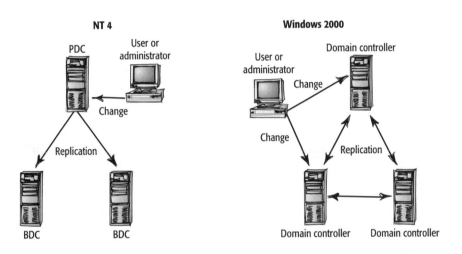

Windows 2000 changes this, allowing for a multi-master domain controller model. PDC and BDC distinctions are irrelevant, as all domain controllers contain a read-write copy of the entire domain's Active Directory. Users in L.A. can now make changes locally and have the L.A. server replicate them outward. The basic functions of a Windows 2000 domain controller are to:

◆ Keep a copy of the security database
◆ Process changes to the database
◆ Alert other domain controllers of changes through replication

NOTE

If you have a network with 10 Windows 2000 servers in a single office, you probably do not want to make them all domain controllers. At least one domain controller is required to create a domain, and a second is recommended for fault tolerance. More than two in a location will probably serve little purpose and just generate unnecessary replication traffic.

Specialized Domain Controllers

Besides the purposes listed above, some Windows 2000 domain controllers also can be assigned specific roles to play on the network. Domain controllers can take on the following roles:

- ◆ Global Catalog Master
- ◆ Schema Master
- ◆ Domain Naming Master
- ◆ Relative Identifier Master
- ◆ PDC Emulator
- ◆ Infrastructure Master

Global Catalog Master

One of the primary functions of a PDC or BDC is the authentication of users, which could be accomplished by any domain controller on the network. In Windows 2000, only domain controllers that have been designated Global Catalog Masters (GCM) can perform this task. The first domain controller in any domain is always a GCM, but additional domain controllers have to be specifically configured if you want them to provide this functionality.

In the example below, for instance, the network on the left has only two GCMs. Users from Fargo, New York, and Atlanta all authenticate to the Fargo GCM, and if the network connection is down, users from N.Y. and Atlanta will not be able to log on to the domain. Because Los Angeles has its own GCM, users authenticate locally, and a break in the WAN connection would not prevent domain logon. Adding Global Catalog Masters can, therefore, increase network performance and save valuable WAN bandwidth. In the example below, a Los Angeles user can authenticate directly to a local GCM, while an Atlanta user must authenticate across the WAN to Fargo.

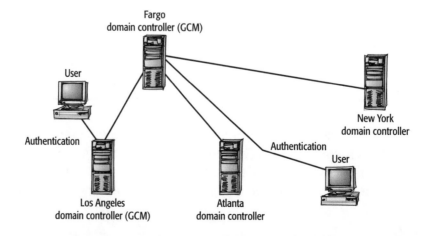

NOTE

The global catalog has information on the entire forest, not on only one domain. On large networks, the global catalog can significantly speed up the process of finding resources in other parts of the forest.

security identifier (SID)
A unique number used by NT to represent a user or a computer on the network.

Operations Masters

Besides GCMs, several other domain controller roles can be assigned to specific machines. Each of these functions must be performed by one—and only one—server within the forest. All are new with Windows 2000. There are five types of specialized domain controllers, collectively known as Operations Masters. Initially, all these roles are given to the first server in the forest, but they may be reassigned to other domain controllers later.

Schema Master   Holds the master reference as to the objects in the directory and the way objects are organized. Also manages all updates to the schema.

Domain Naming Master   Manages the addition or deletion of domains.

NOTE

There is only one Schema Master and one Domain Naming Master in the entire forest. There is one RID Master, PDC Emulator, and Infrastructure Master in each domain.

Relative Identifier Master   In Windows 2000 domains, an object's security identification number is referred to as a **security identifier (SID)**, just as in NT 4. In 2000, though, the SID consists of a domain SID (which uniquely identifies the domain) and a relative identifier (RID) that uniquely identifies the object in the domain. Together, these two numbers distinguish an object from all other objects in the forest. The RID master assigns and tracks these numbers.

PDC Emulator   If users must connect to or from Windows NT domains, the PDC emulator manages replication changes and other server-to-server communication between NT 4 and 2000.

Infrastructure Master   This domain controller manages the update and tracking of domain groups, and which users are in them. Updates then move through the forest as they are replicated to other Infrastructure masters.

279

Review Questions

Terms to Know
- ❑ physical location
- ❑ share
- ❑ X.500
- ❑ flat directory
- ❑ trust
- ❑ replicate
- ❑ OUs
- ❑ parent domain
- ❑ namespace

1. The Active Directory is based on the _____ directory standard.

2. SNTP is used for _____.

3. Windows 2000 uses a _____ replication model.

4. After all domains on your network are upgraded to Windows 2000, you may choose to convert to a _____ mode domain model.

5. True or false: All clients on the network must be upgraded from Windows 98/NT to Windows 2000 Professional before converting to native mode domains.

    _____

6. Which protocol must be installed with the operating system in order for a Windows 2000 domain to be created?

    _____

7. Which contains more objects, the Active Directory or the global catalog?

    _____

8. Two considerations when planning where to place sites on the physical network are geographical location and _____.

9. True or false: In Windows 2000, all domain controllers can authenticate users.

    _____

10. The _____ ensures that new objects in a domain receive a unique ID to identify them on the network.

11. True or false: If five domains in a forest all need to access NT 4 domains through trusts, only one PDC emulator is needed in the forest to accomplish this.

_____

12. The connector used to manage traffic between two geographical locations is a _____.

13. The first domain you create in a new forest also creates a new tree, known as the _____ of the forest.

14. True or false: If you have a domain called foo.com and a domain called foofoo.com, they can reside in the same tree, as they share the foo.com namespace.

_____

Terms to Know
❏ root tree
❏ child domain
❏ schema
❏ global catalog
❏ transitive
❏ LAN
❏ Site Link
❏ replication cycle
❏ SID

Chapter

16

Windows 2000
Account
Management

group *n* **: an object created to represent a number of users in assigning rights and permissions**

A ccount management is the process by which an administrator configures the network to allow users to access what they need and to prevent them from accessing what they shouldn't have. Sounds simple, right? Actually, it pretty much is. Each user is represented on the network by an object (their username) that has membership in one or more groups. An administrator assigns these group objects permissions to use other objects (files and printers, for example).

This chapter explains the first part of that process—the creation of the users and groups that enable you to identify and organize users on the network. Chapter 17, "Windows 2000 Resources: File and Print Management," then finishes the process by showing you how to give permissions to network resources. In this chapter, you will be introduced to the following topics:

 Structuring the Active Directory

 Types of groups

 Creating and configuring groups

 Creating and configuring user accounts

Structuring the Active Directory

An old saying warns us, "A stitch in time saves nine," and the basic premise underlying the statement still holds true: A bit of extra work in the planning stages of any job is the best way to save yourself trouble and embarrassment later. Planning a network is no different, and when you are setting up your new Active Directory, you should resist the urge to simply start adding users and other **objects** immediately. The Windows 2000 Active Directory is very forgiving of this—moving objects from place to place is extremely easy. Still, why make an account and move it, when you can just wait a bit and put it in the right place to start with?

You should have two organizational elements in place before adding other objects: organizational units and groups. These objects will be created based on an analysis of the network, its resources, and its users, and will provide the foundation on which all other permissions rest. If you find yourself upgrading from an NT 4 domain, you may find your hands a bit tied in this, as groups and users will already exist. In such a case, you will have even more planning to do because you will need to decide what to do with the existing objects.

Organizational Units

An organizational unit, as shown in Chapter 15, "Windows 2000 Active Directory," provides a way of organizing resources logically within the domain. Your first step in doing this is to identify any groups or resources within your organization that need to be kept separate from other areas.

Good examples of areas that are often given their own organizational units are accounting and personnel departments. Rather than allow all administrators of the domain to have **admin access** to accounting and personnel resources, you may find it preferable to assign a specific user the role of personnel administrator or accounting administrator. To do this, you create organizational units, and then create users and assign them administrative **rights**.

A real-world example of this is shown in the following exercise.

TIP

Remember that you can divide a domain in two ways—physically and logically. A physical division uses sites and site links. It is generally used to control traffic over WAN links. A logical division uses organizational units, and is used to organize users and break up administrative authority.

---

object

Every element of the network—from people to machines—is represented in the Active Directory by an object. These objects each represent one specific element of the network and have their own properties and configuration elements.

---

admin access

Rights that require membership in the Administrators group.

---

rights

A right is different from a permission. Rights allow you to do a task, whereas permissions concern a particular resource. For instance, in order to access a particular file, a user must have the right to log on to the network and must also have permission to use that particular file.

TEST IT OUT: DESIGNING A DIRECTORY

A company with 400 employees wishes to upgrade its NT 4 network and is planning on completely redesigning its domain structure for use with the Active Directory. The company has four locations: Los Angeles, Chicago, New York, and a Fargo headquarters. Fargo has 175 users, and each of the branches has about 75. There are four major divisions within the company as well: manufacturing, personnel, accounting, and sales. Each division is active at all sites.

1. How many Windows 2000 domains would you recommend?

2. Would you use organizational units? If so, would you make them geographic or administrative?

3. How would you break up administrative control?

Answer: Any of a number of options may be acceptable, but one answer is closest to the spirit of how the Active Directory is intended to be configured. This option would create only a single domain with four organizational units based on company departments. There is no reason why the domain would have to be split up, and organizational units based on the company divisions will provide administrative separation between the divisions.

To create a new organizational unit, open **Active Directory Users and Computers**, which is located in the Windows 2000 Administrative Tools group. Right-click the domain in which you wish to create the new organizational unit and select New ➢ Organizational Unit. You will be asked to supply a name for the new **container**. When you are finished, the new name will appear under the domain and will be ready to have resources such as printers, computers, and even groups added to it.

Active Directory Users and Computers

This is the tool, found in the Administrative Tools, that enables you to manage users, groups, and other elements of the Active Directory. Based on the Microsoft Management Console model, it replaces the User Manager for Domains tool of NT 4.

---

container

Any object in the directory into which other objects can be placed. Objects that do not have this capability are called leaf objects.

Groups

Creating groups also requires planning. Groups are objects that enable a number of users to be administrated as a single account. Whereas users are created to identify individuals on the network, groups are created for the purpose of assigning permissions for a particular task or role. Users can be given permissions to resources directly, but this is not recommended; groups are the standard mechanism for granting access. Therefore, you will want to create a number of groups, some of which may even have only one member!

local groups

Groups that are created on Windows NT workstations and Windows NT servers and allow for local administration of resources. Global groups or domain users could be placed into these groups to give them permissions on the NT machine.

global groups

Groups that hold users in the domain and that are placed into local groups. Global groups are primarily used to group users with similar network roles.

TIP

Creating a group of one may seem like a lot of unnecessary work, but this process has a number of advantages over simply giving that user permissions to resources directly. For instance, if the user who performs backups goes on vacation, you can simply put the user who is covering for that person into the backup group temporarily. If you did not have a group, you would have to assign the temporary backup user rights and permissions equal to the original backup user. This would take time and be confusing to administrate. Once again, plan early and avoid trouble later!

Types of Groups

Windows NT 4 featured two types of groups: **local groups** and **global groups**. Windows 2000 expands on this, allowing four types of groups: global, domain local, universal, and local. Each of these has a particular scope (area of use), and Windows 2000 is stocked by default with a number of built-in groups of each type.

In general, the use of groups in Windows 2000 is similar to the use of groups in Windows NT domains, and indeed many of the built-in groups listed in this section are identical to Windows NT 4 groups. A user is created and placed into one or more global groups based on their job function. These global groups are then placed into domain local groups, and the domain local groups are given permissions to resources.

If you are looking for a process to remember this by, Microsoft has two acronyms it recommends:

AGLP This stands for Accounts into Global groups, into Local groups, which are given Permissions to resources.

UGLR Users are placed into Global groups, which are placed into Local groups, which are given permissions to Resources.

TIP

Neither of the "official" acronyms is especially catchy, and you might find this works better: Remember that setting permissions is one of the U-G-L-ie -R tasks you will need to perform!

Besides the standard built-in groups, there are also five other default groups that are not based on who the user is, but on how they are connected to a resource. These are the Everyone, Authenticated Users, Creator Owner, Network, and Interactive groups. The Interactive group, for instance, includes only those users who are logged on locally to a machine. If the same user accesses a share across the network, they are considered to be in the Network group. These last five groups cannot be configured through the Active Directory Users and Computers tool, but they can be used while setting permissions on resources.

Global Group

Only users from one domain can be added to this group, but the group can be used to access resources in any domain. Global groups are generally used to organize users with similar roles in the organization. One user may be in a number of global groups.

Built-in Global Group	Description
Domain Users	Includes all users created in the domain.
Domain Admins	Accounts added to this group gain full administrative power of the domain.
Domain Guests	Only default member is the Guests user, which is disabled. Users can be added to this group to allow them temporary, low-level access to the network.
Enterprise Admins	Administrators on the domain who need to administrate other domains as well can be added to this group, which must then be given rights in the other domains (usually by being added to the domain local Administrators group in those domains).

Domain Local Group

This group allows users from any domain to be members, but can be used to access resources only within the domain they are created in. These are generally used to identify resources that have a similar function on the network.

Built-in Domain Local Group	Description
Account Operators	Allows members to create and configure user and group information, but not network resources.
Server Operators	Allows members to create, configure, and delete network resources such as printers, files, and shares. Members can also set permissions on these resources, but cannot create or modify users or groups.
Administrators	The Domain Admins global group is placed into this group, and it is this Administrators domain local group that wields power on the domain. Members can add users and groups as well as create and configure resources.
Guests	Guests global group is a member. Any permissions granted to Guests will be available to all Guest users (if Guest is enabled).
Backup Operators	Allows members to perform backup and restore procedures.
Users	Contains the Domain Users global group and, by extension, all users on the domain.

Universal Group

Users from any domain can be members of this group, and they can be given permissions to resources in any domain. This group is generally used only in large multidomain networks. There are no built-in universal groups.

Local Group

The local group is used to assign permissions only to resources that are on the machine that the group was created on. These groups are available on Windows 2000 Professional workstations and on Windows 2000 servers that do not have Active Directory installed on them. For the most part, these mirror the domain groups they are named for, but their scope does not extend past the machine they are created on.

Built-in Local Group	Description
Administrators	Allows full access to all machine configuration and resources
Power Users	Allows users to install software and hardware, and do some admin tasks
Backup Operators	Allows access to file resources for backup
Users	Includes accounts that need non-admin access to the machine
Guests	Can be used to grant low-level guest access to the machine

Power Users

Intended to allow Workstation 4 and 2000 Professional users greater authority over their workstations. Power Users are not as powerful as the Administrator, but can do far more than just Users, in that they can install software and configure more workstation options.

Creating a Group

Although the built-in groups can help get you started, you will likely want to create groups of your own. Creating a group is relatively straightforward. Within the Active Directory Users and Computers tool, select a container for the new group and create the group by using the New Object–Group window shown below. After you have created a group, you can add users to it as they are created. You can also add users from the group's Properties window later.

289

Configuring a Group

After you have created a group, you can configure a number of elements concerning that group, including adding users to the group. To do this, right-click the group in Active Directory Users and Computers and select Properties. Using the Members tab, you can select users and add them to the list of members. You can also add the group to other groups, select a manager for the group, and add other information regarding the group object.

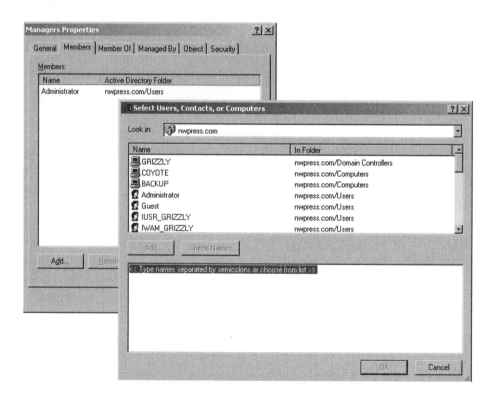

Reasons for Using Groups

Organizing permissions in groups is easier than organizing them on an individual basis. Here are two other reasons for getting used to using groups:

- ◇ If you create a network by using standard Microsoft techniques (remember A-G-L-P?), another administrator who knows the same techniques can easily manage the network when you go on vacation—or when you take a more lucrative position elsewhere!

- ◇ Microsoft MCSE tests expect you to assign permissions the "right" way, meaning the Microsoft way.

User Accounts

After you have created your organizational units and groups, it is time to add user accounts and begin matching users with the resources that they need to do their jobs. The first factor that you should consider at this point is, *just what is a user account, and what is it good for?* This is a slightly more difficult question than it may seem at first.

When you create a new account for Ulysses Grant in your accounting department and another for Teddy Roosevelt in the sales department, you put each of them into separate groups, with permissions to various resources. Remember, though, that in truth you are not assigning *them* access, but rather you are assigning *their role in the company* access. A user account, in other words, represents a particular job in the company—not an individual. If Teddy decided to leave the company and run for president, all you would have to do is rename the account and give it to the person hired to replace him. That person would then fill the role and would have all the rights necessary to do their work.

The other point to remember is that in a well-implemented network, users actually have permissions to no resources at all. This is not to say that users should not be able to access files or printers! A user is created, given particular configuration options and rights based on their network role, and is then placed into groups that provide access to the resources needed. In other words, groups, not individual users, have the permissions.

You should never have to give a user **explicit permission** to a resource (file, directory, or printer). Doing so can cause significant confusion and raise questions such as, "Why can that user print to the color printer? None of the groups she is in has rights to it." The answer may be that another administrator gave the user explicit permission to the printer for a particular task and then forgot to take it away. Although it is certainly possible to give users permissions directly, in general you should remember to use the groups. That's what they're there for.

Other than the users you create, two built-in users are created with the domain:

Administrator   The most powerful account on the domain, the Administrator account cannot be deleted or disabled, and effectively has access to all resources and configuration options on the domain. Access to the Administrator account password should be kept to a small number of people. Oh, and don't forget the password...

Guest   The Guest account is used to provide anonymous access to certain resources on the network. This is obviously a low-security option, and the Guest account is disabled by default. It can be useful for visitor access in a kiosk or for allowing read-only access to certain materials on the network.

explicit permission
Occurs when a user is given permissions to a resource without any groups involved.

Creating User Accounts

If possible, a user account should be created for every individual on the network. Shared accounts (for example, Interns) can certainly be created, but if all interns use the same username and password to log on to the network, it is difficult to maintain any real distinction between them in a security context. It would be far better to create separate accounts—Intern1, Intern2, etc.

To create a new user, simply go to Active Directory Users and Computers and select the container you wish to create the user in. The default is the **Users folder**, but you can also place the user in an organizational unit. Right-click the container and select New ➤ User. When you create a new user, you will be able to configure the following information.

Users folder

One of a number of default folders in the Active Directory. In most cases, using this default location is fine. Users in this folder can later be placed into groups in other folders or organizational units.

Data	Description
First Name	User's first name.
Last Name	User's last name.
Name	Full name.
User Logon Name	Unique name within the Active Directory.
Downlevel Logon Name	Username used to log on to non-Windows 2000 computers. Also must be unique in the domain.
Password	Authentication information used to log on the user.
Confirm Password	The initial password, assigned by the administrator, is retyped here to ensure it is correct.
User Must Change Password at Next Logon	If assigned an initial password by the administrator, this option ensures that the user will create their own password when they first use the account.
User Cannot Change Password	Prevents a user from changing a password. Good for shared accounts.
Password Never Expires	Overrides password expiration options.

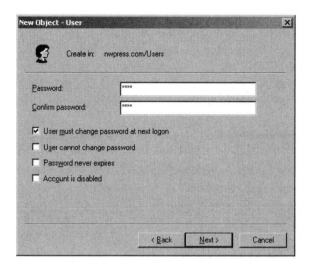

TIP

Before you start creating users, make sure that you have worked out an acceptable naming convention, or policy. For instance, will you use ugrant and troosevelt or ulyssesg and teddyr? If the company is small enough, perhaps just Ulysses and Teddy will do. Regardless, make sure you create a naming strategy that works for the organization and can expand. What happens when a second Ulysses Grant is hired, for instance?

You can require specific password lengths, expiration times, and password reuse policies. Although these provide greater security, don't make the policy so draconian that users can't remember their passwords. Users writing their passwords on sticky notes and leaving them on their monitors is usually a good clue you have gone too far!

Configuring User Accounts

After you have created an account, you will be given a number of additional options that will add to or restrict the power of the account on the network. To access an account's configuration information, select the account in Active Directory Users and Computers and right-click it. Select the Properties option. The User Properties window has a number of tabs, including those shown below.

profile
A record of the user's personal configuration data and preferences. You can store a profile locally or you can store all user profiles on the server and allow them to roam, which means a user could log on to any machine in the domain and get their own profile.

Tab	Configuration Options
General	Name, display name, description, office, phone, e-mail, Web page
Address	Full mailing address
Account	Logon name, logon hours, workstation restrictions, account options, account expiration
Profile	**Profile**, logon script, and home folder locations
Telephones	Additional phone numbers and comments
Organization	Title, department, company, manager, and direct reports
Member Of	Group and Primary group memberships
Dial-in	Remote access, callback, and IP address info

Many of these fields are simply informational, such as the Address and Telephones fields. Others serve specific network security or organizational purposes. The Account and Profile tabs are extremely important to understand, as they allow an administrator to set network locations and user options, including:

◆ Through the use of a logon script, an administrator can map drives for a user, attach printers, and set system or user variables.

◆ Profiles can be used to standardize the Windows Desktop and to restrict which programs or options a user can access.

◆ Home folders can be set up to ensure that all users have their own place on the network to store files. Home folders are secured so that only the user who owns the folder can access its information.

◆ Logon Hours and Workstation Restrictions options enable the administrator to specify the times that a user can use the network, as well as the machines that they are allowed to use.

◆ Account options enable the administrator to set password options, such as how the password is saved for the user, and when it expires.

294

These options give you a great deal of power over the way that users access and use the network. Thus, the end of this chapter returns us to the same idea that we started with: Taking extra stitches here means taking enough time to figure out what your users need, and how you can best configure the network to make their job easier and their work secure. You will therefore want to think carefully about the consequences of implementing any of these options. Using home folders, for instance, allows for easier network backup of user files, but also means that if the home folder server ever fails, users will not be able to access their files until the server is available again.

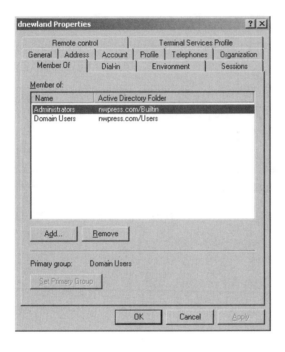

Terminal Services

Whereas normal servers provide file or printer access, a terminal server provides full desktop access. Terminal services allow a single machine to be used by multiple users at once. Each individual uses their own keyboard, mouse, and monitor, and is presented with a Windows desktop, but all programs run locally on the terminal server.

TIP

Depending on which options you have installed, you may see more than just the eight tabs described here. **Terminal Services**, for instance, adds four tabs to the User Properties page when installed (Advanced Server or Datacenter Server only).

Review Questions

1. Each user on the network is represented in the Active Directory by a user _____ object.

2. Windows 2000 accounts are created and managed by using which tool?

   _____

3. An object that can hold other objects is known as a _____.

4. _____ are used to logically divide a domain.

5. True or false: A user may be in only one group other than the default Domain Users group.

   _____

6. A user who needs to administrate multiple domains should be made a member of the _____ group.

7. Users who need to set permissions on files, but do not need to modify user accounts should be placed into the _____ group.

8. In general, should users be placed into global groups or domain local groups?

   _____

9. Which type of group usually is assigned access to resources?

   _____

10. Groups created in the Active Directory to allow e-mail to be sent to multiple users are known as _____ groups.

11. True or false: A user account in Windows 2000 should be thought of as representing a role in the organization, not an individual employee.

_____

12. The hours when a user may log on to the network can be configured from the _____ tab in the User Properties window.

13. Permissions give you access to resources, whereas _____ let you perform tasks.

14. True or false: Users can be prevented from changing their own password in Windows 2000.

_____

15. If you wish to share files from your Windows 2000 Professional machine, but have no server to provide Active Directory services, you can use only _____ groups to provide this access.

Chapter

17

Windows 2000 Resources: File and Print Management

share *n* : an access point to a resource or set of resources on the network

In Chapter 16, "Windows 2000 Account Management," you looked at one half of the process of allowing users to access resources—creating users and groups. The other half of the process, covered here, is creating and making available network resources for these users to access. Numerous hardware and software components can be made available on the network, but by far the most commonly shared resources are printers and data directories.

In general, this second half of the process requires two steps. First, you need to create the resource and prepare it for use by network users. Second, you need to make it available through the process of sharing. This chapter takes you through both steps. You will also examine the creation and sharing of a printer in Windows 2000. You can use printers locally or share them through the network. Just as you can apply permissions to folders, you also can apply security to printers.

This chapter will cover these topics:

 Sharing folders

 Assigning permissions to users and groups

 Using NTFS

 Assigning NTFS permissions

 Understanding how share permissions interact with NTFS

 Accessing resources

 Sharing printers

Sharing Folders

If more than one user needs access to the same data, the easiest way to provide access is to create a network share. In 2000, you create a directory on a Windows 2000 machine, place the information you wish to share into the directory, and then make the directory available to other users. The information is stored on the **local drive** of the Windows 2000 server, but is then accessible by all users to whom you choose to give permissions.

NOTE

The term *server* is usually used to describe a *dedicated server*—a powerful machine reserved for use by administrators. In this chapter, though, *server* simply means a machine that shares resources. All Windows 2000 machines have the capability to share resources, and if the Windows 2000 Professional workstation at your desk is sharing a directory, then it is acting as a server.

By applying security to shared folders, you can control how users access the folders. For example, assume you have a folder called DATA on the Sales server. You might assign members of the Sales group **full access** to the share, assign members of the Accountants group **read access** to the share, and not allow any other users any access to the share.

Local users can see which folders are shared on their computer through My Computer or 2000 Explorer; a hand underneath the folder indicates shared folders.

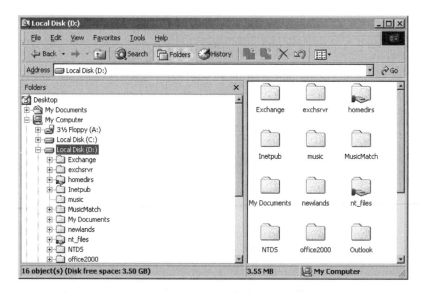

After a folder is shared, network users access the share through the My Network Places utility (assuming the user has been given sufficient permission).

---

local drive

Storage that is physically located on the user's own machine. Often the only local drives are the primary hard drive (C drive) and the CD-ROM (D drive).

Full access

General term meaning that the user has Full Control permissions on the resource.

Read Access

Permissions that allow a user to view a resource but not modify it.

Creating a New Share

To share a folder in 2000, you must be logged in to the computer as a member of one of these groups:

- ❖ Administrators
- ❖ Server Operators
- ❖ Power Users (on 2000 Professional or a non-domain controller 2000 server)

To create a network share, right-click My Computer and select Explore. Browse the folder you want to share and right-click it. Select Sharing from the menu. At this point, you will see a dialog box with several options. These options are outlined in the table below.

This table defines the Sharing tab options.

Option	Purpose
Do Not Share This Folder or Share This Folder	Indicates whether the folder will be available for network access. You must select one of these radio buttons.
Share Name	Specifies the name to be displayed through My Network Places that users will see when they access the share.
Comment	Enables you to provide a description of the folder. Users will see this description through My Network Places.
User Limit	Specifies how many concurrent users can access the share. In 2000 Professional, the maximum number is 10. In 2000 Server, the number of connections is unlimited, but you must have sufficient Client Access Licenses to legally support the number of connections you set.
Permissions	Assigns which permissions users and groups have when accessing the folder over a network share.
Caching	Configures offline access settings for the folder.

caching
A process whereby information is retrieved from the network and is then stored locally for use later, when the network is not available.

Applying Permissions for Accessing Folders

When a folder is shared, all users have Full Control to the share by default. You have the option of changing share permissions to restrict access to the folder for specific users and/or groups. Share permissions include:

- **◇** Full Control
- **◇** Change
- **◇** Read

For each of these three permission options, you have three choices: You can allow a group access, you can leave the group out of the list (the group is neither allowed nor denied), or you can specifically **deny** them access at any of the permission levels.

Share Permission	Description
Full Control	Allows a user to read and make changes to files within the folder. In addition, a user can change the share permissions for other users and groups and **take ownership** of files on NTFS partitions.
Change	Allows a user to read files, add files and subfolders, edit the data within existing files, delete files and subfolders, and edit file attributes within the shared folder.
Read	Allows a user to display files, read the contents of a file, execute program files, copy files to other folders, and display file attributes.

NOTE

Be extremely careful when using the Deny permission. Deny not only prevents a group from using the resource, but also keeps all members of the group out even if they are given access in another group!

---

deny

To prevent a user from using other permissions to access a resource. It is far stronger in its effects than simply not giving them permissions.

---

take ownership

Each file on an NTFS drive has an "owner"—a user account or group that is given complete access to that file. Taking ownership is the process of becoming the owner of a resource.

Assigning Permissions to Users and Groups

You can apply share permissions to folders either to individual users or to groups. As noted in Chapter 16, it is recommended that you use the group strategy, but either way the processes are similar. When a user attempts to access a shared resource, the operating system must determine what access the user should have.

Windows 2000 creates an **access token** each time users log on to a 2000 workstation or a 2000 domain, and this token is the key to determining whether the user can access network resources. The token specifies the user's unique user identification and any groups that the user belongs to. This information is used by the network to verify that the user has share access permissions to the share that they are attempting to access.

If the user has access permissions applied through user and group permissions, or if the user belongs to multiple groups that have access permissions assigned, the user's **effective permission** will be the most permissive permission that has been assigned. The exception to this rule is if the user has Deny permission through user or group assignment. If Deny has been assigned, the user has no access to the resource at the level they have been denied, even if they have been granted that permission through other assignments.

For example, assume that you have two users, Kate and Magda. Kate is a member of the groups Sales and Execs, and Magda is a member of the groups Sales and Temps. These permissions have been assigned:

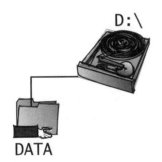

D:\

DATA

Share Permissions

Temps – Deny Read
Sales – Read
Execs – Full Control

In this case,

- ❖ Kate has Full Control permission, because it is most permissive.
- ❖ Magda is denied access, because she is a member of a group with Deny permission.

---

access token
A set of credentials that represent you on the network and that contains information about who a user is and what groups they are in.

---

effective permission
A user's effective permission is the permission that they are actually able to use on an object after all permission elements have been added together (or denied, as the case may be).

Applying Share Permissions

In the exercise below, you will experiment with setting share permissions. Make certain that you are logged on to a Windows 2000 machine with sufficient permissions to share folders. Note that in this section, you will first be shown exact steps for sharing a folder, and then you will create test users and experiment with permissions levels.

Sharing a Directory and Setting Permissions

1. From 2000 Explorer, right-click the folder that is or will be shared.
2. Click the Sharing option.
3. From the Sharing dialog box, select the Permissions button. You will see the dialog box below.

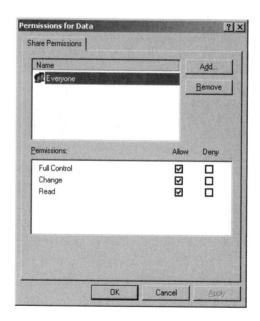

4. If you do not want to leave group Everyone with Full Control permission, highlight this group and click the Remove button.
5. To add new share permission assignments, select the Add button.
6. You add groups by double-clicking them. After the group is added, select them in the Permissions dialog box list and add the proper permissions levels. To add user assignments, complete the same steps that you used to assign the group permission.

TEST IT OUT: SHARING AND SECURING A FOLDER

1. Start by creating two users on which you can test share permissions. Make sure you are logged on as Administrator, and open Active Directory Users and Computers. Create a user named Kate and a user named Magda.

2. Next, create a folder that the users will share. Right-click My Computer and click Explore. Create a folder. Name your new folder SHAREME.

3. To share the folder, single-click the SHAREME folder. Select Sharing. Click the Share This Folder radio button. The folder is now shared. If you go back to Windows 2000 Explorer, you will notice that the folder has a hand underneath it, indicating that the folder is shared.

4. From the Sharing dialog box, click the Permissions button. Remove group Everyone from the permissions list by clicking Everyone and then the Remove button.

5. To add users and groups to the shared permission list, click the Add button. Add Kate with Full Control permission and click OK. Repeat the same steps to add the local group Administrators with Full Control permission and Magda with Read permission.

6. You can test share permissions by **logging on** as Magda and accessing the share through My Network Places. If you try to create a file in the shared folder, you should be denied access, because Magda has only Read permission to the share.

7. Log on as Kate and repeat the test.

logging on
The process of authenticating to the network and gaining access to the network as a particular user.

TIP

It is important that you use My Network Places for this test, because this accesses the resource as a share. If you use Explorer or My Computer, you access the resource locally, and no share permissions are applied.

TIP

Besides folders that you share, Windows 2000 also makes a number of administrative shares, and some applications also create shares. Be sure to research these and to account for them in your security planning.

Using NTFS

There are two ways of protecting the files on your Windows 2000 system. You have already seen security applied at the share level, and now you will look at a second method: NTFS security. The basic differences between these are:

NTFS	Share
In effect regardless of where the user connects to the resource	Only takes effect if the user accesses the resource using the share
Permissions include Full Control, Read, and Deny	Has more complex permissions, including Read Write, List Folder Contents, Read and Execute, Modify, and Full Control

NTFS is more than just a security system, though. It is a file system that offers enhancements over the traditional FAT system used by Microsoft DOS and Windows. It is also significantly different from the FAT32 system utilized by Windows 95/98. This section will examine what NTFS is, and the services and options it gives you when configuring your system.

NOTE

FAT 32 support is new to Windows 2000. Windows NT 4 machines support only FAT or FAT32.

To determine the type of file system that is installed on an existing Windows 2000 drive, right-click the drive in the Explorer and select Properties. Information will be presented about the drive, including its file system and size.

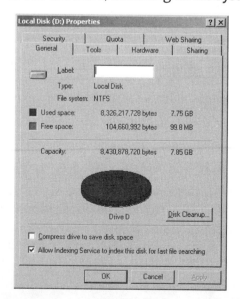

Selecting a File System

Each local drive on Windows 2000 must be formatted with a file system before it can be used to store data. A file system defines how information is stored on the disk and defines the properties that can be applied to files. Windows 2000 supports four file systems:

◆ FAT (File Allocation Table)

◆ FAT32 (File Allocation Table for Windows 95/98)

◆ NTFS (2000 File System)

◆ CDFS (Compact Disc File System)

When you format your disk partition, you use FAT/FAT32 or NTFS. This table describes some of the major differences between them.

FAT/FAT32	NTFS
Operating systems such as DOS, OS/2, Windows 3.*x*, Windows 95/98, and Windows 2000 all support FAT. If you require dual-boot capability to one of these other operating systems, you must use FAT. Windows 95/98 and Windows 2000 support FAT32. If you require dual-boot capability to Win95/98, you may choose to use FAT32.	Windows NT and 2000 are the only operating systems that can access an NTFS partition. If your computer uses only 2000, this partition type will be accessible, but if you wish to dual-boot to DOS or Windows 95/98, you must use FAT.
FAT/FAT32 offers no local security. This means that if multiple users share the same computer, all data stored on the FAT partition is available to all users.	One of the main advantages of NTFS is that you can specify local security. Because logon is mandatory, you can specify what rights users and groups have to NTFS folders and files.
No file compression or encryption is available.	File compression and encryption is supported.
No support is available for Macintosh files.	You can store and share Macintosh files on NTFS partitions.
You can convert FAT/FAT32 to NTFS at any time.	The only way you can go from NTFS back to FAT is to reformat your partition. This means that you will lose all data, and you must restore it from backup.

Understanding the Basics of NTFS

NTFS is the native file system of the Windows 2000 operating system. You can format a disk partition to use NTFS through the 2000 installation or with the **Computer Management utility**. To convert an existing FAT disk partition to NTFS, you use the CONVERT command-line utility as seen here:

```
CONVERT [drive letter]: /fs:NTFS
```

For example, if you want to convert the C drive, you use this syntax:

```
CONVERT C: /fs:NTFS
```

The main advantage of the NTFS file system is that you can apply **local security**, also referred to as local permissions. For example, assume that you have two users, Terry and Ron, who share the same computer. Each user has a folder at the root of C:\ called TERRY and RON, respectively. With NTFS permissions, you can specify that only user Terry has permission to the TERRY folder and only user Ron has permission to the RON folder. This is possible only with NTFS and cannot be defined on FAT partitions.

When you format a partition as NTFS, permissions are applied in two ways:

❖ To any user who accesses the computer locally, meaning that user is logged on to the computer where the resource is located

❖ To any user who accesses an NTFS folder that has been shared over the network

NOTE

NTFS permissions are different from share permissions in that you can apply them to folders and files.

WARNING

As with shared folders, the default NTFS permissions for any newly created NTFS drive is that the group Everyone has Full Control.

Computer Management utility

Used to monitor and configure the Windows 2000 computer. System tools, system drives, and services can all be configured from here.

local security

Permissions settings that take effect even if the user is working locally on the machine where the resource is located.

Assigning NTFS Permissions

NTFS permissions allow for far more specific permission assignments than share permissions.

NTFS permissions can be set at two levels: the file level and the folder level. As you have seen, share permissions are set only on folders.

Folder Level   Setting a permission at the folder level changes the attribute for the folder object, and also changes the default permissions of any new files or subfolders created in the folder. Existing files in the folder may also be set to the new permissions. Folder-level permissions include the following:

Permission	Allows
Read	View folder and files within it.
Write	Create new files and subfolders.
List Folder Contents	See the contents of the folder.
Read and Execute	View and run programs from the directory.
Modify	Change properties or delete the folder.
Full Control	Change permissions and ownership. Can create, modify, or delete folder and files.

File Level   Permissions set at the file level are generally best left the same as the folder they reside within, but this does not have to be the case. Each file has the capability to support security on its own. The following permissions can be set at the file level:

Permission	Allows
Read	View file and its attributes.
Write	Change the content of the file.
Read and Execute	Used on a program file, it allows the user to run the program.
Modify	Includes Read as well as Read and Execute, but also allows file to be deleted.
Full Control	Change permissions and ownership. Can modify or delete the file.

You apply NTFS permissions in a similar fashion to share permissions. One difference is that you apply share permissions to folders, and you apply NTFS permissions to folders and files.

Combining NTFS and Share Permissions

NTFS is similar to share permissions in the sense that if a user belongs to multiple groups that have been granted access to the same resource, the least restrictive access permission is applied. The exception to this rule is if the Deny permission has been specified. A user given Deny through any user assignment or group membership has no access to the specified resource.

If a user has a different set of permissions for a folder and the files within the folder, the file permissions are applied.

As an example, assume this directory structure:

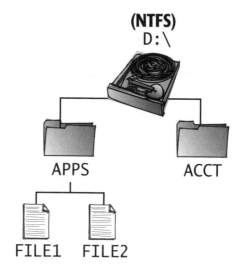

These assignments have been made:

Resource	Assignment	Permission
D:\APPS	Everyone	Read
D:\APPS\FILE2	Everyone	Modify
D:\ACCT	Temps	Deny Read, Deny Modify
	Accountants	Modify
	Managers	Full Control

These assignments mean:

- ◆ When accessing the D:\APPS folder locally, all users have Read permissions to the files in the folder except for FILE2, which has been explicitly assigned a different permission.

- ◆ A user belonging to Temps and Accountants would still have no local access to D:\ACCT, because Deny overwrites any other permission assignments.

Applying NTFS Permissions

To implement NTFS permissions, you must first format the disk partition as NTFS. If you have an existing partition, you use the CONVERT command to save existing data.

To access the Directory Permissions dialog box, which you use to assign NTFS security, complete these steps:

1. From 2000 Explorer, single-click the folder you want to apply permissions on.

2. Right-click the folder (click the secondary mouse button) and select Properties.

3. Select the Security tab to view the Permissions area, shown below.

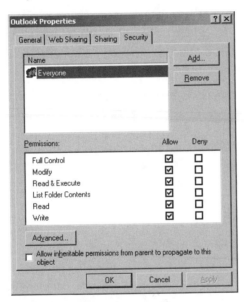

4. You will notice that the group Everyone has Full Control permission by default. To remove this assignment, highlight Everyone and click the Remove button.

5. To make a new assignment, click the Add button to see the Select Users, Computers, or Groups dialog box.

6. For each group you want to assign permissions to, highlight the group in the Name box and click the Add button. Click the OK button.

7. Back at the main permissions window, select each group and set the permissions they need.

NOTE

To manipulate NTFS permissions, you must be logged on as a user with Full Control to the folder whose permissions you want to manipulate.

Understanding Share and NTFS Permission Interaction

Remember that by default the permissions on both NTFS and share resources are set to Everyone—Full Control. If you leave these permissions, any folder you share will be exposed to the network with no security at all in force. Any user on the network will be able to open the share, view files, and even modify or delete them!

To prevent this, you must either apply local security to the files (using NTFS permissions) or you must use share-level security on the shared folder itself. In deciding which of these to use, you will need to take a few key elements into account:

- ◆ When accessing files locally, only NTFS permissions are considered.
- ◆ When accessing resources across a share, share permissions are considered first. If a user has only Read access to a shared file, they cannot modify it, even if they have Full Control of the file at the NTFS level.
- ◆ If NTFS permissions are more restrictive than permissions across the share, the more restrictive NTFS permissions will be used.

If you are concerned about providing maximum security for your shared resources, you will usually want to use NTFS permissions because they are more powerful and flexible than share permissions.

Consider this example:

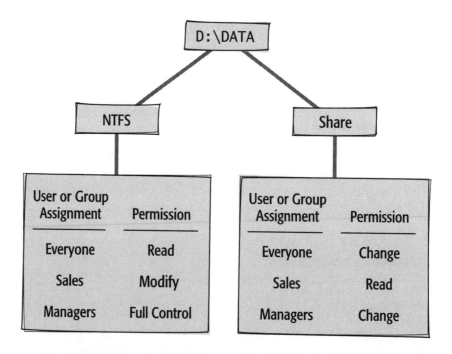

Scenario 1: Lars is a member of the Sales group and wants to access the DATA folder. If he accesses the folder locally, he will have only NTFS security applied and will have Modify access. If Lars accesses the DATA folder over a network share, the system will look at his NTFS access, which is Modify, and his share permission, which is Read. Because Read is more restrictive, this is the permission that will be applied over the share.

Scenario 2: Peter is a member of the Everyone group and the Managers group and wants to access the DATA folder. If he accesses the folder locally, he will have only NTFS security applied and will have Full Control access. If Peter accesses the DATA folder over a network share, the system will look at his NTFS access, which is Full Control, and his share permission, which is Change. Because Change is more restrictive, this permission will be applied over the share.

Accessing Resources

Flow of resource access is what happens when a user tries to access any Windows 2000 object. The object can be a share, a file, or a network printer. By understanding resource access, you can more effectively troubleshoot access problems.

As stated earlier, when a user logs on to a Windows 2000 machine, an access token is created. The access token is created only at logon. The access token identifies the user and any groups that the user belongs to. If the user is added to a group after they have already logged on, the user has to log off and log on again in order for the access token to be updated.

When the user attempts to access a resource, Windows 2000 checks the **Access Control List (ACL)**, which identifies the users and groups that can access the resource. The ACL is part of the object and determines whether the user has permission to access the resource from a user or group permission assignment.

If the user is on the ACL, the system checks the **Access Control Entries (ACE)** to see which permissions the user should be granted based on user and group assignments. If the user has a Read-Deny listed in the ACE, Windows 2000 will not even check for other Read permissions.

Access Control List (ACL)

List of users with permissions to a specific resource.

Access Control Entry (ACE)

List of permissions a specific user or group has to a specific resource.

TIP

A common error in access assignment occurs when a user fails to log off and then log on again before accessing a resource for which they have a new permission. Whenever you make new group assignments, you should advise users to log off and log on again. Many users do not realize that this is required to update the user's access token with the new group assignment.

Sharing Printers

In addition to files, printers are another common resource that users share over a network. Without printer sharing, any user who needed to print hard copies of information would have to have a printer attached directly to their own machine—a significant expense for companies and an administrative problem as well. With Windows 2000, you can install a single printer on a machine on the network (usually referred to as a print server) and then allow numerous users to access it for printing services. This section covers the installation and sharing of printers on a Windows 2000 system.

switch box

A device that enables multiple machines to share a single device, such as a printer or a monitor. The disadvantage is that only one machine at a time can use the device.

Understanding Network Printing Basics

To understand how network printing works, you should first contrast network printing with local printing. With local printing, you attach a physical printer to your computer (usually through your parallel port) and install the software that comes with the printer. This process is generally straightforward. But, as noted before, in a large computing environment, this can be an expensive way to manage printing because each computer requires its own printer.

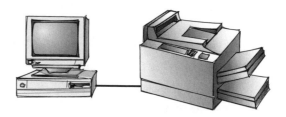

The next evolutionary step in shared printing was to allow multiple computers to access a single printer through some kind of device such as a **switch box**. With an A/B/C switch box, three users can share a printer. The first user is assigned port A; the second user is assigned port B; and the third user gets port C. In order to print, a user must walk over to the switch box and turn the dial to their port. This also was an inefficient way to manage printing for a large number of users.

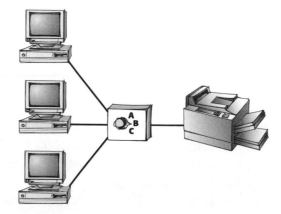

Network printing works in a different fashion. In this case, a special computer is designated as a print server. The print server runs a service called a print spooler that stores print jobs in a queue until they can be printed.

An analogy for network printing is that the print spooler is like the air traffic controller of printing. The spooler processes all jobs and determines when print jobs are printed. The print queue is like the take-off taxi and is a place where print jobs can wait before they are actually printed. The print queue is a special directory on the print server, so you need to make sure that your print server has enough disk space to accommodate all the print jobs that potentially could be submitted at any one time. After a print job has completed, it is deleted from the print queue.

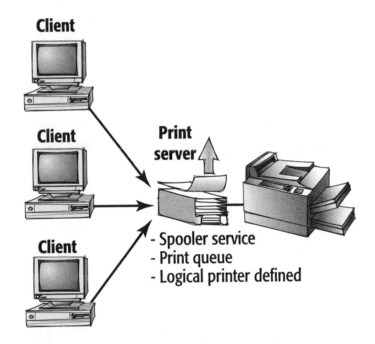

Here are some important terms that you should know for Windows 2000 printing:

Printer   The software installed on the Windows 2000 machine that enables it to format and manage information that needs to be printed. The printer is specific to a particular print device.

Print device   The actual physical printer or hardware device to which you print.

Print server   The computer on which the printer has been defined. Print jobs are sent to print servers before they are sent to the print device.

Print spooler   The service on the print server responsible for managing incoming print jobs and passing the print jobs to the print device.

Print queues   Special directories that reside on print servers and store print jobs until they are sent to the print device.

Creating a Printer

To create a printer, you must be logged on as an Administrator, Server Operator, or Print Operator. The Windows 2000 Workstation and Server software provides a Printer Wizard to help facilitate the creation of printers. To access the Printer Wizard, click Start ➢ Settings ➢ Printers. After you are in the Printers folder, double-click the Add Printer icon.

This table describes the printer configuration options.

Windows Update
A set of online updates and drivers provided by Microsoft that allow users to locate current files for their system, and for new devices.

Configuration Option	Description
Local or Network Printer	Specifies whether you will create a new printer (Local) or connect to an existing print queue (Network Printer).
Locate Your Printer (network only)	Enables you to find the printer in the directory, to browse to the printer, or to find it at a TCP/IP URL.
Select the Printer Port (local only)	Specifies whether the print device will be connected to a local computer port (a parallel or serial port) or whether the printer has a network card and will be directly attached to the network.
Printer Manufacturer and Model (local only)	Defines the printer so that the correct printer driver will be installed. You can use a default driver provided with Windows 2000, a driver provided by the manufacturer, or a driver obtained over the Internet by using **Windows Update**.
Printer Name (local only)	Enables you to define a name that will be used for the printer locally and to determine whether this will be the default local printer.
Printer Sharing (local only)	Specifies whether the print device will be configured as a local printer or a network printer. If it will be shared, you should provide a friendly name to identify it on the network.
Location and Comment (local only)	Used to help further identify the printer.
Select Operating Systems That Will Print to This Printer (network only)	If your printer will be accessed by Windows 95/98 computers, you can install print drivers for these platforms on your print server through this option.
Print Test Page	Prints a sample page so that you can verify that you properly installed and configured the printer.

Configuring Printer Properties

After you have created a printer, you can change the settings of the printer through printer properties. To access printer properties, you highlight the printer you want to manipulate, right-click it, and select Properties.

This table shows some options you can configure. Because different printers may have specific options not available on other models, you might find that not all printers have the same Property tabs. One good example is the Color tab, which is shown only on color-capable printers.

Configuration Option	Purpose
General	Specifies the general properties of the printer and includes comment information, location information, the driver that the printer will use, whether a **separator page** will be used, and the **print processor** that will be used. It also gives you the option of printing a test page.
Sharing	Configures the printer as a local printer or a network printer.
Ports	Configures the port that the printer is attached to. Ports can be local ports or network ports.
Advanced	Configures many options. You can specify which hours the printer is available, set the priority of the printer, specify whether jobs must be completely spooled before they are printed, and bypass network printing and print directly to the printer.
Security	Configures the printer's permissions.
Device Settings	Enables you to configure print properties that are unique to your printer (based on the print driver you select). Device settings include options such as form assignments to paper trays and font cartridges used by the printer.

separator page
A page that is used to show where one print job stops and another one starts.

print processor
The print processor and the default data type determine how much of the formatting of a document is done by the printer, as opposed to the application.

Sharing a Printer

One option available under the Printer Properties window is the Sharing tab. To share a printer on the network, simply click this tab and select Shared As. Type a network name for the printer—something people can easily identify. For instance, "3rd-Floor Color Printer" is easily distinguishable, whereas "Printer_02" is a bit vague.

drivers

Software that shows a particular operating system (Windows 2000, for instance) how to access and interact properly with a specific device (an HP Color LaserJet 4000, for instance). Each piece of hardware therefore may require a different driver for every operating system it is installed in.

The List in the Directory option is checked by default and should normally be left checked. Whereas NT 4 listed printers and shares only under the server that was hosting them, the Windows 2000 Directory enables you to browse resources from many machines at once.

The last sharing option is an important one. Unlike files, printers are not accessed in the same way by every operating system. Windows 2000 and Windows NT share **drivers**, but Windows 95/98 use a different driver type, and DOS/Windows machines use yet another. Because of this, the Additional Drivers check box enables you to install drivers for some other operating systems, so that when users on those systems print, the server can offer them the correct driver and make sure they are able to print properly. Some operating systems (DOS, for instance) cannot use this, but Windows 95/98 certainly can.

TIP

As with folders, after a printer has been shared, it will have a hand under it in the Printers window.

Establishing Print Permissions

In Windows 2000, a printer is an object, like a share or an NTFS folder. Because printers are objects, you can assign permissions to printers as you do to shares. For example, if you have an expensive printer that is intended for the marketing department, you can share the printer as a network printer but allow only the Marketing group to have Print permission. As with files, you can either grant or deny any of the three permissions levels shown below. Unlike files, which have two sets of permissions, printers do not. The Security tab sets the permissions that are available both for local use of the printer and use through the share.

This table defines the print permissions.

Print Permission	Description
Manage Printers	Enables you to create, manage, and delete printers. Equivalent to Full Control file permissions.
Manage Documents	Enables you to manage documents that are submitted to the printer. With this permission, you can pause, restart, resume, and delete print jobs.
Print	Enables you to submit print jobs to a network printer and to manage your own jobs.

To manipulate printer permissions, you highlight the printer and click Printer ➤ Properties ➤ Security tab. The graphic below shows a printer that a number of groups have been given permissions to.

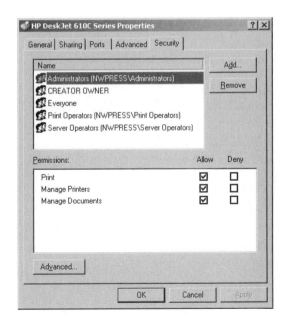

Review Questions

Terms to Know
- ❑ local drive
- ❑ Full access
- ❑ Read Access
- ❑ caching
- ❑ take ownership
- ❑ deny
- ❑ access token
- ❑ effective permission
- ❑ logging on

1. Which groups can share folders on Windows 2000?

   _____

2. What is the default permission assigned when a folder is shared?

   _____

3. Sam is a member of the Sales and Managers groups. These share permissions have been assigned to the \\SALES\DATA share:

Sales	Change
Managers	Full Control
Peons	Deny Full Control

   What permission will Sam have when he accesses this share?

   _____

4. Dianne is a member of the Sales, Peons, and Managers groups. These share permissions have been assigned to the \\SALES\DATA share:

Sales	Change
Managers	Full Control
Peons	Deny Full Control

   Which permission will Dianne have when she accesses this share?

   _____

5. True or false: You can apply local permissions to a FAT partition.

   _____

6. Which command do you use to change a FAT partition to NTFS while preserving existing folders and files?

   _____

7. True or false: When you apply NTFS permissions to a folder, they are applied to the folder's subfolders by default.

_____

Terms to Know
- ❑ Computer Management utility
- ❑ local security
- ❑ ACL
- ❑ ACE
- ❑ switch box
- ❑ Windows Update
- ❑ separator page
- ❑ print processor
- ❑ drivers

8. What minimum NTFS permission would you assign to a user who needed to create, edit, and delete files within a folder?

_____

9. If a user's combined share permissions to a resource are Change and their combined NTFS permissions to the resource are Read, what access will the user have to the resource when it is accessed over the share?

_____

10. If a user's combined share permissions to a resource are Read and their combined NTFS permissions to the resource are Full Control, what access will the user have to the resource when it is accessed locally?

_____

11. The _____ is used to store print jobs before they are sent to the printer.

12. Which default permissions are assigned when a printer is created?

_____

13. True or false: A Windows 2000 print server can provide print drivers for Windows 95 and Windows 2000 clients.

_____

14. In Microsoft terminology, a _____ is the actual physical printer.

Appendix A

Answers to
Review Questions

Chapter 1

1. Intel 8088

2. The 8-bit 8088 provided a more cost-effective product for IBM to release, replacing the true 16-bit 8086 processor.

3. The number of operations that are processed in one second

4. SDRAM can transfer data at 100MHz.

5. Real mode accesses memory in a linear format, whereas protected mode can allocate memory to a specific task.

6. Clock cycles represent the internal speed of a computer or processor expressed in megahertz. The faster the clock speed, the faster the computer performs a specific operation.

7. Virtual Real Mode is software built into Windows 95/98/NT that enables DOS programs to run. Virtual Real Mode creates a software-based memory space called conventional memory that is needed for DOS programs to run.

8. PROM stands for Programmable Read-Only Memory and is a special type of chip that is manufactured without any configuration. Manufacturers can then *burn in*, or program, the chip to contain whatever configuration is needed.

9. Clock doubling refers to the mechanism that enables the internal system clock to run at twice the normal rate of speed.

10. 3.1 million

11. Asymmetrical multiprocessing uses a separate processor to run the operating system and a second processor to run the applications. Symmetrical multiprocessing shares the tasks equally among the processors.

12. A math coprocessor, or Floating Point Unit (FPU), is a secondary processor that speeds operations by taking over some of the main processor's work. It typically performs mathematical calculations, freeing the processor to tend to other tasks.

13. The Pentium II contains on-board cache within its cartridge to increase performance, whereas the PII Celeron has no on-board cache.

14. Microsoft recommends 256MB of physical RAM for Windows 2000 Server.

15. RAM is dynamic, meaning that its contents constantly change. Permanent information, such as the BIOS, is stored in ROM.

16. PCI has a wider data path of 32 bits and runs at 33MHz. Much faster than any other bus architecture before it, PCI also improves CPU performance by relieving the CPU of many tasks that are handled by the PCI-Host bridge.

Chapter 2

1. IDE
   SCSI

2. False. IDE drives can use either the controller that is integrated with most motherboards or a simple paddleboard, which facilitates the connection but is not considered an adapter.

3. 40

4. 50

5. SCSI

6. A physical drive is the physical drive itself; for example, drive 0 or drive 1 in a two-drive configuration. A logical drive is based on how you partition your physical drive and is assigned a logical drive letter; for example, C.

7. A volume set is two or more partitions that have been combined into a single logical drive.

8. Disk mirroring (including duplexing)
   Disk striping with a parity stripe
   Disk striping with a parity drive

9. Disk mirroring uses a single controller and two drives to mirror data. Disk duplexing uses two controllers and two drives to mirror data.

10. False. You can regenerate a stripe set only if a single drive fails. If two or more drives fail, you must restore data from the most recent backup.

11. True

12. Online storage is available without any user intervention. Offline storage requires the user to access the data from media that is not immediately accessible.

13. 640MB

14 SuperDisk and HiFD are backward compatible with 1.44MB floppy disks.

15. A DVD disc holds 13 times the amount of data as a CD, enabling DVDs to store several high-quality, full-length digital movies. DVD players also are backward compatible with CDs.

16. True

Chapter 3

1. Serial communication is the process of transmitting and processing data one bit at a time.

2. Data that is transmitted serially is transmitted one bit at a time; parallel data is transmitted eight bits (one byte) at a time.

3. False. Refresh rate signifies the number of times that the beam of electrons shot from the electron gun redraws the screen.

4. Super Video Graphics Adapter (SVGA) will support the most colors and highest resolution of all adapter types.

5. Serial
   Bus
   PS/2
   USB

6. False. Digital data represents discrete voltage values. One value is represented at a given moment in time.

7. A modem uses a standard telephone line to dial out to another modem or Internet provider. A cable modem uses the CATV network and maintains an active connection to the Internet.

8. Traditional modems must convert digital signals to analog signals (modulate) to send data over phone lines. The maximum transmission speed of data in analog form over phone lines is 56Kbps. DSL is all digital and therefore is not bound by the same physical restrictions as modems.

9. True

10. False. Motherboards are manufactured to support more than one bus type to accommodate various add-in components.

11. Printers are networked to provide many users access to a single print device and therefore save money by sharing the resource.

Chapter 4

1. You use a DIP switch or jumper to accomplish the physical configuration of a hardware device.

2. Interrupts
   Base memory
   I/O memory
   DMA

3. An interrupt enables a hardware device to interrupt the microprocessor to request attention. When the request is satisfied, the microprocessor is free to carry out its responsibilities.

4. IRQ 5

5. False. Not all devices need a reserved area of memory in which to operate.

6. 1F0–1F8

7. DMA enables a device to transfer data directly to RAM without involving the processor.

8. DMA channel 2

9. A software driver is a special program that tells the computer how to communicate with and control a hardware device.

10. False. There is no such thing as the Software Driver Association. Drivers are written for specific operating systems.

11. True, provided that each device has a different I/O address.

12. Direct memory access

13. input/output

14. Interrupt request

Chapter 5

1. Disk Operating System

2. Graphical user interface

3. Windows for Workgroups 3.11

4. False

5. A feature in operating systems where multiple tasks running simultaneously each have equal access to the processor.

6. Windows 2000

7. Windows 95

8. DOS 6.22

9. Windows 98

10. Plug and Play

11. X Windows

12. USL System V UNIX
    BSD Unix

13. Linux

14. False

15. POSIX

Chapter 6

1. FORMAT

2. SYS

3. All of these options are valid answers:

   Create DOS partitions or logical drives
   Set the active partition
   Delete partitions or logical drives
   Display partition information
   Change the current fixed drive

4. FORMAT /Q

5. FORMAT /S

6. COMMAND.COM
   IO.SYS
   MSDOS.SYS

7. CD\

8. DEL C:\TEST\TEST.DOC

9. To copy whatever is written on the screen to a text file

10. B

11. False. You use the TYPE command.

12. REN

13. You use ? to represent a single character, while * can represent any number of characters.

14. With COPY, you maintain a copy of the file in both the source and destination directories. With MOVE, you maintain a copy only in the destination directory.

15. ATTRIB TEST.DOC +H

Chapter 7

1. The Recycle Bin

2. The Internet

3. My Computer

4. The Taskbar

5. The Start button

6. Documents

7. Settings

8. Help

9. Standby
   Shut Down the Computer
   Restart the Computer
   Restart the Computer in MS-DOS Mode

10. True

11. They enable you to create a pointer that you can use to quickly and easily access another object.

12. A Wizard is a program that steps you through the installation of a particular item.

13. Windows Explorer explores the local computer and network, and Internet Explorer explores the Internet.

14. The right mouse button

Chapter 8

1. It makes networking easier to understand.
   It makes it easier to replace modular components as technology changes.

2. Session

3. Data-Link

4. Application

5. Network

6. Physical

7. Presentation

8. Transport

9. Logical Link Control (LLC)
Media Access Control (MAC)

10. Router

11. Connection-oriented services establish a connection between the sender and the receiver and are more reliable. Connectionless services send data without establishing a connection and are more efficient.

12. A physical address is identified at the Data-Link layer of the OSI model and is hard coded on the network interface card. A network address is associated with the Network layer of the OSI model and is a logical address that the network administrator assigns.

13. Physical
Data-Link
Network
Transport
Session
Presentation
Application

Chapter 9

1. Peer-to-peer networks do not use dedicated network servers for authenticating users and providing secure access to network resources. In this model, clients share resources, and other clients have access to whatever has been shared.

2. The role of the primary domain controller, or PDC, is to store the domain accounts database, called the Security Accounts Manager, or SAM. The PDC also sends updates of the SAM database to any BDCs within the domain.

3. BDCs offload logon authentication from the PDC. They also provide fault tolerance if the PDC is offline.

4. Directory services model

5. False. Each network model has its own strengths and drawbacks. No one network model meets the needs of every network.

6. Peer-to-peer network

7. An object is a logical representation of anything that can be managed on the network, including user accounts, servers, and printers.

8. False. In a client-server model, you need an account on each server on which you want to access resources.

9. False. You can add users to the PDC or the BDC. The account information is automatically updated to the other server.

10. The directory services network model

Chapter 10

1. Star
   Bus
   Ring

2. A physical topology is the way that the network is physically arranged and is cabled, and a logical topology is the way that the data is transferred through the network.

3. Carrier Sense Multiple Access with Collision Detection

4. 10Mbps and 100Mbps

5. 4Mbps and 16Mbps

6. The star topology

7. False. The standard you choose defines the topology. For example, Token Ring cannot use a physical or logical bus topology.

8. A

9. The star topology

10. Ring, star

11. True

12. Ethernet

13. IEEE 802.3

14. IEEE 802.5

Chapter 11

1. IP address
   Subnet mask
   Default router or gateway

2. DHCP

3. IPX/SPX

4. Providing each attached device a unique address

5. Network layer

6. SPX

7. Class C networks

8. C

9. A

10. True

11. DNS maps domain names to IP addresses, which makes accessing resources easier for people.

12. The subnet mask

13. True

14. It needs no configuration.

Chapter 12

1. Reliability, scalability, performance, interoperability

2. Two or more CPUs can be used to simultaneously process a single instruction.

3. Servers in the domain share the same database of users and security-access levels.

4. Configuration changes often require the server to be rebooted.

5. Microsoft developed Active Directory services for managing objects on a network, including servers, user accounts, and other devices.

6. True

7. Client-server

8. Directory services

9. NetWare 5.1

10. NetWare Loadable Module. An NLM loads and unloads server and network services dynamically.

11. NetWare 5.1 adds completely pure IP protocol support.

12. Unix is the most reliable, stable, and fastest NOS.

13. Both can be difficult to learn because of the vast number of commands.

14. Besides the effort involved in learning commands, there is very limited support for Linux.

15. It has characteristics similar and in some cases, equal to Unix.
    It is free.

Chapter 13

1. Provide flexibility in OS code
   Be reliable
   Offer high performance
   Use portable code
   Be compatible with existing standards

2. Windows 2000 Professional
   Windows 2000 Server
   Windows 2000 Advanced Server
   Windows 2000 Datacenter Server

3. NT 4

4. NT 3.5

5. NT 3.51

6. Microsoft Cluster Server

7. Windows 2000

8. MMC, or Microsoft Management Console, provides a common interface and utility for all administrative tasks. The administrator can customize this utility.

9. Windows 2000

10. A group of computers running together that appear as if they are one system to clients and applications. Clustering improves performance by distributing tasks across multiple computers. It also provides reliability by allowing a computer in the cluster to be removed for maintenance without stopping service.

Chapter 14

1. Windows 2000 Professional
2. Server, Advance Server, or Datacenter
3. True
4. Microsoft Management Console
5. One million
6. Windows 2000 Server
7. 128 MB
8. Windows 2000
9. Offline
10. Kerberos, smart cards
11. Datacenter Server; no
12. Internet Explorer 5

Chapter 15

1. X.500
2. Timekeeping and time synchronization
3. Multi-master
4. Native
5. False
6. TCP/IP
7. Active Directory
8. Bandwidth
9. False
10. Relative Identifier Master
11. False
12. Site Link
13. Root tree
14. False

Chapter 16

1. account
2. Active Directory Users and Computers
3. Container
4. Organizational units
5. False
6. Enterprise Admins
7. Server Operators
8. Global groups
9. Domain local group
10. Distribution
11. True
12. Account
13. Rights
14. True
15. Local

Chapter 17

1. Administrators, Server Operators, Power Users
2. Everyone—Full Control
3. Full Control
4. Change
5. False
6. CONVERT
7. True
8. Modify
9. Read
10. Full Control
11. Print queue
12. Everyone—Print
13. True
14. Print device

Appendix

B

Glossary

Numbers

10BASE2   A network communication standard that uses Ethernet on thin coaxial cable in a linear bus topology at 10Mbps.

10BASE-T   A signal capable of transmitting at 10Mbps over twisted-pair cable by using baseband signaling.

A

Accelerated Graphics Port (AGP)   A bus technology developed by Intel to replace PCI. In addition to controlling the transfer of data between expansion cards, the CPU, and RAM, the AGP chip set boosts the transfer of data to RAM and the accelerated graphics port to 528MBps.

Access Control Entry (ACE)   List of permissions a specific user or group has to a specific resource.

Access Control List (ACL)   List of users with permissions to a specific resource.

access token   A set of credentials that represent you on the network and that contains information about who a user is and what groups they are in.

Active Directory   A replacement for the Windows NT domain structure, the Active Directory stores all information about users, computers, and the network in Windows 2000.

Active Directory Users and Computers   The tool, found in the Administrative Tools, that enables you to manage users, groups, and other elements of the Active Directory. Based on the Microsoft Management Console model, it replaces the User Manager for Domains tool of NT 4.

active matrix   Sometimes referred to as Thin Film Transistor (TFT), active matrix LCD displays offer superior clarity and color. This is due mostly to faster refresh rates and more powerful LCD cells.

active partition   The partition that the computer identifies as the one that will be used to boot up the computer and load the operating system.

admin access   Rights that require membership in the Administrators group.

American National Standards Institute (ANSI)   An organization that seeks to develop standardization within the computing industry. ANSI is the American representative to the ISO, or International Standards Organization.

American Standard Code for Information Interchange (ASCII)   A 7-bit coding scheme that translates symbolic characters into the ones and zeros that are stored as data on a computer. Extended ASCII uses an 8-bit coding scheme.

array   A set of objects, all of which are the same size and type.

ASCII file   Text file that uses the ASCII character set. ASCII is a standard for encoding letters and numbers into the ones and zeros that the computer understands.

Asymmetric Multiprocessing (ASMP)   A computer architecture that uses multiple CPUs to improve the performance of the computer. In the ASMP model, one CPU is dedicated to managing tasks (which usually includes managing the other CPUs) for the computer system. The remaining CPUs process user tasks.

asynchronous communication   Begins transmission of each character with a start bit and ends transmission of each character with a stop bit. This method is not as efficient as synchronous communication but is less expensive.

Asynchronous Transfer Mode (ATM)   A network technology that uses fixed-size cells to transfer data. The fixed-size cells enable it to provide better performance.

authentication A process that requires a user to enter an ID and a password and then be verified by the software to gain access to resources.

B

B channel Stands for bearer channel; a 64Kbps circuit-switched channel. Used to carry voice and data.

backbone A network segment that uses high-speed transmission media and handles the majority of network traffic between two areas or LANs.

BackOffice A suite of server applications built by Microsoft to run on the NT server platform.

backup The copying of all your data to a secondary storage option. If your primary storage option becomes unavailable, you can use backups to restore the operating system, application, and data files.

backup domain controller (BDC) Used in NT domains, it has read-only copies of the PDC accounts database. BDCs serve two primary functions: They offload logon authentication requests from the PDC and they provide fault tolerance. If the PDC fails, the BDC can be promoted to PDC.

bandwidth The capacity of a network line to carry information. Bandwidth is best thought of as a highway; four lanes support more traffic than two and have fewer slowdowns.

base memory Memory addresses that are reserved and used to store low-level control software that is required by an add-on device.

baseband A technology that permits a single transmission of data at a fixed frequency on a wire at any given moment.

Basic Input/Output System (BIOS) Software located in a ROM chip that is responsible for communicating directly between the computer hardware and the operating system.

Basic Rate Interface (BRI) The basic ISDN service offered by telecommunication companies. BRI consists of two B channels and a single D channel.

batch file A file that contains a set of commands to be executed by the operating system. AUTOEXEC.BAT is one example of a batch file that is executed during the final stages of the boot process. All batch files end in BAT.

baud A measurement of the number of signals that are transmitted each second.

bit A binary digit. The digit is the smallest unit of information and represents either an off state (zero) or an on state (one).

bit depth A value representing the number of bits that are used to make up a pixel. The higher the number of bits, the more colors that can be displayed.

bits per second (bps) The number of bits, or ones and zeros, transmitted each second.

boot partition Synonymous with the active partition on a disk. The boot partition contains the necessary files to start the operating system on the computer.

bridge A layer 2 netowrk device that enables networks using different layer 2 protocols to communicate with one another. A bridge can also minimize traffic between two networks by passing through only those packets that are addressed to the other network.

broadband A type of transmission that can use a single wire to transmit multiple streams of data simultaneously using different frequencies. This method is similar to the method used by radio stations all sharing the airwaves to send their signals.

broadcasts Data transmitted to all devices on the same network.

browser service   In NT networks, broadcasts the availability of network services such as network shares or printers.

burst mode   The temporary increase in data transmission speeds beyond what is normal. The increase is not sustainable and usually prevents other devices from transmitting.

bus architecture   Any linear pathway on which electrical signals travel and carry data from a source to a destination.

bus speed   The rate at which data can be transferred between the CPU and the rest of the motherboard. Typical bus speeds are 50, 60, 66, or 100 MHz, with 133 MHz-based motherboards entering the market.

byte   A unit of measurement representing eight bits.

C

Cable Modem Termination System (CMTS) device   A device used to forward user data to the Internet. Downstream data from the Internet is forwarded to the cable television equipment in that neighborhood, where it is then forwarded to the home user.

cache memory   Very fast memory that sits between the CPU and the main RAM. Cache memory can be as fast as 5 to 10 nanoseconds, whereas main RAM is usually not faster than 60 to 70 nanoseconds. (Yes, a lower number is better here because it takes less time.)

caching   A process whereby information is retrieved from the network and is then stored locally for use later, when the network is not available.

central office   A building in a given neighborhood where all local phone lines in that neighborhood are terminated.

Central Processing Unit (CPU)   The microprocessor, or brain, of the computer. It uses logic to perform mathematical operations that are used in the manipulation of data.

child domain   A tree created under the namespace of an existing tree.

client   A computer on the network that requests network services.

client-server network   Uses a dedicated server to centralize user and group account management. Users at a client, or workstation, log on to a server where they have user accounts and access resources on the server to which their user account has permission.

clock cycles   The internal speed of a computer or processor expressed in MHz. The faster the clock speed, the faster the computer performs a specific operation.

clock signal   Controls the rate at which synchronous data is transmitted.

clustering   Connecting two or more computers to make them appear as one system. Clustering is used to take advantage of the processing power of multiple computers.

coaxial   A type of media that has a single copper wire surrounded by plastic insulation, is wrapped in metal braid or foil, and finally protected by a plastic cover.

collisions   A problem on Ethernet networks that occurs when two computers transmit on the wire simultaneously, causing a electrical spike twice the strength than is normal for the network.

COMMAND.COM   A DOS operating system file that receives and executes commands as they are entered at the command line by the user.

command-line   The prompt in a DOS screen from which a command is executed by typing letters and characters.

compact disc (CD)   A plastic or optical disk that can be read by using lasers. All compact discs have a maximum storage capacity of 650MB.

compact disc- rewritable (CD-RW)   A compact disc that can have data rewritten to it several times by using lasers. Lasers record data to the disc like a CD-R, but slightly less powerful lasers are used to erase the data. Even weaker lasers are used to read the data.

compact disc-recordable (CD-R)   A compact disc that can have data recorded onto it once with a laser and can be read many times.

Complex Instruction Set Computing (CISC)   A full complement of instructions used by a processor to complete tasks such as mathematical calculations. Used in the most common type of processors produced; most Intel processors are based on this standard.

compression   A method of reducing the size of data by using a mathematical calculation.

Computer Management utility   Used to monitor and configure a Windows 2000 computer. System tools, system drives, and services can all be configured from here.

concentrator   See hub.

`CONFIG.SYS`   A DOS or OS/2 file that contains special configuration settings in the form of line statements. The file is stored in the root of the C drive and is one of the key files read when an operating system boots.

connection-oriented   A method of communication that is considered reliable because the sender is notified when data is not received or is unrecognizable.

console command   A command that is input directly from the keyboard and monitor of the server instead of remotely.

container   Any object in the directory into which other objects can be placed. Objects that do not have this capability are called leaf objects.

conventional memory   The first 640KB of memory, which is required by the Disk Operating System (DOS) to run. Memory above 640KB was used by operating systems such as Windows 3.1.

cyclic redundancy check (CRC)   A form of error detection that performs a mathematical calculation on data at both the sender's end and the receiver's end to ensure that the data is received reliably.

D

D channel   Stands for delta channel; a 16Kbps circuit-switched channel. Used to manage control signals.

daisy chain   To connect a series of devices, one after the other. When signals are transmitted on a daisy chain, they go to the first device, then to the second, and so on, until termination is reached.

data path   The number of bits that can be transported into the processor chip during one operation.

data warehouses   Through modern database technology, companies are able to store and access tremendous amounts of business data. A data warehouse is the hardware and software that provides this functionality.

database server   A type of computer that maintains information records that can be added, deleted, changed, or searched. Database servers play a major role in most companies and on the Internet.

defragmentation   The reorganization of data on a hard disk to optimize performance.

demodulate   To convert an analog signal back to digital data. This is typically done on the receiving end of a computer transmission using standard phone service.

deny   To prevent a user from using other permissions to access a resource. It is far stronger in its effects than simply not giving them permissions.

dialog control Manages the dialog between the sender and receiver. It consists of managing the transfer of data, determining whether an acknowledgment is required, and determining the appropriate responses to the sender.

Dial-Up Networking A feature of Windows 95 and 98 that guides the user through setting up a network connection by using a modem, a phone line, and the pre-installed Microsoft software.

differential backup Uses the archive bit to determine which files have changed since the last normal backup. Files that have changed are backed up. The archive bit is not reset until the next normal backup. If you have to restore data, you need only your last full backup and your last differential tape.

Digital Subscriber Line (DSL) A digital signaling method used to transmit data over regular phone lines at speeds up to 6Mbps. DSL uses Asynchronous Transfer Mode (ATM) to pass data in fixed-size cells.

digital video disc or digital versatile disc (DVD) Based on the same technology as CD-ROM, DVD uses a much smaller laser and is able to copy many times more the amount of data. DVDs can hold at least 4.7GB of data and as much as 8.5GB.

DIN Deutsch Industrie Norm—a German standards organization.

direct memory access (DMA) A process wherein data moving between a device and RAM bypasses the CPU. The CPU is then free to complete other tasks.

directory services model Uses a hierarchical database to logically organize the network resources. This model scales well to small, medium, or large enterprise networks.

disk controller Manages floppy and hard disks. It can be a separate piece of hardware, or it can be integrated with the hard drive.

disk imaging Disk imaging technologies enable the contents of a hard drive to be copied and then reused on other machines. This enables administrators to quickly and efficiently prepare large numbers of computers.

disk partitioning The process of creating logical disks from a physical disk. You can then format the logical disks and use them to store data.

distributed processing Sharing the task of processing instructions between a server and a client CPU.

domain model Logically groups computers, users, and groups into a domain. Users log on to the domain and have access to any resources within the domain to which their user account has permission.

Domain Name System (DNS) A system that resolves domain names to IP addresses by using a domain name database.

DOS An operating system developed by Microsoft. DOS predominantly uses command lines to manage the operating system, applications, and files.

DOS shell The name that is used to describe the software that makes up the DOS user interface.

DOSKEY A DOS utility that enables the user to customize settings for DOS and add key commands for DOS.

dot pitch Measures the distance, in millimeters, between two dots of the same color on a monitor.

drivers Software that shows a particular operating system (Windows 2000, for instance) how to access and interact properly with a specific device (an HP Color LaserJet 4000, for instance). Each piece of hardware therefore may require a different driver for every operating system it is installed in.

Dual Inline Memory Module (DIMM)
Memory that has a board with memory chips on both sides to increase the capacity of the module. DIMMs have 168 pins for connecting to the RAM sockets in a motherboard.

dual in-line package (DIP) switches   A set of tiny switches attached to a circuit board that are manually configured to alter the function of a chip for a specific computer or application.

dual-boot   Having two or more operating systems on your computer. At system start-up, you can select which operating system you will boot.

Dynamic Host Configuration Protocol (DHCP)   Automates the assignment of IP configuration information.

Dynamic Host Configuration Protocol (DHCP) server   Automates the assignment of IP configurations.

E

EDIT   A DOS text editor.

Extended Data Out (EDO) RAM   Memory that uses dual-pipeline architecture, allowing the unit to store data (write) at the same time it sends it out (read). EDO RAM is limited to a bus speed of 66MHz, due to its non-parity design. EDO RAM can be purchased in 72-pin SIMMS or 168-pin DIMMS.

effective permission   The permission that a user can actually use on an object after all permission elements have been added together (or denied, as the case may be).

electron gun   The device that shoots electrically charged particles called electrons toward the back of the monitor screen.

encryption   The process of encoding data to prevent unauthorized access.

Enhanced IDE (EIDE)   An extended version of the IDE standard. The benefits of EIDE include the support of hard drives over 528MB, the capability to chain devices other than drives (for example, CD-ROM drives and tape drives), faster access time, and the capability to chain up to four devices.

Enhanced Parallel Port (EPP)   The standard developed for parallel communication by Intel, Xircom, and Zenith Data Systems to allow for data transfer rates of more than 2MBps. It supports bidirectional operation of attached devices and an addressing scheme.

enterprise   A large network, generally involving thousands of users, many servers, and extensive wide area network links.

Erasable Programmable Read-Only Memory (EPROM)   Maintains its contents without the use of electrical power. The stored contents of an EPROM chip are erased and reprogrammed by removing the protective cover and using special equipment to reprogram the chip.

error control   A mechanism for assuring that data received is in the same condition and format that it was sent.

Ethernet   A network communication technology developed by Xerox that encloses data with a destination and source address along with other information. The enclosed data is called a frame. Additional information for Ethernet is also added to the frame.

expansion card   An add-on device, such as a sound or video card, that is installed directly into an expansion slot built into a motherboard. The card must be of the same bus architecture as the slot on the motherboard.

explicit permission   Occurs when a user is given permissions to a resource without any groups involved.

Extended Binary Coded Decimal Interchange Code (EBCDIC) The 8-bit character set used by IBM mainframes.

Extended Capabilities Port (ECP) The standard developed for parallel communication by Hewlett-Packard and Microsoft to allow for data transfer rates of more than 2MBps. In addition to the high data transfer rates, it allows for bidirectional operation.

extended partition A non-bootable partition that can contain multiple logical partitions that are then assigned drive letters. An extended partition is created from the hard drive space remaining after creating the primary partition.

F

FAT32 File Allocation Table 32. A 32-bit version of the FAT file system that will recognize drives larger than 2GB. FAT32 can adjust the size of the clusters (individual cells that are used to organize the data) on a hard drive to accommodate larger-sized drives.

fault tolerance The use of hardware and software to prevent the loss of data in the event of a system, hardware, or power disruption or failure.

Fiber Distributed Data Interface (FDDI) A network specification that defines a logical ring topology of fiber transmitting at 100Mbps. FDDI provides similar network connectivity as Ethernet and Token Ring, and functions at the same layers of the OSI model.

fiber-optic A type of media that uses glass or plastic to transmit light signals. Single-mode fiber optic contains a single fiber. Multi-mode fiber cable has two individually protected fibers.

File Allocation Table (FAT) A table stored on the outer edge of the hard drive that indicates the location and order of files on the hard drive.

file server A computer that is dedicated to the task of centrally sharing files and folders for access by users.

File Transfer Protocol (FTP) An application layer protocol for transferring files between two computers. FTP involves the use of FTP client software and an FTP server.

File Transfer Protocol (FTP) Server Transfers files between the FTP server and FTP clients. Most Web browsers use FTP client software to download and upload files to Internet servers running the FTP service.

flat directory Used in many simple directory schemes, a structure that does not allow for compartmentalization of resources, users, or other accounts. It also has no hierarchical relation between directory elements.

Floating Point Unit (FPU) Also known as a math coprocessor, it is a secondary processor that speeds operations by taking over math calculations of decimal numbers.

flow control A feature of the Transport layer that manages the amount of data being transmitted between sender and receiver. If the receiving computer is unable to accept more data, it notifies the sending computer to pause transmission.

FORMAT A DOS utility used to prepare a floppy disk or hard disk to store data.

format To initialize a floppy disk or logical drive and prepare it so that you can store data on it.

frame Data that has been encapsulated by the layer 2 protocol before being transmitted on the wire.

freeware Software that you can use without payment.

Full access General term meaning that the user has Full Control permissions on the resource.

fully duplexed Means that simultaneous two-way communication can take place.

fully qualified domain name (FQDN)   The complete name registered with InterNIC that is used to identify a computer on the Internet. It includes the computer name (hostname) and the domain name. For example, `mycomputer.sybex.com`.

G

global catalog   A fast-access copy of the full directory that includes only those objects that are commonly used, such as usernames and logon names.

global groups   Groups that hold users in the domain and that are placed into local groups. Global groups are primarily used to group users with similar network roles.

graphical user interface (GUI)   An application that provides intuitive controls (such as icons, buttons, menus, and dialog boxes) for configuring, manipulating, and accessing applications and files.

H

H0   Another ISDN channel that includes 6 B channels. Other H channel definitions include H-10 and H-11, which are just another way of identifying the 23 B channels of the Primary Rate Interface.

hard drive   Stores data as a series of ones and zeros on a series of magnetically coated disks. A positive charge indicates a one, and the absence of a charge indicates a zero.

Hardware Compatibility List (HCL)
Provided by Microsoft, the HCL lists all hardware that has been tested by Microsoft and has proved to work with a particular operating system. Hardware not on the HCL might work, but is not certain to.

hexadecimal   A numbering system that uses 16 instead of 10 as its base; it uses the digits 0–9 and the letters A–F to represent the decimal numbers 0–15.

hidden file   A file that is not viewable using the DIR command in DOS or viewable in a folder. The hidden file attribute can be set to on or off by using the attribute command in DOS or by setting the file properties in Windows.

hop   The number of foreign gateways (routers other than your own) that a packet must pass through between the source and destination computers.

hub   A Physical layer device that connects computers and other devices to make a network. A hub regenerates an incoming signal from one device and broadcasts the signal out all other ports.

Hypertext Markup Language (HTML)   A text-based scripting language that is used in the creation of Web pages to control the presentation of text and graphics. It can also be used to add functionality to the Web page for navigation or for interfacing with other technologies such as databases and multimedia.

I

I/O memory   Memory addresses that are reserved and assigned to add-on devices. Each assignment tells the CPU about the location of a specific device.

IEEE 802.3   The IEEE standard that is also known as Carrier Sense Multiple Access with Collision Detection (CSMA/CD) and defines how most Ethernet networks function.

IEEE 802.3ab   The IEEE standard for 1000MBps Gigabit Ethernet over unshielded twisted-pair cable (UTP).

IEEE 802.3u   The IEEE standard for 100MBps Fast Ethernet. Defines the specifications for implementing Fast Ethernet at the Physical and Data-Link layers of the OSI model.

IEEE 802.3z   The IEEE standard for 1000MBps Gigabit Ethernet over fiber-optic cable.

incremental backup Uses the archive bit to determine which files have changed since the last incremental backup. After the incremental backup is complete, the archive bit is cleared. Incremental backups occur between each normal or full backup.

input/ouput (I/O) Refers to any device or operation that enters data into or extracts data from a computer.

Input/Output (I/O) channel A circuit that provides a path for an input or output device to communicate with the processor.

Institute of Electrical and Electronic Engineers (IEEE) Pronounced *I triple E*, an international organization that defines computing and telecommunications standards. The LAN standards defined by IEEE include the 802-workgroup specifications.

Integrated Drive Electronics (IDE) A drive technology that integrates the drive and controller into a single piece of hardware. IDE drives are an inexpensive data-storage solution.

Integrated Services Digital Network (ISDN) A technology that combines digital and voice transmission onto a single wire.

International Standards Organization (ISO) An organization dedicated to defining global communication and informational exchange standards. The American National Standards Institute (ANSI) is the American representative to the ISO.

Internet Explorer A World Wide Web browser developed by Microsoft for viewing Web pages on the Internet.

Internet Service Provider (ISP) A company or organization that provides the user with access to the Internet, typically for a fee. Users may gain access by using any one of many remote connection technologies, including modems, DSL, ISDN, cable modems, and others.

internetwork Two or more networks that are connected by using a router.

interrupt A type of signal that is used to get the attention of the CPU when I/O is required. An interrupt tells the CPU that the operating system is requesting that a specific action be taken. Interrupts are prioritized; higher-numbered interrupts are serviced first.

interrupt request (IRQ) The method used by a device to inform the microprocessor (CPU) that the device needs attention. Through this method of interruption, the microprocessor can function without needing to poll each device to see whether it needs service.

`IO.SYS` A DOS system file that is the first to load from disk during the boot process. This system file contains the software that facilitates interaction between attached hardware and the ROM BIOS.

IP Security (IPSec) A protocol standard for encrypting IP packets.

J

jumpers Plastic-covered metal clips that are used to connect two pins on a motherboard. The connection creates a circuit that turns the setting to "on."

K

Kerberos An industry-standard authentication protocol.

L

LAN Manager One of Microsoft's first network operating systems.

level 1 (L1), or internal, cache   Memory in the CPU that is used to temporarily store instructions and data while it is waiting to be processed. There are typically at least two L1 caches of 16 or 32 kilobytes in modern CPUs, like the Pentium II processor.

level 2 (L2), or backside, cache   Memory that is used by the CPU to temporarily store data that is waiting to be processed. Originally located on the motherboard, recent CPU architectures such as the Pentium II and III have incorporated L2 cache directly on the same board as the CPU. The on-board L2 cache can be accessed by the CPU at two to four times the speed as L2 cache on the motherboard.

load balancing   Distributing similar tasks (such as accessing an application or assigning an IP address) equally across multiple computers.

local area network (LAN)   A LAN is contained within a single building or campus and can operate independently of any outside connection.

local drive   Storage that is physically located on the user's own machine. Often the only local drives are the primary hard drive (C drive) and the CD-ROM (D drive).

local groups   Groups that are created on Windows NT workstations and Windows NT servers and allow for local administration of resources. Global groups or domain users could be placed into these groups to give them permissions on the NT machine.

local loop   The two-wire copper telephone cable that runs from a home or office to the central office of the telephone company.

local security   Permissions settings that take effect even if the user is working locally on the machine where the resource is located.

logging on   The process of authenticating to the network and gaining access to the network as a particular user.

logical drive   Based on how you partition your physical drive, the area of the extended partition can be organized into multiple drives. Each drive is assigned a DOS identifier from D to Z.

Logical Link Control (LLC)   A Data-Link sublayer that establishes whether communication with another device is going to be connectionless or connection oriented.

loopback   A special function for testing a device's capability to communicate by making it communicate with itself.

M

managed hubs   Similar to hubs, but with the exception that the device can be managed by using software to monitor and control network communication.

Management Console (MMC)   A Microsoft application framework for accessing administrative tools, called consoles.

Manchester encoding   A method of identifying the beginning and end of a bit signal (one or zero) when it is transmitted on the network.

master   A device that is responsible for controlling one or more directly connected devices.

Media Access Control (MAC)   The sublayer of the Data-Link layer that adds the destination and source addresses to a frame before sending to the Physical layer.

Media Access Control (MAC) address   A hexadecimal number that is allocated by an international organization and is burned into the network interface card by the NIC manufacturer.

megabits per second (Mbps)   A measurement of the amount of data, in the millions of bits per second, being transferred.

megabytes per second (MBps) A measurement of the transfer speed of a device in terms of millions of bytes per second.

megahertz (MHz) One million cycles per second. The internal clock speed of a microprocessor is expressed in MHz.

member server In NT and Windows 2000, a server in the domain that does not provide security services—it does not keep a copy of the SAM or the Active Directory.

microcode The smallest form of an instruction in a CPU.

microcode efficiency The capability of a CPU to process microcode in a manner that uses the least amount of time and completes the greatest number of operations.

millions of instructions per second (MIPS) A measurement of the number of microcode instructions that a CPU or microprocessor can complete in one second, or cycle.

modulate To convert digital data into analog signals. Modulation enables digital computer data to be transferred over standard telephone lines.

motherboard The main board in a computer that manages communication between devices internally and externally.

MSDOS.SYS A DOS system file that is loaded by IO.SYS and contains the primary DOS routines.

MultiMedia Extension (MMX) A processor technology that dramatically improves the response time of games and multimedia-based applications. The technology was introduced through the MMX-equipped line of Intel Pentium chips.

multipoint A shared link between many devices.

multitask To perform several operations concurrently.

N

namespace The part of the naming structure occupied by a certain domain or tree. If the domain is foo.com, all machines and subdomains of foo.com exist within its namespace: www.foo.com, accounting.atlanta.foo.com, etc.

NetWare A popular network operating system from Novell and a competitive product to Windows NT.

NetWare Loadable Module Software that is added or removed to a NetWare server to provide additional functionality. Examples include adding support for Macintosh computers and print services.

network Two or more computers connected for the purpose of sharing resources such as files or printers.

network drive A mapping to a network path that appears to the user as a drive letter. You access it the same way that you access a local drive.

network interface card A device that connects a computer to the physical cable media and produces signals for transferring data.

New Technology File System (NTFS) Developed by Microsoft for the NT operating system, this feature added better file management, larger disk compatibility, and file-level security on the local computer.

node A connection point on a network. Nodes include computers, servers, and printers.

O

object Every element of the network—from people to machines—is represented in the Windows 2000 Active Directory by an object. These objects each represent one specific element of the network and have their own properties and configuration elements.

object linking and embedding (OLE) A technology that enables applications to share data. Each document is stored as an object, and one object can be embedded within another object. For example, an Excel spreadsheet can be embedded within a Word document. Because the object is linked, changes through Excel or Word will be updated through the single linked object.

octet One of four parts of an IP address. Each number in an octet is created using 8 bits.

offline storage Holds data that is currently unavailable. You use offline storage to store large amounts of infrequently accessed data or to store computer backups.

online data storage Holds data that is immediately available and can be quickly accessed, as is the case with hard disks.

open source The free distribution of source code (software) for the purpose of improving the software by the programming community. Regardless of modifications or adaptations of open source software, the code is still protected by the Open Source Definition.

organizational units (OUs) Organizational units are new with Windows 2000, and are compliant with the X.500 directory. They break the directory into subdivisions and are one of the enhancements that has added administrative depth to the previously flat domain directory structure.

original equipment manufacturer (OEM) A term used to describe the device or software that is sold to a reseller who then passes the product on to a consumer. OEM versions of software can sometimes be altered by the reseller in an effort to make the product integrate with the reseller's hardware.

OS/2 A 32-bit operating system originally developed by Microsoft and IBM. OS/2 can support DOS, Windows, and OS/2 applications. Since Microsoft's abandonment of the program in the late 1980s, OS/2 has been produced and sold exclusively by IBM.

Outlook Express A free Internet e-mail client application developed by Microsoft.

P

packet Data that has been encapsulated with information from the Transport and Network layers of the OSI model.

parallel communication The process of transmitting and processing data one byte (eight bits) at a time.

parent domain The domain from which all other domains in a tree take their name.

parity An extra bit found on some memory modules. Non-parity memory has eight bits. Parity adds an extra bit that is used to keep track of the other eight bits. This can help prevent memory errors and is recommended for use in servers.

parity In the context of a stripe set, a series of mathematical calculations based on the data stored. If a disk fails, the stored parity information can be used to rebuild the data.

passive matrix A flat-panel LCD display technology that uses horizontal and vertical wires with LCD cells at each intersection to create a video image. Passive matrix is considered inferior to active matrix but is less expensive to produce.

PC card Small, thin device the size of a credit card. PC cards follow the PCMCIA (Personal Computer Memory Card International Association) standard and can be of three types. Type 1 supports RAM or ROM expansions for mobile computing devices. Type 2 is slightly thicker to accommodate modems and network cards. Type 3 is the thickest and was designed for mobile storage.

peer-to-peer network Does not use dedicated network servers for logging in users or providing secure access to network resources. Instead, clients simply share resources, and other clients have access to whatever has been shared.

Peripheral Component Interconnect (PCI)
A bus standard for the transfer of data between the CPU, expansion cards, and RAM. PCI communicates at 33MHz.

physical hard drive   The physical (or real, as opposed to conceptual) drive; for example, drive 0 or drive 1 in a two-drive configuration.

physical location   The actual location of a resource. Each resource must be homed on a server somewhere on the network. Windows 2000 enables you to organize resources logically, rather than physically.

pipeline   A place in the processor where operations occur in a series of stages. The operation is not complete until it has passed through all stages.

pixel   Short for picture element; a pixel is one dot in an image.

platforms   The hardware or software that supports any given system. The term *platform* can be used, for example, to reference a Pentium III–based computer or Windows 98.

plotter   A special type of print device that draws high-resolution diagrams, charts, graphs, and other layouts.

point-to-point   A direct link between two devices without any intermediary network devices in between.

port address   An address used by the computer to access devices such as expansion cards and printers.

POSIX   A standard originally developed for Unix that defines the interface between applications and the operating system. It is now more widely used for the development of other operating systems, including Windows 2000.

PostScript   A page description language used to convert and move data from an application to a laser printer.

Power On Self-Test (POST)   A set of diagnostic tests that are used to determine the state of hardware installed in the computer. Some components that fail the POST, such as bad RAM or a disconnected keyboard, will prevent the computer from booting up properly.

Power Users   Intended to allow Workstation 4 and 2000 Professional users greater authority over their workstations. Power Users are not as powerful as the Administrator, but can do far more than just Users, in that they can install software and configure more workstation options.

primary domain controller (PDC)   Is used in an NT domain. The PDC contains the read-write copy of the domain accounts administration database, called the Security Accounts Manager, or SAM.

primary partition   The first and bootable partition you create on a hard drive.

Primary Rate Interface (PRI)   The high-end ISDN service offered by telecommunication companies. PRI provides 23 B channels and one D channel. This is equivalent to the 24 channels of a T1 line.

print processor   The print processor and the default data type determine how much of a document's formatting is done by the printer, as opposed to the application.

print server   A centralized computer that manages printing of user documents to one or more printers. Print servers store documents temporarily when the printer is busy.

processor   See Central Processing Unit.

profile   A record of the user's personal configuration data and preferences. You can store a profile locally or you can store all user profiles on the server and allow them to roam, which means a user could log on to any machine in the domain and get their own profile.

Program Information Files (PIFs)   Files for a non-Windows application that include settings for running the application in Windows 3.*x*.

Programmable Read-Only Memory (PROM)   A special type of chip that is manufactured without any configuration. Manufacturers can then "burn in," or program, the chip to contain whatever configuration is needed.

protected mode   A mode available in Intel 80286 and 80386 processors. Added the capability for the processor to allocate each application its own separate memory space. In the event that an application crashed, the rest of the system was protected.

protocol   A set of rules for communication between two devices.

PS/2   Also known as the mouse port and DIN 6, PS/2 was developed by IBM for connecting a mouse to the computer. PS/2 ports are supported for mice and keyboards alike.

R

random access memory (RAM)   A temporary memory location that stores the operating system, applications, and files that are currently in use. The content in this type of memory is constantly changing. When you shut down the computer, all information in this type of memory is lost.

RDISK   A critical management utility that is used to create a recovery disk that can be used in conjunction with the NT CD or disks. RDISK copies the system configuration information and the SAM database to the disk for use during the recovery process.

Read Access   Permissions that allow a user to view a resource but not modify it.

read-only memory (ROM)   A type of memory that has data pre-copied onto it. The data can only be read from and cannot be overwritten. ROM is used to store the BIOS software.

Reduced Instruction Set Computing (RISC)   A reduced set of instructions used by a processor. PowerPC and Alpha processors are manufactured using this standard. The reduced instruction set enables a microprocessor to operate at higher speeds.

Redundant Array of Inexpensive (or Independent) Disks (RAID)   A method of using a series of hard disks as an array of drives. Some RAID implementations improve performance. Others improve performance and provide fault tolerance.

refresh rate   A measurement of the number of times that an image is redrawn to the screen per second. Measured in Hertz; a higher number is better.

Remote Access Service (RAS)   Allows computers to access the network remotely; for example, through a phone, ISDN, or Internet connection.

removable drive   A disk that can be removed from the computer and replaced. Floppy disks, rewritable CDs (CD-RW) and Zip/Jaz/Ditto drives are examples.

repeater   A network device, similar to a hub but with only two or three ports, that can be used to extend the transmission distance of a network signal or to join two networks.

replicate   The process by which a machine sends a copy of its databases to another machine. This usually occurs on a scheduled basis.

replication cycle   The means by which a group of machines synchronize their information; replication is usually done on a pre-configured schedule that can be adjusted due to network or organizational need.

resolve   To convert from one type to another. In relationship to IP addresses and domain names, it is the conversion of an IP address to a domain name on the Internet or vice versa.

rights   A right is different from a permission. Rights allow you to do a task, whereas permissions concern a particular resource. For instance, in order to access a particular file, a user must have the right to log on to the network and must also have permission to use that particular file.

root tree   The top domain within a newly created namespace. All other domains in the tree must fall within the root tree's namespace.

route   The path that a packet takes to reach its destination.

route table   A table created by a router that contains information on how to reach networks that are directly attached to the router and networks that are distant.

routers   Devices that connect two or more networks. Routers work at the Network layer of the OSI model, receiving packets and forwarding them to their correct destination.

RS-232   An interface standard for use between data communications equipment (DCE) and data terminal equipment (DTE).

S

scalable   Capable of expanding to accommodate greater numbers of users and resources.

schema   The set of configuration elements that defines a particular directory. The schema contains information about all objects in the directory.

Security Accounts Manager (SAM)   A database on NT servers that contains the relationship between who a user is and the level of security access that the user has to resources on the network.

security identifier (SID)   A unique number used by NT to represent a user or a computer on the network.

separator page   A page that is used to show where one print job stops and another one starts.

serial communication   The transmission of data one bit at a time.

server   A computer that provides dedicated file, print, messaging, application, or other service to client computers.

share   A resource, such as a directory or a printer, that is made available to network users. A share can have permissions associated to it to control which users can access the resource.

shareware   Software that is generally available for trial use. If you like the software, you should pay a small licensing fee.

Silicon-On-Insulator (SOI)   The microchip manufacturing innovation that IBM invented. It is based on the capability to enhance silicon technology by reducing the time it takes to move electricity through a conductor.

single-edge cartridge (SEC)   An advanced packaging scheme that is used for the Intel Pentium II and later models. The processor is encased in a cartridge module with a single edge that plugs into a 242-pin slot on the system board, much as an expansion card plugs into the system board.

Single Inline Memory Module (SIMM)   Memory that has a board with memory chips attached on one side. SIMMs typically come in 72 pin configurations.

Site Link   A logical connection that links two sites and controls the flow of traffic over WAN links. Just as a trust regulates the flow of permissions and resources, a Site Link regulates the speed and type of traffic that is allowed across the WAN. Site Links therefore enable an administrator to optimize bandwidth usage.

slave   A device that is controlled by another device called the master.

Small Computer System Interface (SCSI)
An interface that connects SCSI devices to the computer. This interface uses high-speed parallel technology to connect devices that include hard disks, CD-ROM players, tape backup devices, and other hardware peripherals.

smart cards   A small device–about the size of a credit card–that can hold various types of personal information.

standard   An agreed upon set of rules, procedures, and functions that are widely accepted.

start bit   The bit that synchronizes the clock on the computer receiving the data. In asynchronous data transmission, the start bit is a space.

stop bit   The bit that identifies the end of the character being transmitted so that the character is clearly recognized.

superscalar   The use of two parallel 32-bit pipelines that allow the CPU to execute twice the number of instructions.

switch   The modern name used for a multi-port bridge. Like a regular bridge, each port on a switch represents a separate network. Traffic on each port is kept isolated except when the packet is destined for another device on a different port or if the packet is a broadcast. Broadcasts must be sent out all ports.

switch box   A device that enables multiple machines to share a single device, such as a printer or a monitor. The disadvantage is that only one machine at a time can use the device.

symmetric processor   Two or more processors in a computer that are each capable of completing processes simultaneously, which maximizes performance. Windows NT and 2000 Server support SMP.

Symmetrical Multiprocessing (SMP)   A computer architecture that uses multiple CPUs to improve a computer's performance. As performance demands increase on an SMP-capable computer, additional CPUs can be added to boost performance. During operation, if one CPU is idle, it can be given any task to perform.

synchronous communication   Transmits data by synchronizing the data signal between the sender and receiver and sending data as a continuous stream. This is the most efficient way of sending large amounts of data but requires expensive equipment.

Synchronous Dynamic RAM (SDRAM)
Similar in design to EDO RAM in that it writes at the same time that it reads, vastly accelerating the flow of data. SDRAM is a popular choice over EDO RAM due to its high bus speeds of 100MHz and its low cost.

Systems Network Architecture (SNA)
Defined by IBM, a standard that specifies how devices can interface with IBM software.

T

take ownership   Each file on an NTFS drive has an "owner"–a user account or group that is given complete access to that file. Taking ownership is the process of becoming the owner of a resource.

telecommuter   Someone who remotely connects to their office to work from home or a remote location.

terminal   Terminal servers allow multiple users to access them at a single time through "thin clients" or other software. The users input information, but all processing is done on the server.

Terminal Services   Whereas normal servers provide file or printer access, a terminal server provides full desktop access. Terminal services allow a single machine to be used by multiple users at once. Each individual uses their own keyboard, mouse, and monitor, and is presented with a Windows Desktop, but all programs run locally on the terminal server.

353

termination   The use of a terminator at both ends of a SCSI daisy chain to keep data signals from bouncing back on the SCSI bus after they reach the end. The terminator is a small plastic connector that has a resistor (ceramic-based material that absorbs electricity) inside of it.

throughput   The amount of data that can be transferred in a set period of time.

token   A special packet that signifies that a user can transmit data to a Token Ring network.

token passing   Developed by IBM, the transmission of data in a token that is passed from computer to computer on a Token Ring network. Only one token can exist on the network at once. When one computer is done using the token, the next computer in line that needs to transmit gets the token.

Token Ring   A layer 2 protocol developed by IBM that uses a token passing method for transmitting data. Each device on the ring takes turns using the token. The token can be used by only one device at a time.

topology   A physical or logical configuration. A physical topology defines the way that a network is physically laid out, and a logical topology defines the way that data is transferred through the network.

transistor   A microscopic electronic device that uses positive electrons to create the binary value of one, or "on," and negative electrons to create the binary value of zero, or "off." Modern CPUs have millions of transistors.

transitive   Trusts that are transitive allow a domain to act as an intermediary for two other domains. If A trusts B, and B trusts C, there is a physical path between A and C. Even with that physical link, though, directory information will pass from A to C only if B acts as a transitive link.

trust   A trust is configured to allow two Windows NT domains to share user authentication information and to allow users from one domain to access resources in another domain.

U

Uniform Resource Locator (URL)   The address that is used to identify and access a Web server on the Internet. www.greenpeace.org is one example.

Universal Serial Bus (USB)   A standard for connecting up to 127 peripheral devices, such as mice, keyboards, printers, and modems. Devices connected to the USB bus share a maximum bandwidth of 12Mbps.

unshielded twisted-pair (UTP)   A type of media that can contain four, six, or eight wires. Pairs of wires are twisted together to prevent signal interference. The wires are then wrapped in a plastic cover. UTP is identified by the category nomenclature.

Upper Memory Area (UMA)   The area of memory between 640KB and 1MB in an IBM-compatible computer. This area of memory was originally reserved for system and video use.

USB hub   A connectivity device that provides multiple USB connections so that several USB devices can communicate with the computer.

Users folder   One of a number of default folders in the Active Directory. In most cases, using this default location is fine. Users in this folder can later be placed into groups in other folders or organizational units.

V

Virtual Address eXtension (VAX)   The technology built by Digital to run the VMS platform computers.

virtual circuit   A logical connection between two devices that transmits and receives data.

virtual private networking (VPN) Using encrypted envelopes to securely transmit sensitive data between two points over the unsecured Internet.

virtual RAM A function of the operating system that is used to simulate RAM by breaking computer programs into small units of data (called pages) and storing the pages in a page file on the hard disk.

volume A part of a physical disk that is identified by a single drive label. See logical drives.

W

wide area network (WAN) A relatively low-speed data connection (typically 1.546 Mbps) that uses the telephone company to connect two locations separated by a large geographical area.

Windows Internet Naming Service (WINS) A Microsoft proprietary protocol that runs on a Windows NT server. The protocol is used on NT severs to resolve NetBIOS names, the workstation name on Windows computers, to IP addresses. WINS is similar in concept to DNS.

Windows NT Diagnostic A utility in Windows NT 3.51 and 4 that displays system configuration information in a graphical format. System settings can be changed and informative reports generated from this utility.

Windows operating system An operating system developed by Microsoft that provides a graphical user interface for DOS.

Windows Update A set of online updates and drivers provided by Microsoft that enables users to locate current files for their system, and for new devices, and to download them automatically from the Internet.

Wizard A configuration assistant that walks the user through a short series of guided steps to complete a task.

workstation Another name for a computer that is used by users. It is sometimes used to describe powerful computers that are used for completing complex mathematical, engineering, and animation tasks.

Y

X.500 An industry-standard directory structure used by Windows 2000 to organize and name network elements. Other network operating systems, such as Novell's NetWare Directory Services, also use X.500.

Appendix C

C

Common Acronyms

Acronym	Meaning
ANSI	American National Standards Institute
API	Application Programming Interface
ARPA	Advanced Research Projects Agency
ARPANET	Advanced Research Projects Agency Network
ASCII	American Standard Code for Information Interchange
BIOS	Basic Input/Output System
BNC	British Naval Connector
bps	bits per second
Bps	bytes per second
CCITT	Consultative Committee for International Telephony and Telegraphy
CD	Change Directory
CD	compact disc
CDFS	Compact Disc File System
CD-R	Compact Disc-Recordable
CD-ROM	Compact Disc Read-Only Memory
CD-RW	Compact Disc-Rewritable
CMOS	Complementary Metal-Oxide Semiconductor
CNE	Certified NetWare Engineer
CPU	Central Processing Unit
CRC	cyclic redundancy check
CSMA/CD	Carrier Sense Multiple Access with Collision Detection
DHCP	Dynamic Host Configuration Protocol
DNS	Domain Name System
DoD	Department of Defense
DOS	Disk Operating System
EBCDIC	Extended Binary Coded Decimal Interchange Code
EEPROM	Electrically Erasable Programmable Read-Only Memory
EPROM	Erasable Programmable Read-Only Memory
FAT	File Allocation Table
FDDI	Fiber Distributed Data Interface

Acronym	Meaning
GB	gigabyte
Gbps	gigabits per second
GBps	gigabytes per second
GUI	graphical user interface
HPFS	High Performance File System
IC	Integrated Circuit
IDE	Integrated Drive Electronics
IEEE	Institute of Electrical and Electronic Engineers
I/O	input/output
IP	Internet Protocol
IPX	Internetwork Packet Exchange
IPX/SPX	Internetwork Packet Exchange/Sequenced Packet Exchange
IRQ	interrupt request
ISDN	Integrated Services Digital Network
ISO	International Standards Organization
ISP	Internet Service Provider
Kb	kilobit
KB	kilobyte
Kbps	kilobits per second
KBps	kilobytes per second
LAN	local area network
LLC	Logical Link Control
MAC	Media Access Control
MAN	Metropolitan Area Network
Mb	megabit
MB	megabyte
Mbps	megabits per second
MBps	megabytes per second
MCP	Microsoft Certified Professional
MCPS	Microsoft Certified Product Specialist
MCSE	Microsoft Certified Systems Engineer

Acronym	Meaning
MCT	Microsoft Certified Trainer
MD	Make Directory
MHz	megahertz
MODEM	Modulator/Demodulator
MSAU	Multi-Station Access Unit
MS-DOS	Microsoft Disk Operating System
NetBEUI	NetBIOS Extended User Interface
NetBIOS	Network Basic Input/Output System
NIC	Network Interface Card
NOS	network operating system
NT	New Technology
NTFS	New Technology File System
OEM	Original Equipment Manufacturer
OS	operating system
OS/2	Operating System/2
OSI	Open Systems Interconnection
PC	Personal Computer
PCMCIA	Personal Computer Memory Card International Association
POSIX	Portable Operating System Interface Extension
PROM	Programmable Read-Only Memory
PSTN	Public Switched Telephone Network
RAID	Redundant Array of Inexpensive (or Independent) Disks
RD	Remove Directory
RFC	Request For Comments
RIP	Router Information Protocol
RJ	Registered Jack
SMP	Symmetric Multiprocessing
SNMP	Simple Network Management Protocol
SPX	Sequenced Packet Exchange
SQL	Structured Query Language
Tb	terabit

Acronym	Meaning
TB	terabyte
Tbps	terabits per second
TBps	terabytes per second
TCP	Transmission Control Protocol
TCP/IP	Transmission Control Protocol/Internet Protocol
THz	terahertz
URL	Uniform Resource Locator
USL	Unix System Laboratories
WAN	wide area network
WINS	Windows Internet Naming Service
WORM	Write Once—Read Many

Index

Note to the Reader: Page numbers in **bold** indicate the principle discussion of a topic or the definition of a term. Page numbers in *italic* indicate illustrations.

JumpStart Your Career!

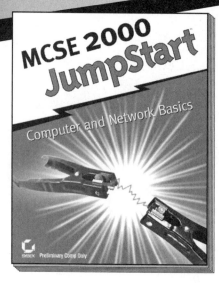

**MCSE 2000
JumpStart
Computer and
Network Basics**
ISBN: 0-7821-2749-5
$19.99 US

**CCNA JumpStart
Networking and
Internetworking Basics**
ISBN: 0-7821-2592-1
$19.99 US

Anxious to take your career in high-tech to the next level but uncertain about where to begin?

The JumpStart™ series from Sybex™ has the answers.
JumpStart books provide the firm grounding in computer and
network topics you'll need to approach certification training
with confidence. In each JumpStart book you'll find:

- Clear and concise explanations of complex
  technical topics
- Review questions to help reinforce your understanding
- Real-world insights from expert trainers

Once you've covered the basics, you'll be ready to start down
the road in pursuit of certifications such as Microsoft's MCSE,
Cisco's CCNA, and others.

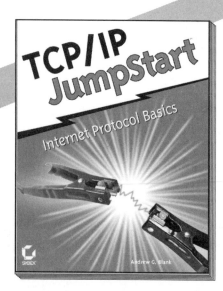

**TCP/IP Jumpstart
Internet Protocol Basics**
ISBN: 0-7821-2644-8
$19.99 US

SYBEX
www.sybex.com

The most comprehensive and accurate
Windows® 2000
books available!

Mastering™
Windows 2000 Server, 2nd Ed.
Mark Minasi, et al
0-7821-2774-6 · $49.99 US

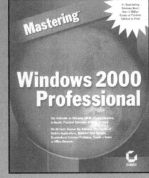

Windows 2000 Professional
Mark Minasi, et al
0-7821-2448-8 · $39.99 US

Mastering™
Windows 2000 Registry
Peter Hipson
0-7821-2615-4 · $39.99 US

Windows 2000
Instant Reference
Jutta VanStean
0-7821-2572-7 · $19.99 US

Mastering™ Active Directory
Robert King
0-7821-2659-6 · $39.99 US

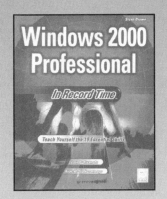

Windows 2000 Professional:
In Record Time™
Peter Dyson & Pat Coleman
0-7821-2450-X · $29.99 US

$45 savings!

Mark Minasi's
Windows 2000 Resource Kit
0-7821-2614-6 · $124.96 US
Includes 4 Mastering books:
Server, Professional, Registry,
and Active Directory.
Plus CD includes PDFs of the books!

Your #1 Resource
for Windows 2000 books!

SYBEX®

SYBEX BOOKS ON THE WEB

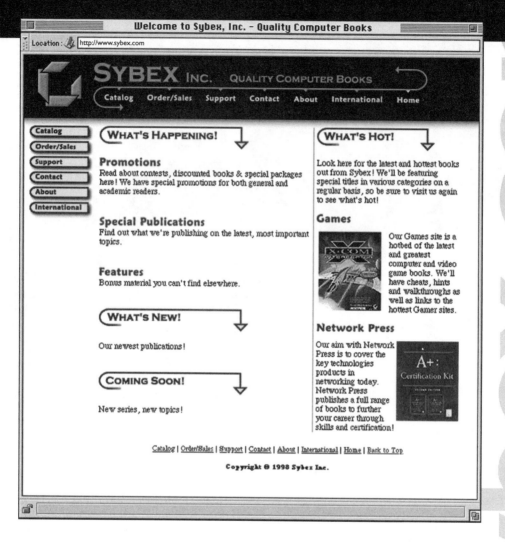

At the dynamic and informative Sybex Web site, you can:

- view our complete online catalog
- preview a book you're interested in
- access special book content

- order books online at special discount prices
- learn about Sybex

www.sybex.com

SYBEX Inc. • 1151 Marina Village Parkway, Alameda, CA 94501 • 510-523-8233

SYBEX®

Boost Your Career with Certification

2nd Edition
Completely revised and updated for 1999–2000!

Detailed information on all the key computer and network certification programs, including:

- Computer hardware

- Operating systems

- Software

- Networking hardware

- Network operating systems

- Internet

- Instructor and trainer certifications

ISBN: 0-7821-2545-X
640pp • 5 7/8 x 8 1/4 • Softcover
$19.99

Learn why to get certified,
when to get certified,
and how to get certified.

SYBEX
www.sybex.com

Build Your Own Networking Reference Library

with Sybex™ books

The Network Press
Encyclopedia of Networking, 3rd Ed.
ISBN: 0-7821-2255-8 • 1600pp
7 1/2" x 9" • hardcover
1 CD • $84.99

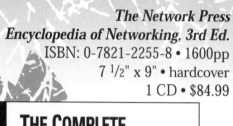

The Network Upgrade &
Maintenance Guide
ISBN: 0-7821-2259-0
1600pp • 7 1/2" x 9"
hardcover • 1 CD • $49.99

Dictionary of Networking,
3rd Ed.
ISBN: 0-7821-2461-5
512pp • 5 7/8" x 8 1/4"
softcover • 1 CD • $29.99

Available
in April 2000: *Cabling: The Complete Guide to Network Wiring*
ISBN: 0-7821-2645-6 • 960pp • 7 1/2" x 9"
hardcover • $49.99

SYBEX®

www.sybex.com

SECURE YOUR NETWORK

Sybex™ provides the information you need to

- Assess the security of your network
- Devise a workable security plan
- Implement effective security measures

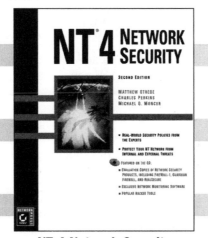

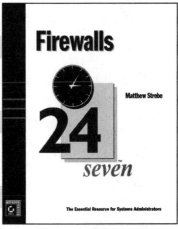

Mastering Network Security
0-7821-2343-0 • US $59.99
704 pages • Hardcover

NT 4 Network Security
0-7821-2425-9 • US $49.99
960 pages • Hardcover

Firewalls 24seven
0-7821-2529-8 • US $34.99
496 pages • Softcover

www.sybex.com

www.24sevenbooks.com

Get MCSE Windows® 2000 Certified!

Sybex Study Guides & Exam Notes™ Provide the Most Comprehensive Solution Available.

$49.99 US

$24.99 US

MCSE STUDY GUIDES

Authoritative and in-depth Study Guides give you everything you need to know, both for the exam and the real world:

- **Assessment Tests** allow you to check your level of knowledge before you study.

- **Key Terms** sections at the end of each chapter highlight crucial vocabulary.

- **Review Questions** for each chapter reinforce what you learn.

- **Practice Exams** give you the chance to test your understanding of the material covered in the entire book.

- **CDs include** pre-assessment exams, program simulators, electronic flashcards, bonus review questions, and a copy of the entire book in electronic format.

EXAM NOTES

The perfect companion to the Study Guide and an excellent quick review, Exam Notes will help you gain and retain the information you need, objective by objective.

- **Critical Information** sections provide you with detailed analyses of the key issues for each exam.

- **Necessary Procedures** sections give you the nuts and bolts of each topic with concise step-by-step instructions.

- **Exam Essentials** sections highlight crucial subject areas you need to know for the exam.

- **Key Terms and Concepts** sections define words and concepts vital to passing the exam.

- **Sample Questions** sections allow you to preview the types of questions found in the exam and give you answers and explanations.

Sybex offers Study Guides and Exam Notes books for each MCSE exam offered. For a complete list, visit us at
www.sybex.com

Sybex – Leaders in Certification